CHRIST'S WITCHDOCTOR

CHRIST'S WITCHDOCTOR

FROM SAVAGE SORCERER TO JUNGLE MISSIONARY

by Homer E. Dowdy

HODDER AND STOUGHTON
LONDON · SYDNEY · AUCKLAND · TORONTO

To the untold numbers who
prayed through the years,
thereby giving substance to
this story

Contents

Note on pronunciation of names:

Wai Wai is pronounced like the letter
"Y," as though it were spelled "Y-Y."
Most names are accented on the final
syllable (EL-KAH).

I will not give sleep to mine eyes, or slumber to mine eyelids, until I find out a place for the Lord, an habitation for the mighty God of Jacob.

—Psalm 132:4 and 5

And he stood between the dead and the living; and the plague was stayed.

—Numbers 16:48

For God hath not given us the spirit of fear; but of power, and of love, and of a sound mind.

—II Timothy 1:7

Preface

The story of how Elka and his people exchanged fear for faith in Christ could have been told from several perspectives; for example, from that of the missionaries who have lived more than a dozen years among them. I chose to tell it from the Wai Wais' own standpoint, especially through the experiences of their chief. His and their testimonies to the grace of God are living witness to the dedication and skill of those who brought the news about God to the jungles of British Guiana.

The singleness of the missionaries' purpose stands out in this story: to present Jesus Christ. They did not endeavor to impose the trappings of a Western culture on Indians whose forest and river, whose manner of dress, served their temporal needs well. Rather, they planted, watered, nurtured the Gospel seed. Changes have come, but they have sprung from within, where Christ now dwells.

It has not been simply what the missionaries did—evangelizing, teaching, attending to physical ills, learning the tribal tongue and giving it back to the people in mysteriously wonderful written form—not the influence of their considerable abilities alone, or even the loving spirit in which they have served, that explains what happened in the villages and along the trails of Wai Wai land. The hand of God has been evident. To cite one instance, the original plan of the mission called for a school for Indian boys. But somehow the prospective students never seemed to be there; they were carried away by their fathers, or died, or repeatedly ran away. Through such unexplained interventions the missionaries finally saw that if they were to win the people, they would have to begin by reaching the men—and through them the women and children. Proof of the correctness of this different approach came again and again in later months, starting with the conversion of the most unlikely man in the tribe.

This and other interventions—some recognizable as divine guidance only by hindsight—came by prayer. One man began praying for the Wai Wai in 1926, when to the world the tribe was only a name listed in the musty journals of nineteenth-century explorers. Helping to unlock the power of God for these people have been concerned Christians in America, Britain, and other places—relatives, personal friends, home churches of the missionaries, and the constituency of their sponsoring board, Unevangelized Fields Mission of Bala-Cynwyd, Pennsylvania. None have been more productive in recruiting prayer support than the Rev. and Mrs. William E. Hawkins of Dallas, Texas, parents of the three brothers who made the original contact with the tribe. Through their widespread radio contacts they regularly solicited prayer for the needs of Elka, Kirifaka, Yoshwi, and others—not the usual general prayer for far-off natives, but specific intercession for real people with real problems and real destinies.

The Wai Wai people themselves were seemingly prepared by God for the work he was ready to do in and through them. This was evident as the degradation and decline in their old life became known. Since no man exists in a vacuum, they were being readied for the inner change that was offered them.

In short, the amazing story of Wai Wai transformation goes back not to the missionaries and their consecrated efforts entirely, nor to Elka and his people, but to God Himself, who would redeem some (and a large percentage of the total in this case) "out of every kindred, and tongue, and people, and nation."

To tell this story has required the reading of nearly a thousand letters and diaries that the missionaries sent home over the years, subjection of the missionaries to a reporter's brand of psychiatric couch, search among nearly forgotten books and unpublished journals of old-time adventurers, and, most important, interviewing nearly three dozen men and women in the tribe to obtain their life histories.

What has been attempted is not a report as it might be submitted to mission headquarters, not the bones of statistical fact, but the flesh and blood of vibrant reality that have made these occurrences what they are. Thus, while telling a story of true if amazing facts, it has been the writer's task to recreate the atmosphere in which those facts occurred. Usually, this required nothing more than absorbing the details recited by the person being interviewed. Sometimes it required coupling the typical generality with the specific event of the moment. Above all, it meant delving into the mind and memory of Elka. For this I am indebted to the patience and understanding that this most unusual man displayed, as hour after hour I was astounded at his precise recollections (owing perhaps to the lack of written language until recent years) and his keen comments while we talked during hunting trips, at the desk in his palm-thatch house, or on the high clay bank of the river.

I am similarly indebted to Mawasha for introducing me to the ways of the jungle, even though his rapid pace along the hunting trails made me more than ready for my hammock at sundown. Kirifaka, Yakuta, Tamokrana, Seshwa, Shirifa, Yoshwi, and many others submitted with the best of grace to the most personal interrogation by one who could not "catch" their language without an interpreter and who must have seemed to them incredibly ignorant of Wai Wai ways.

This story could not have been written had not Claude Leavitt, one of the missionaries, given untold hours to interpretation. And to Barbara Leavitt, his wife, I am grateful for her remembrance of things past and for her delicious breakfast rolls and pumpkin dishes when monkey meat and alligator steak began to pall.

I owe an enormous debt to Robert Hawkins and his wife, Florine, who have worked among the Wai Wai longer than any others. Their over-all guidance and close scrutiny of detail have been keen and incisive and, of course, indispensable.

Special recognition is due Nurse Florence Riedle, who was able to teach me to know the Wai Wai as real people because no one has known or loved them more than she. My thanks go, too, to the personnel of the Missionary Aviation Fellowship and Door to Life Ministries, which for several years served in Wai Wai territory, for the air lifts they provided.

I would be ungrateful if I did not mention at least a few of the many at home who encouraged me in writing this story or made it possible for me to go to Wai Wai land:

Mr. John Galbraith, a hometown friend; Dr. Russell T. Hitt, editor of *Eternity* and himself a writer of books on global evangelism; the Rev. Ralph B. Odman, general secretary of Unevangelized Fields Mission; Dr. Henry R. Brandt, who has often given me a "push" when needed; Mr. Fred Renich, whose color slides introduced me to the Wai Wai; Dr. Kenneth Pike, anthropologist and linguist extraordinary of the University of Michigan; Mr. Ralph B. Curry, under whom I received my reporter's training at *The Flint Journal*.

The parents of the missionaries co-operated unstintingly in assembling hundreds of letters and making even the most personal available to me. And I can never express adequately my appreciation to Melvin Arnold and Frank Elliott of Harper & Row, and to Edward Sammis, all of whom had a large part in this book's becoming what it is. To my wife, Nancy, and my six children I am indebted for their listening to my telling and retelling elements of this story and for their letting me have a quiet corner in a bustling house in which to write undisturbed.

The Wai Wai are a happy, purposeful people today; how they got that way is a story from which I have had to step aside and marvel and say simply, "God did it." If I have been successful in capturing this story on these pages, with the help of those mentioned and others, it is God, too, who is responsible for that.

H. E. D.

1

Must a Baby Die?

In the blackness just before dawn Elka shot his canoe from one fish trap to another on the familiar jungle stream. The young Indian boy of the Wai Wai tribe begrudged every moment of his chore. He *must* get back to the village, where his mother was about to give birth. His stepfather, the ill-tempered Tumika, was standing by to kill the child. Who would prevent the killing if not Elka himself? And how could he when he still had rounds to make, inspecting traps on the black river?

Breaking the darkness ahead of him, ever so faintly, was the glow of the firebrand propped in the prow of his dugout. By its light he strained to see whether a trap had been sprung, whether one of the bent-over sticks now stood straight in the water holding a basket aloft with its heavy catch. In the swampy backwaters there were more traps than all his fingers. He might have to look at every one before finding a big fish that would provide breakfast for the village. Maybe he would have to return empty-handed; then the old men would grumble and elbow him away as a pot of starchy cassava drink passed from hand to hand around the hungry circle.

Although Elka cared nothing about breakfast this morning,

the others did, and so he had to tend the fish traps; there was no way out. No matter how fast he tried to work, his pace seemed terribly slow. Would he never reach the last trap?

And always his thoughts turned back to his mother. What would he find when he finally got back to the village? His mother still in agony? A baby, all pink and crying—the brother he longed for? Or a tiny, lifeless body, its head smashed in? Would he get there in time? Would he? The question surged rhythmically with each motion of the paddle.

He paused to rest his aching muscles. A new question came, more disturbing than the first: If he did get back in time, could he really stop his stepfather? Elka was pitifully small to thwart a man bent on killing. Only seven big-rain seasons had come and gone since he was born. A seven-year-old seemed hardly worth his stepfather's notice. Yet in the boy was something of a man. There had been other times when his determination and courage had reduced his stepfather to frustrated rage.

Twice Elka slowed his paddling and waved the brand to renew its flame. The flickering gleam picked out on his light-brown face the broad flat nose, the wide mouth, the dark, penetrating eyes. As he moved, the light caught the mass of lustrous black hair falling on his bare shoulders. It winked from the beads strung around his neck and from the shiny bobs that plugged the lobes of his ears. It gleamed on his smooth brown body, naked except for the beads and a loincloth.

Elka maneuvered expertly on the swift water. Yet his quick, sure skill was no more than the Wai Wai people expected of their boys. Living in the heart of the dense rain forest of British Guiana, he was skilled in the many arts of survival. The harsh facts of jungle life he knew firsthand. He had watched and heard the suffering of women in childbirth. And he knew that a birth today would mean a quick death if he could not get there to stop it.

"Shall I snatch up a club and beat the old young thing when

he comes?" Tumika had asked just the day before, grinning like a madman. (Elka had never seen him smile—only that demonic grin.) "Or shall I tie a cord around his neck, or hold his face in the dirt until he no longer sucks in breath?"

Young Elka had seethed with anger, but said nothing; he dared not show his contempt for an elder. In the pit of his stomach he ached for the baby; he wanted a brother more than he wanted arrows or a red-handled knife. For days he had searched for a way to save the baby.

Ill luck had brought his mother's first pains late the previous day, and they had come again in the night hours before Elka left for the river. Why must the pains strike when he had to be away from the village? He might not have to be away again for several days, certainly not if a hunter brought in a couple of wild pigs, making it unnecessary to trap fish for a while.

Even worse, on this day Elka had to make the rounds alone, so that the going was slower. Usually a kindly old man, Fehwe, whom he called "Uncle," came along on this early morning duty, if only to hold the light. But his uncle had wakened hot—feverish—unable to lift himself from his hammock.

"Never mind the trap where we saw the anaconda," he told Elka, knowing the boy was afraid of the spot. He rolled over then, to bury his aching head in the crook of his arm. Elka set out by himself.

A member of the tribe did not like to be alone—not to work or to hunt or to fish or even to eat. Yet this morning he was hurrying—and thinking—too much to mind it. He was recalling how he had wakened in the night and looked beyond the family fire. Where his mother's hammock usually hung, and Tumika's, there was nothing. Then, fuzzily, he remembered. The evening before, she had left the big communal house for the shelter he had helped to raise at the edge of the village where the thick jungle began. He lay half-awake, trying to recall to his fogged mind why she had gone. A low moan came to him through the night air and

wakened him fully. That was it: She was going to give birth!
And he could do nothing but listen, helpless, to her suffering
until it was time for him to leave. How the pains kept up! Would
this child never come? Now, out on the river, he was afraid it
would come too soon—afraid that even now his mother might
be at the final moment, with only his stepfather on hand.

Tumika was a silent, sullen, suspicious man. He did not like
to work with others or to sit and talk with them, even when the
men all gathered on their small, carved stools in the cool evening
after the sun dipped behind the curtain of tall, shadowy trees.
He was a rare one to stand aloof, and not to care how others
felt or what they said of him—at least he said he did not care.
People avoided this quick-tempered man. If they took their dogs
in the waning daylight for a swim in the river and happened
to meet him on the path, he would snarl at them,

"Why are you coming near me? Why do you send your dogs
on me? You mean to kill me. I know it."

But *he* was the killer. People said he had often killed by
witchcraft. He had many enemies, and some of them had died
because he "ate their spirits." To kill by spirit-eating, Tumika
would find something belonging to the hated one—maybe a
fishbone from his meal or a footprint caked in the mud—and
carefully take up whatever it was, wrap it in a leaf, and blow his
breath on it, *koosh koosh koosh!* Then he would pierce it with
the thorn of a palm, hang it on a branch, and wait for his enemy
to die.

But killing a baby was much simpler and more direct. Painfully Elka's mind went back to the year before when he had stood
by while his mother gave birth to another child. He could still
see Tumika glowering at the infant boy lying where it had come
forth on the earth floor of the birth hut. As long as it lay untouched, death from an angry parent was possible. To lift a baby
from the ground, however, was to save it; the danger of killing
was then past.

Elka remembered Tumika saying to the villagers who witnessed the birth,

"The old young thing is not to be lifted up."

If any villager had wanted to save the child, none offered; all were afraid of Tumika. They had already turned away, a few muttering an idle threat about "next time," before Tumika took a piece of split wood and struck one swift blow.

That night Elka had cried for the dead infant that had so briefly been his brother. There was no comfort from his mother, who still lay under the three-cornered roof of the birth hut, her hammock slung beneath her husband's. In the big house no one seemed to care that Elka cried as he lay in his hammock. What did it matter to them that a baby was dead; they went on in their usual way—piping on their wooden flutes, gossiping with one another, or snoring contentedly next to a warm night fire. The whimpering dogs, tied on shelves next to the walls, seemed more sympathetic.

Toward dawn Elka had jumped from his hammock, unable to lie with his grief any longer. By the last light of a sinking moon he stole across the clearing to a pile of litter behind a leafy outbuilding. He poked around until he found what he was looking for. Picking it up, he ran to the birth hut. By the dim firelight he could see Tumika sleeping heavily. Elka stared for a long moment, raging inwardly and trembling with fear and hate. As he tried to speak all that came out was a sob, but this freshet released a flood and then a torrent of shouted grief.

"He killed him! He killed him! Why did he kill my little brother?"

The boy screamed his accusation, not *at* his stepfather, but *about* him; a Wai Wai child dared not be more direct.

Tumika awoke with a start. He sat up and turned in his hammock, his feet dangling over the side. Rubbing his eyes, he felt he must have been dreaming. But in the faint light he saw Elka holding the dead body tightly in his arms.

"Gicha!" he swore, spitting on the ground in disgust. "Why do you bring that dead one here?"

"He killed him," Elka mumbled.

In the lower hammock the unsleeping mother had seen her son come in and had watched silently. It was time she spoke.

"My son would like to have a brother for himself," she said.

In one swift motion Tumika jumped from his hammock and snatched the cold body from Elka's arms.

"He wants a brother?" he asked heatedly. "Let him take the anaconda for his brother and embrace *him*! I will bury this old young thing. Then he'll have a brother—under the dirt."

He drew a long knife from the roof and stalked out to chop ground for a grave.

Elka walked slowly back to the big house. Those who had been talking were now asleep; the flutes were silent. The village dogs still growled and whimpered as they bit at their fleas. Elka climbed into his hammock.

It was dawn before sleep had closed his tear-filled eyes.

Now, a year later, with the rains due once more, young Elka had made up his mind that Tumika would not kill again. Emerging from the swampy gloom of a backwater, the boy looked up into the first light of dawn, which was turning the black river to green, except where the water boiled white at the base of two giant rocks.

Kiricici—Old Bead—was the name of the stream on which Elka lived, so called because of a man who had drowned in it long before. The man was soon forgotten; the precious beads that sank with him lived on in the name of the stream. It was a remote tributary of the Amazon, cutting a meandering path two canoe-lengths wide through the endless forests that covered northern Brazil and the southern edge of the Guianas. Its source lay many days' travel above the village and its mouth was two full days downstream, where it emptied into the Mapuera—the

Kum-Kwow or "Palm Fruit," as the Wai Wai people called the larger river. The Mapuera rose in the high mountains away to the north and (so Elka had been told by older and wiser ones) followed a rocky course into the still bigger Trombetas; this in turn poured into the biggest of all rivers, the mighty Amazon.

The towering rocks, each as big as the communal house of the village and bare of vegetation except for mud-plastered leaves from the previous year's floods, gave the name to Elka's village: Tohmiti Pona, Big Rocks in the River. They broke Old Bead's vine-covered banks and provided a protected landing place for canoes.

Elka had not always lived in Big Rocks. He had been born where it flowed into the Mapuera. Remnants of other tribes besides the Wai Wai had settled there. All were a part of the scattered peoples of the vast rain forest. The jungle walled them in, yet let them live in no great want. If animals and birds were elusive and fish did not always bite, they survived on the fruit of the palm, nuts, and a few staples from their garden fields wrested from the jungle growth.

Yet nature's bounty did not provide them with a tranquil life. Pitted against the best of their wits were evil spirits determined to destroy them. Strict rules and taboos and the pleadings of witchdoctors were their only salvation.

No occasions were fraught with more evil and danger than birth and death. Death contaminated a house. Usually it required that the house be burned. Birth also contaminated a house. So the villagers built small birth huts that could be ripped down when no longer needed. Elka had been born in such a house, like the one he had helped put up for his mother the day before. Such a shelter kept off most of the falling rain but, lacking walls, failed to deflect the cold, blowing mists of early morning.

Parallel to, and a step above, the ground was a thin pole, lashed to the supports holding the roof. Another pole was tied several feet above it. In giving birth to Elka, his mother had stood on the lower pole and clasped the upper one with her hands, slumping in a half kneebend. Feeling the pangs, she pulled hard overhead until her burden dropped onto the pallet of banana leaves beneath her.

Elka had then been bathed from a giant clay pot in the hut and handed to his mother on her hammock over a warming fire. She cuddled him, enjoyed him, just as at other times she snuggled a favorite puppy to her breast. In a few days luxury was ended and she resumed her duties. In a barkcloth slung over her shoulder she carried her infant son as she worked. Riding in the sling he could feed at her breasts at will, and she could paddle a canoe, gather firewood, and dig cassava tubers with no thought of her baby as a hindrance.

His mother had returned to her chores almost immediately, but tribal custom dictated that Elka's father avoid strenuous labor, keep out of tall trees, and refrain from eating with anyone who had shot a tapir—that shy and gentle creature, largest of their jungle animals. Had he broken the rules of *foi*, the taboos for childbirth, his child would have died.

Elka's father had killed a child born the year before Elka. But Elka had been picked up, his life spared. Why? he often wondered. His own father had been hated by the people, just as they now hated his stepfather. Elka did not remember his father, but who among the villagers had not told him that the man made bad talk about others, more than the usual gossip, starting wicked rumors about this one and that? After his father died his mother did not want another husband. But Tumika, his father's friend, was without a wife, and against her wish he bargained with her older brother. For the sleek skin of an otter and five newly feathered arrows the brother was willing to let her go. Tumika carried his new wife and Elka and Elka's sister up from the mouth of Old Bead to the village of Big Rocks.

Elka doused his firebrand and by the growing light of dawn sped toward his final trap. Fortune awaited him.

In the long, upraised basket was a *haimara*, a giant fish half Elka's own weight. It had entered the submerged basket, and nipped the taut line that held it, releasing the bent-over stick attached to one end. Standing in his canoe, Elka reached for the basket hanging atop the stick and dumped the big fellow into the dugout. Then, paddling with all his might, he raced for the village landing. There he dragged the fish to the top of the steep bank and, heaving it to one shoulder, set off as fast as his legs and heavy burden would allow along the winding path to the village.

The trail led through a thickness of jungle, then burst upon an old garden field, long abandoned and now sprouting a scrubby second growth. The remains of trees felled and burned years ago in preparation for the garden lay there still. The boy picked his way over and around the charred timbers. Shifting the fish to his other shoulder, he quickly threaded his way through a thicket of tall, slender cane from which the men made their long arrows. Before he reached the clearing he heard the chorus of barking dogs, telling him the village was awake.

Breaking upon the village clearing he saw another sign of morning activity. From the big round house with the conical roof the smoke of many cooking fires seeped and hung oppressively over the hulking, windowless dwelling. Elka sped toward its single black opening, skirting around the entrails of a wild pig that lay in a heap, left by someone who had butchered the day before and now covered with flies and flesh-eating ants. His toughened bare feet did not feel the litter of broken pottery and cracked gourd bowls. He hardly noticed the village men sitting on their carved stools combing out their waist-long hair or binding it into queues or painting designs on their faces with red annatto-seed pulp and oil, and outlining them with soot. He ducked around two or three women scurrying across the clearing with pots of the cassava drink or bent over with firewood on their backs—too busy to be concerned with their appearance, except to tie on their aprons of tiny colored beads. One had pulled her hair back into a bun; the others let theirs hang loose and scraggly.

As Elka neared the big house, his eyes darted to the birth hut at the edge of the clearing. He could make out shadowy figures under the shelter, but not what they were doing. Then a sudden cry told him that he might yet be in time.

"*Achi*, Big Sister!" Elka shouted in panic. An older woman stuck her head through the doorway and the boy dropped the fish before her startled gaze and raced toward the hut.

That cry! The baby had come. Was that his stepfather bending over the tiny form on the ground? Was he about to strike or had he already struck; was he even now looking at his handiwork? How Elka wished he could have hurried faster on the river!

The cry came again—*there had been no blow*. If only the baby kept on crying . . .

Elka pulled up short at the hut, his eyes searching the scene under the leafy roof. He saw his mother, still trembling from her ordeal, and grasping the rail on which she had pulled desperately in giving birth. Supporting her was the old village granny. He saw a few paces from them a small girl, his sister, and next to her Tumika, who leaned slightly forward and appeared almost enraptured by an object at his mother's feet. Elka followed his gaze, and there before his mother lay a pinkish boy kicking and wailing on the red-stained leaves of a banana tree.

Elka had his brother!

It was a handsome boy, Elka could see, even through the bloody, wet mass that covered the infant. The sharp-toothed jaw of a wild pig lay on the ground close by, but no one had used it as yet to cut the umbilical cord. The baby had not been lifted up. Elka knew that it still lay under the threat of Tumika's murderous will.

He looked quickly at his mother, whose eyes were closed in pain, and at his sister, who stood motionless, peering straight at the baby. The old granny stared, muttering angrily, but made no move. Elka did not have to look at Tumika again to know that because of him they did not stir. He did not have to see that face to know the hatred in it.

"I will kill the old young thing," Tumika was muttering to no one in particular, working himself into a rage. "There are too many of us in the village now. People are talking. They say, 'Look at old Tumika. He is bearing like the Brazil nut tree.' Such talk is bad to my ears."

So Tumika did not care what people thought and said? This silent, sullen one did care, and he hated them for it.

Elka's mother opened her eyes and looked at Tumika. The girl, too, turned to watch as he raved. But Elka's eyes were only for his infant brother, his ears only for the baby's urgent cry. The scene before him—the helpless, wet baby—swam crazily in his tears. Once he had been thrown from a canoe into the rapids; he had fought the churning waters, not knowing whether he was near the surface or at the bottom of the river. He felt the same way now. *Why did they not lift up the baby?*

Who would protect the baby? He would—but a child did not lift up babies to save them. There was one thing, though, that he could do: He could protect his brother's body from the blow he knew was about to fall. With a spring as sudden and swift as his fish trap when the line snapped, Elka bounded past his ranting stepfather to the boy. He sank on his knees and laid his hands on the tiny face. Astonished at this boldness, Tumika broke off his mouthings. Elka touched his own naked breast to that pinkish skin. It was warm, so warm. Not like the clammy, cold body he had nestled the year before. Drawing back to look at his prize, he dropped a tear on the small chest.

The baby's cry stopped for an instant. In the brief stillness Elka smiled down at his brother, and as he did his mouth caught and tasted a tear. He looked up at his mother, his whole body shaking with sobs.

"Mother, I want my brother! I don't want him to die!" His eyes pleaded what he dared not say, *Can't I pick him up?*

Tumika still stood, half crouching, frozen by Elka's boldness. When he did move he took an angry stride toward the pair on the ground and bent low over them. He raised his arms, clenching his fists.

"You don't want him to die," he mimicked. Tumika's lips could hardly form the words that rolled from his throat. "Caress him! Caress him all you can! You will not have him for long. I'm going to kill the old young thing!" His voice rose to a scream with the last words.

The mad screeches carried across the village and seemed to hover like the morning smoke. A man taking his basket of feathers and paint to the big house to get it out of a coming rain threw it in the doorway and clutched his cheeks in shock. Women preparing cassava roots for bread dropped their graters and squinted toward the hut. In the birth house the old granny, still supporting the weary mother, waved a wrinkled fist.

"Don't you kill this child!" she shrieked.

Elka bent lower over the small form. If a blow came to kill, it would have to strike him first. From the corner of his eye he saw a man running into the hut. A woman followed, then another man, then—it seemed—all the people.

"Lift up your child," they commanded Tumika, almost in unison. "Lift him up!" Somehow they had lost their fear of him.

Tumika stood defiant. He looked at one, then another. Elka raised his head to look, too. Would they drop their eyes under his stepfather's gaze? Would they turn to leave one by one, as they had done last year, refusing to interfere? He waited an endless time for the answer.

But the sun did not rise a hand's breadth behind the passing rain cloud during the interval that it took Tumika to look into a dozen pairs of eyes set with fire, into a dozen faces determined that he should not kill.

It was Tumika who, in defeat, lowered his head.

He shot out a fist and with a fierce blow sent Elka sprawling. Hesitating a moment, again he swept his eyes over the silent faces and saw they had not softened. He reached down, picked up the baby, and shoved him at the granny. Then he strode to the edge of the hut and as he went spoke with contempt to Elka.

"If I had been there the day you were born, I would have killed you," he said. "You would not be a caressing one today."

A woman in the crowd picked up the sharp-toothed pig jaw and severed the baby's cord. Elka's sister took a slender piece of vine from her waistband and tied the stub. She took the baby from the granny for washing, then handed him back and helped her mother to her hammock. The mother clasped the baby to her breast.

Only two or three villagers remained in the hut. The others had filed after Tumika to talk about his meanness. Elka's mother said to the granny,

"We must pierce his ears and tie on his legbands."

To Elka she said,

"We'll call him Yakuta, after our dead uncle."

Elka, suddenly a child again, started to cry.

"Little Body," his mother continued, using the term of tenderest endearment for a child, "you have your brother now. He will be a fine boy—if the evil spirits don't spoil him."

2

Someday a Witchdoctor

Eight big-rain seasons had come and gone since Elka saved his brother's life. Despite great odds against any Wai Wai child's survival, Yakuta had lived. But Elka's mother had died a year later in giving birth to yet another baby, and Tumika fell ill and died not long after that. Elka, now an orphan, was sad when, some time after Tumika had died, an older half-brother, Chekema, came to carry him down Old Bead stream and a day's paddling up the Mapuera to a new and larger village called Kashimo, or Big Falls. He liked Chekema—a husky, precise, and exacting man, yet a happy one—but in the move to Big Falls he was taken from the places and people he knew, especially Yakuta, of whom he was very fond.

At Big Falls the time came for Elka to undergo the ordeal which, if passed, would make him strong and handsome as he grew into a man. Belts of stinging ants were to be tied to his legs. He knew the stings would hurt, but he dared not fail the test.

Chekema, who was headman of the village, supervised the ritual. First he wove two belts from reeds and tied them on his wrists. Then he and Elka went in search of a colony of stinging ants. They found one just off the path to the river, an ashen mound spewing out innumerable ants, brown and as long as a thumbnail, carrying vicious stingers in their tails. Chekema took one of the belts from his wrist and, stretching its scores of flexible holes, handed it to Elka.

"Pick them up by their heads," he said, "and stick their fat rumps into the holes." Elka filled each opening with a wriggling ant, careful not to let one sting him prematurely.

They came back to the village with both belts filled. A crowd had gathered in front of the house. Elka was beginning to be afraid; he had been stung before by the ants, but never by so many as this. What if he should cry in front of all those people? Some would laugh at him. Others would say, "He's just a boy—what can you expect?" And that would be just as bad. What if he tore off the belts, unable to bear the stings? If he did, how in the world could he go through life?

Chekema had stooped down and was beginning to tie the belts on Elka, just below his knees.

"Try to keep them on as long as you can," his brother said, not unkindly. Elka bit his lip against the coming ordeal. Stop laughing, he wanted to say to one snickering boy, for your time is coming.

A prickle struck the back of one leg. Instinctively Elka reached down to brush at it, then restrained himself. Soon came another prick, then another. The ants, unable to free their tails from the tightened bands, were stinging furiously in retaliation.

The stings were like arrow points scratching his skin, or like the fangs of a hundred tiny snakes. It was worse than walking through a field of razor grass. His legs began to twitch. He clenched his fists. Thorns were being driven into his flesh. He dug his nails into his palms, determined not to touch his legs!

At first he felt each sting. Soon both legs were burning. They were many stings—no, they were all one. Elka wanted to tear off the bands. Why hadn't he ground the ant nest under his heel when he had had the chance? He must run to the river to cool his burning flesh. He wouldn't, though. The people would laugh all the more and despise him for his cowardice. He would stand fast—for a while yet. Wasn't the magic of those tiny mites getting inside him? Wasn't the strength pouring into his body with each cruel sting? He stood stiffly, holding back the tears.

Did he not, by now, have strength enough to last a lifetime? He wanted to grow up strong, but not to pull trees out by their roots!

The hurt was spreading from his legs, going up and down his whole body. He felt it in the marrow of his bones. Maybe the ants had burrowed into his flesh, as fleas did into the soles of his feet, and were stinging him from the inside.

"Ohhhhh!" What was he doing? He was crying! He wasn't going to cry—but he did. The tears were spilling from his eyes and there was no holding them back. He still clenched his fists, but he could not control them. Savagely they beat at his swollen legs. He couldn't stand still. He began to dance. The villagers roared.

"Take them off!" he screamed at last.

Chekema did. As the older, wiser one stooped to remove the belts, Elka wondered if he had behaved himself so as to bring reward. He had cried, and now he was ashamed of himself.

"Oh, Little Body," his brother said, smiling broadly as he surveyed the puffy skin where the belts had been. "You can boast of many stings. They will make you a strong and desirable man."

This ordeal marked the end of Elka's boyhood. A few days later he became a man by an old but simple rite: Chekema wrapped strings of tiny white beads around his biceps. With his armbands he bore the badge of a youth who could take one of the young girls with growing breasts as his wife, one who could enter freely into the drunken frenzies of the tribal dances.

Growing up had been simple for Elka. Unlike a Wai Wai girl, who spent unending hours helping her mother, he had only to hunt and fish at his leisure, occasionally to help clear a patch of jungle for a new garden field, and to learn to weave a loincloth or hammock or to make palm-leaf shelters and baskets.

His early education had come from Fehwe, the old man at Big Rocks he called "Uncle," avoiding his personal name for fear the spirits would hear it and rain their punishment on one they now knew. The old man took the place of a father. From him Elka learned how to string and shoot a bow longer than himself and how to make the blows of his ax bite into the trunks of hardwood trees. The old man and the eager boy tramped over all the known hunting trails and often rediscovered forgotten ones. Together they studied droppings and half-eaten fruit on the ground to tell what kinds of birds or monkeys nested in the treetops far overhead. From him Elka learned to pick up the scent of the wild bush hogs and to tell whether they were the small breed that ran in pairs and hid in hollow logs, or the bigger and more vicious ones that traveled in packs of forty and fifty and could tear a man to shreds with their tusks.

His uncle taught him the jungle calls: the shrill whistle that lured the night-prowling tapir, the *ki ki ki* that called the big-billed toucan, the throaty *um um* that brought the bush turkey seeking a mate. Man and boy walked long distances to search out the favorite high-ridge spots of the spider monkeys, whose fat red stomachs were a delight to Elka's palate.

On the rivers—first on Old Bead and later on the Mapuera— Elka learned to trap *haimara,* the biggest of their fish, to shoot the sharp-toothed pirhanas, and to kill caiman alligators at night by lighting up their eyes with a firebrand. And with a hook that had come into the village by trade he mastered the art of catching fish that would not stay still long enough for shooting.

At Big Rocks Elka often took his young brother Yakuta with him into the forest. At Big Falls, on the Mapuera, he found a friend in Mawasha, the son of Chekema. This boy was quiet and reflective. Though younger than Elka, he was taller by nearly a head. Together they explored new fishing spots and hunting trails. Sometimes an even younger friend went along, a quick-witted boy named Kirifaka.

As a man Elka now pulled up his stool to sit with the others when they preened and painted themselves every morning. He may not yet have looked much of a man—he was small-chested, his arms and legs were like bamboo, his stomach awkwardly big. A man's ornamentation, though, helped hide these deficiencies of early youth. He pulled out his eyebrows and cut off his lashes. He tied feathers on his loincloth and stuck brilliant plumes in his armbands. His black hair he bound into a queue and stuck into a bamboo tube. As the locks grew longer the tube would become shorter until, someday, he could throw it away and proudly tie feathers on the end of a waist-long pigtail. The final touch was the painting of his own red-and-black design on his cheeks, nose, and forehead. Dark body-paint he merely smeared on by wiping his fingers across his chest and stomach when he had finished.

At field-cutting time Elka went with the other men. They would cut the slender trees half through their trunks, then a man skilled with the ax would fell a large tree, key to the whole cutting scheme. Elka would have to run. As the big tree toppled, it took all the half-cut trees down in its broad swath. Its fall was so great that the ground quaked and the echo rumbled in all directions.

Felling trees was good excitement; so was the burning after they had dried for a season. In one tremendous whoosh the flames leaped as high as a lofty *kechekere*, the tallest tree in the sur-rounding forest. When the dense smoke hid the sun, Elka was overcome with awe. What power of destruction!

One day Elka sat with a work party on a high bluff near Big Falls, overlooking the Mapuera. They were watching the fire devour what once had been majestic trees. Someone remarked,

"Witchdoctors can be like a burning field."

Whatever in the world does he mean? Elka asked himself. He pondered it, and soon he thought he understood.

The fire before him was awesome, but it was good. It was help-ing to clear a field so his people could plant cassava and yams and bananas. Witchdoctors were awesome, too, and they could be good; they could blow their breath to cure the sick. Sometimes fire burned the dry thatch of Wai Wai houses or the flesh of a child who got too close. Witchdoctors, like fire, could also be destruc-tive.

Elka tried not to think of this. But he could not help thinking about it—all about witchcraft, the good and the bad. The thoughts burned in his mind, as the great fire had burned in the field.

He had been irresistibly drawn toward that awesome calling since the day, several years ago, when a celebrated sorcerer had come to his boyhood home of Big Rocks to treat his ailing step-father. Elka was perhaps nine or ten, and had his own basket of feathers and paint to imitate a man's decorating. Putting away his basket one morning he heard Tumika groan in his hammock.

"Are you hot, Father?" Elka asked.

Tumika was. His head, he complained, was about to break open from hurt.

Elka was frightened by the wild look in the man's bloodshot eyes. Tumika began to spit blood. The villagers, summoned by the boy, started whispering in shocked tones,

"The father of the killed one is about to die."

"We must send for Mafolio," the village headman said duti-fully. "Only a witchdoctor with many charms can save him."

If anyone could save Tumika, Mafolio could. He lived at Big Falls on the Mapuera and was the greatest witchdoctor in their land. They were uncertain about his origin and about how he had become a witchdoctor. Some said he wasn't a Wai Wai; this only added to his mysterious character. He was so old that none could recall his ever being young.

They feared him because he was so close to the spirit world. But they liked him, too, and he liked them. He limited his prac-

tice to deeds of helpfulness. He traveled up and down the big
rivers and small streams. People constantly called him to come
heal their sick.

Mafolio had not been up Old Bead in Elka's memory. The
young lad was anxious to see him. But the dawns came and went,
and Tumika grew worse before a runner could locate the sorcerer
and call him to Big Rocks. The day he arrived, Elka was lying
idly in his hammock. Mafolio's approach was announced by the
knocking of paddles against the sides of his canoe. Elka's heart
pounded like the canoe paddles; his excitement was almost more
than he could bear.

"He's coming!" sang out one who heard the knocking.

"Take the children to the field," shouted another.

Yakuta and two or three other toddlers were rounded up and
hustled off. They must not see the witchdoctor; the code of witchcraft warned that if they did they might fall fatally ill. On other
occasions when a witchdoctor had come, Elka was among those
hidden away. It was doubtful whether he was yet old enough to
escape the toxic effect of the visit of a sorcerer in full regalia. But
in the excitement of Mafolio's coming, who was to think about
Elka? Left to follow his own wishes, he preferred to see this man
of renown and take his chances.

He wanted to spring from his hammock and race to the landing, but dared not lest someone see him and send him away. So
he lay still, hoping to remain forgotten.

Shouts were coming from the river. Mafolio must be nearing
the landing. Elka saw men put up the arrow points they had been
carving and women quickly bank the fires under their baking
plates.

"The one who blows good is arriving," someone said. They
hastened out of the house and went quickly toward the river. If
the chief of a distant village had come for a dance, they could
not have been more eager to greet him.

Only Elka and his sick stepfather, forgotten also for the moment, remained in the house. Elka, looking over at Tumika, found him turned to the wall in torment. He jumped from his hammock and sprinted toward the river, keeping off the path and out of sight. As he ran he caught a fleeting glimpse through the trees of the oncoming canoe. Mafolio, he saw, was prowman. He was using a stick to pole the craft toward the landing.

Elka stopped short of where the villagers had gathered and hid behind a wide treetrunk. Peeking out, he saw that Mafolio had draped himself with chestbands made from animal skins. Calling greetings all the while, the old fellow speared his stick to the canoe floor and fished up a basket. This must be his basket of charms, thought Elka. To complete his costume, Mafolio set a feather crown on his head. He turned to one of his paddlers and told him to bring the hammock. Then he leaped from the canoe. Elka knew he was very old, yet he seemed as agile as a boy. With his long pole he vaulted up the bank and started off on a fast hobble along the path.

The trail passed near Elka's tree. The boy bent low, wedging himself in a network of roots, yet managing to keep open his line of sight. Mafolio stumped along toward him, spitting tobacco everywhere. Once, turning momentarily, he let out a loud and cackling laugh. His laugh was contagious; those following him may not have known what had amused him, but they laughed when he did. Elka's mouth, too, stretched into a wide grin.

The sorcerer reached the tree behind which Elka cowered. The old fellow spattered it generously with dark brown juice. His laugh then was even louder; he knew the boy was there.

Elka, however, lost his smile. For the first time he got a close look at Mafolio, and found him hideous. His deeply lined face was kindly and reassuring enough but his feet and arms and legs! Three toes were missing on one foot. He had a gruesome infection on the other foot. No wonder he hobbled! His arms and legs were covered with scaly white sores. How could a great man be so ugly? Yet this was the great Mafolio. In spite of the shock,

Elka was glad he had seen the witchdoctor and he wanted to see and hear more.

The procession passed into the village clearing. Elka left his hiding place and made his way stealthily to the shadow of the big house. Nearby stood a rack, head high, on which cassava cakes were placed to dry. Elka swung himself up onto this to see what would happen next.

Mafolio was all business. Elka watched him crisply direct the preparations for treating Tumika. A few men were sent into the forest to fetch a particular type of palm branch. Other men dug shallow holes in a circle about three long paces across. When the men brought back the palm, they split it into straight poles, which they dropped into the holes and brought together to be tied at the top. Finally, they attached palm leaves to this frame. Mafolio now had a *shurifana*, a witchdoctor's house, in which to work in private over his patient.

The sun had ridden to the middle of the sky. Old Mafolio parted the leaves of his doorless, windowless shelter and entered to work his charms. Elka's stepfather, carried from the big house none too tenderly, was handed through the same opening. The leaves were then put back in place. What went on inside was strictly between the witchdoctor, his patient, and the spirits.

With the sorcerer out of sight, Elka felt the danger of banishment was past. He had seen his elders go back to their hammocks or resume their jobs around the house. He knew they would talk about spirits and charms, and he was curious. He jumped from his perch to go to his hammock where he could listen to the words of Kurum, a sickly, browbeaten old fellow, and his wife, Tochi, who was not so old, but whose tongue was sharp and contradictory. If anybody were going to talk over a subject, they would.

Elka was right. Kurum and Tochi soon started talking about Mafolio's visit. Kurum began by venturing that it was good to have brought the great man to blow on Tumika before it was too late.

"I say, let the spiteful one die," Tochi spat. "He doesn't o̶ any charms."

"The one in the *shurifana* will blow hard," said Elka's old uncle, Fehwe, across the house. "He is really stuck fast to Kworokyam."

All nodded.

Kworokyam was the center of Wai Wai spirit life. Not a person, not a legendary hero, not an individual spirit in the sense that each animal had its individual spirit, Kworokyam was all the spirits of the Wai Wai world wrapped into one all-powerful supernatural being. At mention of his name Elka felt a sudden chill, a stabbing fear in the pit of his stomach. He wished he had not been so eager to eavesdrop.

Kworokyam could be bad or good. He caused sickness, yet he was the one whom a witchdoctor entreated for a cure. Elka knew that he was mostly bad. In this world where every animal, every insect, every rock or tree had a spirit to be reckoned with, the greater number of spirits, by far, were evil. So by the sheer balance of the spirits that composed him, Kworokyam was mostly evil. To induce him to show his good side was a difficult task, reserved for the sorcerers he had chosen to be his servants.

Being a spirit—or was it spirits?—Kworokyam had no body of his own. Sometimes he showed himself in the massive constricting coils of an anaconda, sometimes in the body of a man. At times he lived at the bottom of the river. Nearly always he walked the jungle trails at night. The fluttery whoosh of a vampire bat—that was Kworokyam racing to get somewhere. The thunderous roar of the howler monkeys, the crackling of a tree falling after a rain, the skip-skip of fish breaking the river's surface, the drip-drip-drip from dew or droppings—these all told of Kworokyam's presence. Man had better beware!

Man had a spirit, too. But it had no relation to Kworokyam unless the man was a witchdoctor. Then, on occasion, Kworokyam and the witchdoctor joined to become a single being, whether for good or for evil.

Elka was pleased that Mafolio would use his influence with Kworokyam to plead for Tumika. He wasn't particularly anxious for his stepfather to enjoy good health, but every time death visited their tiny clearing in the forest, that mysterious being could return again and again to plague them all. It was comforting to know that Mafolio would go to great lengths even for a man so despised. For this, Elka took pride in his new hero.

"Maybe he is now putting the smooth little stones of his spiritual pets into his mouth," suggested old Uncle Fehwe. "Maybe he is rolling his tobacco so he can blow its smoke on the sick chest of the angry one."

"I could not help the father of the killed one," Kurum confessed, yet taking a cautious pride in the fact that he had made the attempt. "I scratched his back with many scratches and rubbed in hot peppers. And I fastened belts of stinging ants on his head to make him forget the hurt, but he still kept on being hot."

"Maybe my old husband thinks he is one who can treat diseases?" bristled Tochi. Her bitterness came quite naturally. The only one of her mother's six children saved at birth, she had been picked up not by the child-hating mother but by her grandmother. Her life had been wretched, and none knew it better than her husband. Even to young Elka it was evident that Kurum might well leave the talk to others.

They eventually fell silent, and then Elka had an idea: If he listened while Mafolio worked his charms, might he not learn the songs that were a part of witchcraft? He slipped from his hammock and moved furtively from the house to the shadowy side of the *shurifana*. From inside the sorcerer's house came an incantation:

> Come, little water dog, come, come,
> Spirit of the otter, come—
> Ah yai, ah yai, ah yai,
> Come and take away my brother's hurt!

Elka sat listening to this eerie verse, then to a second song, then to another and another. Such songs he had never heard! One was to the bush chicken, another to the bush hog, still another to the loathsome anaconda. He put his ear to the leaf wall and heard the groans that came from his stepfather and the *koosh koosh* that told that Mafolio was blowing smoke from the stones onto Tumika's arms, legs, head, and body. And he heard a rapid *pt-pt-pt-pt*. Mafolio was dry-spitting over the spot where Tumika hurt most.

The old witchdoctor was going to work through the night. Enthralled, Elka sat until the sun had gone down behind the trees of the forest. He would have stayed longer, drinking in the intoxicating ritual, but a villager bringing the children back from the field caught sight of him and hustled him off to his hammock. But it did not matter. By then Elka had heard enough to fire his imagination until long after quiet finally came to the communal house.

He awoke with the dawn. Tumika was back in the big house, sleeping fitfully and apparently no better. Mafolio was up and making ready to leave. The old sorcerer was tired. Still, he must go—the demands on a witchdoctor, particularly on one of his skill, were great.

Mafolio refused the payment of cotton fibers offered by the village headman. This was indeed a bad omen, for a witchdoctor was paid not so much for services rendered but to use his influence to ward off future sickness. Taking no pay now meant that he thought Tumika was doomed. It would not be worth his effort to intercede further.

All that day Elka sang the songs he had heard through the leafy walls of the *shurifana*. He sang to the hummingbird, to the stingless bee, and to the bush hog—especially to the bush hog. These wild pigs were his favorites. Bathing in the river before sunup, while the air was still chilly and the water warm, he sang. The sun rode high; he hunted turtle eggs in the warm sand, and sang. Late in the day he went into the cane patch to cut shafts for new arrows, still singing. The smooth stiff cane grew too high and thick for him to see old Kurum in the patch, but Kurum heard him.

Knocking over cane to get to him, Kurum accosted him bluntly.

"Whatever in the world are you singing?"

Elka was startled. Knowing nothing else to say, he replied with boyish frankness,

"I'm singing the songs of the spirits, the songs of Kworokyam. I got ears for them as I sat outside the *shurifana*."

Was there anything wrong with that?

Kurum covered his eyes with a scarred arm.

"*Kofi*, oh, how scary!" he said with a shudder.

Then he lowered his arm just a bit to look at the puzzled boy. Innocently Elka wondered what he had said to bring such terror into the old man's beady eyes.

"You must not sing those songs, Little Body!" Kurum whispered urgently. His breath came hard and his voice was unsteady. "Kworokyam will say to you, 'You sing songs like a witchdoctor, but you are not a witchdoctor so I will kill you.'"

He turned hurriedly to go, lest this evil of all evils catch him talking with the presumptuous young singer.

Elka stopped singing the spirit songs aloud. But he hummed and whistled them when alone. And almost all the time, day or night, he continued to sing them inside his head. He could not wipe from his mind the magic chants that Mafolio had unknowingly planted there.

From that time on, Elka was careful to listen to every scrap of talk about spirits and witchdoctors. People often spoke of such things in the big house at night when they thought younger ears were closed by sleep. Elka, wide awake, would lie motionless in his hammock and take it in.

Elka kept on listening and learning about witchcraft after

moving to Big Falls on the Mapuera. There he lived under the same roof with Mafolio and could watch the venerable witchdoctor every day—and every night could peek out at him through the loose mesh of his hammock.

"That Mafolio's a good one," a woman said one night in the house on the Mapuera. Mafolio's fame was even greater up and down this river than on Old Bead. "He's a strong one," she continued. "He woke up my old grandmother when we took her for dead."

"Hnnnn, that's right," another nodded. "And for our keeping well he tells us where to walk and not to walk, and when he blows on our hooks the fish bite with good appetite."

A third thought along other lines:

"You know, if he chooses he can send his spirit away into his pets and bring hurt to those he doesn't like."

"Mafolio likes us all," someone else spoke up quickly. "He's a smiling one."

"But we can't say this of Muyuwa," another asserted.

No, they could not say much of anything good about that other witchdoctor, the crafty old devil who lived on the other side of the high mountains, beyond the place where the rivers were born. Elka knew by reputation this feared and despised Muyuwa. He had heard returning travelers say that Muyuwa had no cackling laugh like Mafolio's. He was no smiling one. Lustful, he walked around at night seeking women. He talked evilly about others and took food from those he disliked. Elka had heard again and again that Muyuwa, chief of all the Wai Wai on the other side of the high mountains and sorcerer without equal there, sent his spirit away into his pet, the jaguar, that vicious jungle cat, and caused him to attack and kill people.

Elka began to find that sleep could no longer give him rest from the world of spirits. Dreams were becoming a disturbing part of his world.

One night Elka lay in his hammock and listened as the howler monkeys roared one after another. He had no fear of the animals themselves, but their spirits made him crouch low in his bed. After the last howler fell silent the rain came. Distant and muffled it started, then advanced slowly but steadily through the broad-leafed jungle. Finally it poured down on the village clearing, striking the thatched roof with a tumult that filled Elka's ears. The rain came down for a long time, and Elka thought—but he wasn't sure—that sleep came only as the storm moved on.

And when he did sleep, it was fitfully. Once, not quite knowing whether he was awake or asleep, he felt a tug on his hammock and heard the snorting of a pig.

"Hee hai yoko," he heard the pig say.

What were those words? He tried desperately to bring up their meaning from his mind. But the more he strained, the stranger they seemed. And then it suddenly seemed odd that he should have tried. Why should he be expected to know the language of wild pigs? This was comforting—to know that their talk was no concern of his. He sank deep into a delicious suspension of thought.

Then, as if he were snatched again from the pleasant submersion, he felt a rushing in front of his face. He tried to lift his arm to brush away an object, a hairy thing with no definable shape. Lifting his arm was a great effort, for it felt heavy and was difficult to move. But he had to brush away that hairy form. When he was able to raise his arm at last, the object was gone.

The rain had passed. The light of the full moon now shone in his eyes. He shielded them with his upraised arm. Peering out just a bit, he found it hard to focus in such brilliance. Gradually he made out, against the moon, the pig that had pulled at his hammock and snorted the strange words. It was a huge one, with stiff bristles. Tusks showed under its snout. Elka thought its face was vaguely pleasant. The pig smiled wryly, as if to coax a bit. And then, all of a sudden, the pig was not alone. Assembled beside it were a hummingbird—a tiny iridescent thing—a giant anaconda, and an armadillo. Elka wanted to run away; his legs would not move. The pig motioned him to listen. He could do nothing else.

"Sing the songs of Kworokyam," the pig said in a tone of command.

The others joined in chorus:

"We will teach you, Little Body."

"No! No!" Elka tried to say. The words stuck in his throat. Only a groan came through his lips, and it was enough to wake him. He uttered a cry of fear.

That cry brought him back, back from another but very real world. He sat up. He looked at the familiar fires and sleeping bodies around him. Still the fear of his dream lingered. Who was that talking in the sky?

He was afraid to sleep again, and waited out the night feeling alone and shaky. With the coming of dawn he went to Mafolio and told him his dream.

"I heard him speak, but his throat never moved," Elka said in amazement. "Who was it that talked in the pig, Grandfather?"

"That was Kworokyam," replied Mafolio, much surprised to hear the boy's recital. He knew Elka as one of the boys of the tribe, but who would pick him out as one to be reached by Kworokyam?

"Kworokyam reveals himself to whom he wills and in the way he wants," he explained to the wide-eyed lad. "To you, Little Body, he is in the wild pig."

Old Kurum had known that Elka was a singer of the spirit songs; now Mafolio knew that Kworokyam had talked to him. One other person was to recognize the fate of this most unusual boy. A few days after his dream he happened to meet the village granny down at the river landing. She had just filled a gourd with water, and now set it on a rock. Pointing a stubby, crooked finger at Elka, she said accusingly:

"You are one who sings the spirit songs within you. Never mind how I know. I know."

Elka averted his eyes from the penetrating gaze of the old crone, who was something of a sorcerer herself. He chose to look at his flea-bitten feet.

"Little Body," she said, leaning to his ear and spitting words into it in a husky, cautious whisper, "someday you will be finding yourself a——a witchdoctor!"

She covered her toothless mouth in horror at her words. They had been shot like an arrow. Now they could not be called back.

The earth spun dizzily around Elka. Maybe he fainted. Maybe he fell into the water and it brought sense back into his head. He only knew that the old granny was shuffling up the path to the village with her water gourd, and he was left alone with her prophecy.

He a witchdoctor, a slave of Kworokyam? Would he be like Mafolio? The thought cheered him. Or would Kworokyam fashion him like Muyuwa? He tried not to think about that. But Elka was a thinker.

Why, asked those who lived around him and knew only a smattering of what went on in his head, why couldn't this boy be an ordinary boy? . . . Why couldn't he? Elka would ask himself. Why did he have to be one to bear the burdens of life, to turn them inside out, to look for answers when there were no answers, to pursue a worrisome quest that never ended? For a long time, before and since coming into his armbands, he had been asking himself these things.

Why was he so concerned with witchcraft?

Only a rare one became a witchdoctor, a real witchdoctor who controlled the spirits and who was, in turn, controlled by them. The life of a witchdoctor was mysterious. It was a life to dread: cruel demands to sacrifice self, wearisome journeys, long days and nights of blowing, being feared and sometimes hated, becoming the slave of a world of spirits.

If it were a matter of winning admiration, he could strive to be the best shot with the bow. Or he could become a leader in the dances. Or he could hope to become headman of a village. He did not have to rely on sorcery.

How terrible to be a witchdoctor, even a good one—to say nothing of the chance of becoming a sorcerer through whom the worst of Kworokyam could be channeled to his people! Busy as he tried to be, the thoughts would come. And the dreams. And the granny's prophecy: "Someday you will be finding yourself a witchdoctor."

Good witchdoctors and bad, blowing to cure and to kill—these were tremendous forces buffeting Elka, giving shape to his future. From that time on, in his thoughts witchcraft, good or bad, would surely be imposed on the changeless patterns of jungle life. Yet his vision went only as far as the tall trees of his forest.

Beyond, unseen, was something more.

3

White Killers Coming

While Elka dreamed of pigs controlled by evil spirits, hundreds of miles away three brothers with another vision were planning a move that would bring them face to face with the Wai Wai. It was 1948; outside the jungle the mammoth tribes of civilization had put away their instruments of war. The brothers saw that ahead lay a battle of another kind—invasion of the Devil's territory its object, the Bible its weapon.

The Hawkins brothers—Neill, 33, Rader, 30, and Bob, 26—each tall, angular, with kindled eyes and compassionate heart, had the background for such a venture. They had grown up in a Texas home in which Father was a hard-hitting champion of the old-time religion of sin and salvation and Mother dedicated her talents to training her sons for foreign missionary service. All three joined Unevangelized Fields Mission to serve Christ among people not yet reached by the Gospel. Neill and Rader, with their families, had spent ten years between them evangelizing the semicivilized Macusi Indians along Brazil's Rio Branco. They had seen their labor bear fruit, and Neill decided that with this experience they should go to the Wai Wai. Little was known about the tribe except that their villages straddled the Guiana-

Brazil border deep in impenetrable jungle and that an occasional explorer had noted they were "a filthy people with many dogs."

Leaving Rader among the Macusi to come on later, Neill journeyed across the savannas—the vast grassy plains of British Guiana—to Georgetown, the coastal capital. There he met Bob, fresh from college and seminary in the States.

They found everything, or nearly everything, right for going inland. A small savanna had been spotted from the air near the tribe's villages along the upper Essequibo River. With work this open space could be made into an airfield. It had recently become possible to charter a plane to the interior, and arrangements could be made to maintain a supply line of 360 air miles from Georgetown to the Wai Wai area. The two-hour flight would be vastly simpler than the water route, with its rapids and tree-strewn reaches which required three weeks to navigate.

But colonial officials were not so convinced as the Texas brothers that the Wai Wai needed Christianity. One commissioner in particular, a tall English civil servant, opposed the Hawkinses' plan. He had been in colonial service elsewhere and did not enjoy his transfer to the sticky, unsophisticated north coast of South America. These Americans pestering him for a travel permit to the interior certainly were not helping him accept the assignment with grace.

"My predecessor visited the Wai Wai and found them a happy, innocent people," he said in the clipped speech of finality during an interview. "I will not allow you to go in and upset their drinking and dances."

Neill had done most of the talking for the brothers. Now soft-voiced, deliberate Bob spoke up.

"We've come to be witnesses for Christ, sir, not to tear down customs," he said.

"But when they become Christians they'll change," the commissioner commented concisely and coldly, convinced that he was right.

He *was* right. Of course he was right. The brothers could not disagree, any more than they could deny that wherever Christian belief had penetrated the world it had changed the world. But despite his repeated refusals the brothers persisted. Eventually they discovered that the commissioner's stand had no legal ground. The law permitted ministers of the Gospel to go anywhere in the colony. Still he refused to grant a permit. But by January 1949 the commissioner had left for a less exasperating post, and Neill and Bob, written permission in hand, were paddling up the Essequibo en route to a three-month stay among the Wai Wai.

They knew nothing of the alarm their impending visit had raised months earlier, on both the Essequibo of Guiana and the Mapuera of Brazil. When Neill had stopped on the savannas between his Macusi post and Georgetown, he made inquiries about the Wai Wai. He had said he and his brothers wanted to visit the tribe. That caused word to be passed through the jungle that white men were coming. By the time the grapevine had sped the message to Muyuwa's village, "white men" had become "white killers."

It was Mapari, the blood brother of Elka's mother, who first brought the ominous word to Big Falls on the Mapuera. Never having seen the man before, Elka did not know it was his uncle who tied his canoe at the village landing one day. He knew only that he was a stranger from over the mountains and that he was old and looked mean. One eye was fogged over. In his effort to see with the other eye, he wrinkled his nose and made an ugly face. Elka decided he did not like him.

Mapari walked the path to the village and quenched his thirst with a bowl of cassava drink in the communal house; by this time most of the villagers had gathered. Several times he hinted he bore momentous news, which he would get around to telling eventually; but his trip, he explained, was first and foremost one of duty.

"I come to claim the son of my dead sister."

Elka poked his friend Mawasha and whispered that he was glad he did not live with the old fellow. Mawasha laughed oddly and said to Elka,

"He's *your* uncle."

Elka felt as if an electric eel had touched him. *His* uncle! Then *he* was the one the man had come to claim, to take over the high mountains to the village where the evil Muyuwa was witchdoctor. He wouldn't go, he said to Mawasha. He would run far into the forest, "where you will never find me."

But darkness was setting in; Elka realized this was no time to enter the forest where he might meet hovering spirits. He would run away tomorrow. Tonight he would sit at his uncle's fire, and without liking the man a whit more he would listen with the rest of the villagers to news from the other side.

The old fellow had news, all right, but he seemed in no hurry to get to it. So long as he kept it to himself, he was the center of attention. During the evening meal, as Elka dipped his cassava bread into the broth pot with the others, Mapari spoke first of everything else. Elka was impatient. What if the news concerned Muyuwa? Had someone eaten his spirit? In that case perhaps he *would* go.

After supper Mapari sat before the fire, enjoying the anxious suspense of his audience. Methodically he unwound the cord from his queue and began combing out his long, glistening hair.

"People are coming," he finally said.

The listeners strained expectantly. He lapsed into silence. What people? wondered Elka. Why didn't he tell them?

His uncle rewound his queue. Elka eyed him as he scooped up oil from a cooking pot and slicked down his bangs and sprinkled them with white down. Only after he had put his paint and feathers away with deliberate care did he tell more.

"Ones with white skins."

He stopped to let that sink in.

"These white ones are bad men. They come to kill the Wai Wai."

It was out. The visitor had told his news. Those who had strained to listen broke their silence. They turned to each other and wailed. The house seemed to quiver with their excited shouts. The shriek of an old woman rose above the cacaphony.

"We'll all be dying ones!" She hopped around the floor lamenting their doom, then groveled in the dirt.

"Wherever can we run to?" a little boy sobbed, clutching his mother's knees.

Elka wanted to cry, too. He felt the coming of his uncle had given him double reason. True, he was in his armbands, a young man in his middle teens. Yet he felt small and helpless, just as he had felt years before at Big Rocks. In the forest there one day he had idly rubbed his itching foot on a tree root, and it turned out to be not a root but a deadly bushmaster. The serpent had reared its head and hissed at him. Elka had run back to the village to the safety of his old uncle, Fehwe, who seemed to know everything about the forest. Fehwe had returned with him and killed the snake.

His life had been spared then—but for what purpose? To face a life of misery under Muyuwa? Or to be destroyed swiftly by an invading white foe?

No sleep came to the village that night. A murky dawn finally crept upon them. Elka hid. But his uncle Mapari, who had lived many more years than he, seemed to know where a frightened young fellow would hide. Pledged to duty toward a dead sister, he flushed him out with dogs as he would the smaller breed of wild pig. He marched Elka from a thicket of thorny palms to his waiting canoe. He pointed to the prow, indicating that Elka was to travel there, serving as front guide for the treacherous upriver journey.

Shoving away from the rock landing, Elka said in an undertone,

"I don't want to live near Muyuwa."

He slapped his hand to his mouth. It was too late. He had already spoken. He looked around to see if he had been heard by the tale-bearing wren, the tiny bird that tattled on where the tapir was feeding and on people's comings and goings—and on their foolish statements.

"I'm scared of white killers," he said in a louder voice, hoping this would cover up his slip.

Elka's fear, though not his dislike, of Muyuwa was lessening. At least the cunning old devil was one of their own, and he could understand the black magic. He feared the white man more. Why didn't his uncle seem afraid? Why didn't he choose to run with the others over trails that only the Wai Wai knew and no outsider could ever follow?

Maybe the old man and Muyuwa had conceived a plan to kill the whites before they could kill the Wai Wai. His people had arrows that could slay a jaguar—why not a man with white skin? And the Wai Wai had other ways of killing. They knew how to kill and smile at the same time.

Years before, they had killed white rubber hunters that way. The story was well known to Elka.

Men had come into the forest seeking rubber. They brought knives and axes for trading. The Wai Wai looked on them as good ones, glad to have these foreigners living among them.

One day the rubber hunters stopped smiling. They refused to give out more knives. They took the Wai Wai women and mistreated them. After hurried counsel, the Wai Wai men climbed tall trees and brought down a vine. They beat it on a rock. They dipped it up and down in a large pot of palm-fruit drink. Ordinarily the milky liquid running from this vine was used in catching fish. This day, however, it was to have a new use.

"*Onhariheh!*" shouted the village headman.

The visitors answered his call to drink and eat and sat down with the Wai Wai. Smiling pleasantly, the headman dipped small bowls into a big pot and passed them to the rubber hunters. The Wai Wai, smiling and talking, drank from another pot. Nothing appeared unusual until the hunters, their bowls drained, slumped over glassy-eyed, as though stupidly drunk. The poison had paralyzed them.

The Wai Wai men grabbed their war clubs and bashed in the white men's heads.

Worried friends came looking for the men. They neither looked nor worried long, Elka had been told. They, too, were served palm drink spiced with poison. More heads were broken open. After that, no more white men came.

As the dugout with man and youth breasted the swift-running stream, carrying Elka to his uncle's home in a new land, Elka had to paddle too hard and fight too many rapids to think much about what lay ahead. But at night, when they camped, he wondered about the world he had known and the strange world of white men. In the stillness the *kok kok* of an old tree frog told him that there would be conflicts between the two worlds.

4

A Trap for Every Man

Elka and his uncle went as far as the dwindling river could take them. They tied their canoe to a sapling, placed their few belongings in quickly woven baskets, shouldered a meager food supply, and struck out on the path that led over the high mountains. This trail would take them up past the Mapuera headwaters and on to the feeder streams of the Essequibo.

Elka had moved from village to village before. But this move, requiring a full cycle of the moon to complete, proved a turning point in his life.

They were heading for the village of Erefoimo, or Old Baking Plate. Its one main house and scattered outbuildings sat on a jungle-clad hill a short way down the Essequibo from Deep Eddy —Mawika in Wai Wai language—the home of the terrible Muyuwa. Elka was sad and afraid. He feared both the wicked Muyuwa and the coming of the white men. He was unhappy over leaving his home on the Mapuera and his friends and favorite forest spots. He had lesser anxieties, but gnawing ones, about what he would find on the other side. The same sun would ride in the sky, he was sure, but where would it rise and set? What were the rivers like? If they did not flow into his Mapuera, where could they possibly go?

The mountains were a divider for Elka as well as for the cold streams. His old life lay on one side; it had been a happy life for the most part. On the other side lay a new one; who knew what its hazards might be? Elka sighed. Trading the known for the unknown was never easy.

The trail was rugged and uncertain. The burden of keeping on it fell to Elka, for old Mapari, having only one good eye, found it hard to pick his way. Although the trail was new for Elka, he felt at home in any part of the forest. Together the two scrambled over rocks and moss-covered fallen trees, slogged through muck, waded waist-deep across mountain streams, climbed up and slid down shadowy, vine-strewn hills—sensing rather than seeing the way. As they moved ahead slowly and almost painfully, Elka grew to like—just a little—this man whom he had first despised.

At the end of the trail was a canoe, the one Mapari had used on his trip over. In it they paddled down the river, which Elka found to be quite like the Mapuera. As they rounded a bend, a high bank loomed before them.

"The path to Muyuwa's village starts there," his uncle told him. "But we must get on to my village before the darkness falls."

Elka had not wanted to stop where Muyuwa lived, for he dreaded meeting the wicked witchdoctor. His uncle had known he did not want to stop. Elka sensed that he knew and liked him the more for it.

Safely past, Elka spoke.

"Let's stop paddling and drift. If darkness catches us we can enter your village at night."

"Hnnnn," replied the old man in the nasal hum the Wai Wai used when musing. "Why do you want to do that?"

"If we enter at night," Elka explained, "we can mingle with the people there and maybe the spirits won't notice that I've arrived."

To this his uncle said no. So they halted just long enough to put fresh paint on their faces. Moving on, they shouted and struck the sides of their canoe at the end of each paddle stroke to warn the villagers of their coming.

Sometimes such warnings brought people to the landing; at other times the villagers would hear the knocking and, feeling safe because enemies did not make noise, they would not bother to get out of their hammocks. No one came to greet Elka and his uncle. Mapari left the youth to secure the canoe and started up the forested hill toward the village. Elka followed as soon as he could. When he reached the clearing at the top and looked across in the dusk, he saw that Old Baking Plate was much like other villages he had known. Its communal house, however, was older and larger than the one at Big Falls. One side sagged; it seemed dangerously near collapse. Going inside, he saw more family fires than his former houses had contained, and many more hammocks. Finding an empty spot beside a fire, he tied his own hammock between posts. He sat down in it and looked around.

As his eyes grew accustomed to the dimness he was able to recognize some of those who gathered around their evening cooking fires. They were people who had moved from Big Rocks shortly after Elka had been taken to live at Big Falls. In fact, most of them had stopped at Big Falls to break their journey. Elka remembered how he had pitied them because they were headed for the land ruled by Muyuwa. They did not look now as if they were any the worse for their move. There was Fehwe, Elka's old teacher of jungle ways; he was the village headman here. There were Kurum and Tochi, the quarrelsome pair, and their two daughters: Ahmuri, who had been Elka's playmate as a child, and a younger girl. Old weather-beaten Kurum still bent with whatever wind blew—mostly the biting breath of his wife. Elka could hear Tochi's scolding voice now.

Ahmuri, the girl Elka had played with at Big Rocks, could rival her mother's sharp tongue, he knew, but she could be sweet, too. Now perhaps thirteen, she had grown very attractive. He looked across the messy floor to where Ahmuri toyed with her cooking fire. Her eyes reflected the dancing firelight. Her breasts were large and rounded. She stood up; Elka could see that her middle was, too.

"She carries your Uncle Mapari's child," a villager explained.

"Is she his wife?" Elka asked.

"Um-hum," came the reply. "But from the way they act around her the young men don't seem to know it."

It was not that Ahmuri was any more abandoned in her conduct than others. Though there was a sense of proprietorship in marriage, it was customary for both men and women to trade or "loan out" marriage partners and for all to take part in occasional sex orgies.

Ahmuri now bent over her fire, blowing needlessly on it. Her gaze was not at the fire; she was looking over it at Elka. Their eyes met. She flashed him a smile of recognition, then quickly turned in search of more fuel.

Elka felt comfortable inside. Her eyes had kindled more warmth in him than any fire had done.

On his first morning at Old Baking Plate, Elka entered the communal workhouse, a small round building without sides, to do his painting and preening. Some villagers were already there, weaving cotton cloth or squeezing sugar cane in a hand press. Shyly Elka would glance at one or another until they looked back at him. Then he would quickly shift his eyes to the palm-leaf shelters built for dressing out wild pigs or to the drying racks for cassava bread standing here and there in the clearing. He stared for some time at a handsome young man who sat on a stool carving arrow points.

Yukuma, perhaps a few years older than Elka, was his cousin, the son of Mapari. On Elka's arrival he had said hardly a word, but this morning he seemed more friendly. Presently he offered to take Elka hunting.

"If you can keep up with me," he added. "I'm pretty fast on the trail. And my arrows get most of the birds."

Elka thought Yukuma was a bit haughty.

On their first hunt Yukuma tumbled two brown monkeys and a toucan from the tops of the trees. Another time Elka did well, but Yukuma's kill was more impressive. Elka envied Yukuma for more than his hunting prowess. His cousin's smile brought answering smiles to the faces of Ahmuri and her young sister. His arms were big, bursting with strength, and there was a look of manliness about him. Elka still looked more boy than man. The stinging ants had made him stronger, but so far they had done little to make him attractive. A front tooth had rotted away, giving him an awkward grin. Smiling or not, he sometimes felt like a gangling frog. But his faith in the ants remained unshaken. Some day Ahmuri would pay attention to him and think of him as more than just the little boy with whom she had played.

Elka began to enjoy his new life at Old Baking Plate. He discovered the favorite feeding places of wild pigs. Frequently he went behind the village to a grove of *ite* palms. There he could sometimes kill as many pigs as he had arrows. In the river he discovered new rapids for shooting fish, and backwaters for trapping the giant *haimara*. Up and down this stream he paddled, finding the watering holes of tapirs, and sometimes the nests of giant anacondas.

Though he often hunted with Yukuma and was thrown with him in other ways, he was not fond of him. He missed his friend Mawasha. But soon he had a companion again in his younger brother, Yakuta. The boy was brought to this side of the mountains by their sister and her husband not long after Elka's own arrival.

Elka did not hunt and fish every day. After he had cut trees in the forest for a garden plot and had repaired his canoe or restrung his bow, and carved new arrow points, what was there for him to do? The women cut the firewood and harvested, carried water up the steep path from the river and prepared the meals. The day might stretch ahead for Elka, as for other men, offering nothing more urgent than to eat a huge piece of cassava bread softened in a bowl of peppered fish broth, and then to climb back into his hammock. When he tired of lolling, he might sit on his carved stool, perhaps roll some silk grass on his thigh to make twine for a hammock, and gossip with his neighbors.

He found the villagers at Baking Plate obsessed in their talk with one subject: the coming of white killers. Some of the men declared that they would fight. Others accepted their obvious destiny with resignation. Still others had their minds set on trading for precious tiny glass beads; they would get as many as they could before dying.

The moon passed through its cycle again and again. The *tali-tali* locust sang the song that gave it its name, and soon the dry season was at hand. Still the dreaded visitors did not come. Some guessed that they might never come, and Elka let himself half believe this. Gradually hammock talk shifted to other, less catastrophic topics.

No day went by without gossip about an absent member of the group.

"The one who went upstream to see his old mother-in-law stole my arrows." "He stole my wife while I was sick and couldn't leave my hammock."

Maybe so, maybe not; Elka knew that truth was no requirement for talk. For this reason he hesitated to be away from the others, for he knew that then he would be the one they talked about. And it was mostly bad talk.

A Wai Wai always smiled to the face—except a man to his wife. He could berate her without mercy or ignore her. But if he wanted help in cutting his field or wished to avoid the danger of a curse, he had to be on good terms with others in the village.

Communal living afforded the comfort of numbers. Elka lived in a constant confusion caused by the incessant chatter of people, blowing of pipes and horns, and barking of dogs. Yet this noise was at least his hedge against the world of spirits, a world at its worst when all was frighteningly silent.

Closeness of living together, however, led to cheating. Food was common property; if the catch of fish was small, Elka, like others, might eat it on the river. That way he would not have to share it back at the house. Sometimes the cheating was found out and built up in the endless gossip until someone used witchcraft to punish the offender.

Elka was particularly interested in the sorcerer's role in witchcraft. Ordinary folk, though not possessed with Kworokyam, could manipulate the spirits to some degree. Anyone could cast a spell by blowing his breath on the belongings of one he did not like, felling that person with a serious illness. And anyone could eat another's spirit by hanging up such a belonging in a prickly palm tree, causing its owner to die. However, one hesitated to eat a spirit because of *farawa,* the dread ceremony of revenge. By magic it killed the one who had killed.

Elka remembered hearing how Mafolio's boy had died on the Mapuera by having his spirit eaten. For once the kindly old sorcerer broke his rule against evil witchcraft. He retaliated with *farawa.* As preparation, he ate only piranha; that little fish with the razor teeth was mean. The night before the ceremony he had to run through the forest—where no man wanted to be after dark—and shout in his cupped hands:

"Fororoʈoro!"

In performing the ritual, Mafolio burned his boy's body. He forked out a bone from the ashes and wrapped it in scarlet leaves from the blood tree. This he stuffed into a bamboo, then buried it all under a giant *kechekere* tree. Waving leaves toward the sky he cried again and again,

"Revenge! Revenge! Let my little son's death be revenged!"

Farawa turned up the killer. Within the limit of six days prescribed by the laws of the ominous rite, death came to a certain man and his evil-minded old sister, proof enough that they had committed the murder.

Elka hoped he would never be caught in the web of *farawa*. But that was not his only worry. There were other plaguing fears. He laughed and joked and pursued pleasure, of course; often with hilarity. But these were interludes in a life dominated by fear. He feared the jungle, sometimes for its physical vastness, more often for its spiritual terrors. He feared everything unusual —a banana that had grown double, a fish with a peculiar spotting. Were they not omens of the spirits' ill-temper? He feared a relative living far up a feeder stream of the Mapuera, a man whom he had never seen. If the relative chanced to think evil toward Elka, maybe because of a parent's long-past misdeeds, he could seek something of Elka's to blow on. Elka even feared his young friend, the clever Kirifaka, whose people had recently crossed to this side of the high mountains. Kirifaka could lift a footprint Elka had left in the mud and, perhaps in self-defense, hand it over to one who would eat Elka's spirit.

Death by spirit-eating was always possible, particularly since his uncle might not bother to perform *farawa*, leaving him without the protection that the threat of retaliation usually afforded. And often Elka became obsessed with the fear of fears: the shadowy uncertainty that lay beyond death.

Much that was not fear was indifference. There was little incentive to seek more than a basic existence. Through trading the skins of animals he had shot, Elka accumulated many strings of beads, one of the Wai Wai yardsticks of wealth. One day Yukuma wrinkled his nose at his insignificant cousin and thrust up his chin a bit.

"You have red beads," he said. "I like red beads."

Elka knew he wanted them.

"I'd kind of like to see your payment," he stammered, feeling reduced to a small boy.

"I don't have any," replied Yukuma, staring strangely at Elka. He was sitting astride his hammock. Then with a curious smile beginning to play on his lips he lay back. He stretched his arms above his head to pull on the cords. He spoke again, hardly moving his lips. Elka strained to hear him.

"Will your old beads make you strong? Will they protect your spirit when I eat it?"

Elka scarcely heard the threatening whisper. With nervous hands he unwound the beads from his neck. Without a word he handed them to Yukuma. If the fruits of labor could so easily vanish, why should he work to gain them?

Elka wished that Ahmuri were his wife. She was, of course, Mapari's wife. But she made it plain that she was too young to bestow her affections on such an old one. Although she was the mother of his newborn daughter, she acted more like a housemaid than a wife.

During these early days at Old Baking Plate Elka was not the only one to cast his eye longingly on this spirited young creature. But none looked more discerningly. Elka found her pretty, not so much for any feature as for her liveliness, and for the laughter that made her full brown cheeks swallow up her eyes. She swung her ax to split wood for a fire, and her supple figure flexed so easily. She knotted her hair in back, but always some strand escaped to exaggerate the constant tossing of her head.

Ahmuri could be gay and companionable. But she could also grow abruptly quiet with the sudden fear of superstition. At other times her pleasantness gave way to scolding. Under the spell of infatuation Elka loved even the vixen in her.

She was inclined to be responsive to Elka's tender words— evidently the ants had made him at least a little attractive. When Elka brought her the meat of wild pigs and bush turkeys, she cooked it over her fire and gave it back to him, in spite of her husband. This was open seduction; it flouted a custom reserved to husband and wife.

But Yukuma also wanted Ahmuri for himself. Already he had taken her younger sister as his wife, and Tochi, mother of the girls, carried his child in her womb. Yukuma was confident of getting Ahmuri as well.

Elka had no such self-confidence. He couldn't think of any victory he had yet scored over his rival. He was living under the same roof with Ahmuri and she was cooking his meat, but always it appeared that Yukuma would get what he wanted. Maybe it was because fate seemed so fixed that Elka busied himself with other things.

If there was anything in which Elka excelled, it was in dancing. He sang dance songs far into the night, his repertory outlasting all others. When he donned a flowing leaf cape and a tall head-dress of riotous feathers and joined in to stamp his feet in rhythm, Elka felt he was a man. It pleased him to hear people say,

"Look at Elka. No one dances better than he."

"Yes," others would respond. "When it comes to dancing, Elka is a leader."

Usually when they danced, guests came from other villages. As much as a full cycle of the moon beforehand the headman would send invitations to distant points, perhaps even over the high mountains. The invitation was embodied in a string tied in several knots, called a *shim-shim*. The knots represented the number of days before the party was to start. If the *shim-shim* was accepted, a knot would be untied to mark the passing of each day until the dance.

While the messengers delivered the invitations, the hosts were busy preparing for their guests. The men went on long hunting trips and roasted each day's kill to preserve it for the coming party. The women baked huge stacks of cassava bread. By chewing the bread and spitting it into a pot, and later soaking

"Be a strong one, not a tired one. Go long distances, work all night. Plead for Kworokyam to hide his badness with good."

That night after Elka fell asleep in his hammock the spirit of the wild pigs found him. He dreamed that he and the villagers had tracked the bush hogs to the *ite* palms and had surrounded them. One pig had separated from the pack. Elka ran after him. Just as he lifted his bow to aim, the pig looked up at him and spoke:

"Little Brother, why do you want to shoot me? I am one you ought not shoot."

Elka lowered his bow. The talking pig, alone of all the pack, nodded his thanks and then ran off with the others unharmed.

Elka awoke in a sweat.

"*Kofi!* How scary!" he whispered hoarsely. "I thought it really happened."

The dawn came. Yukuma smelled a pack of wild pigs. Elka ran with the rest to track the pigs to the *ite* palms. Sure enough, a fat pig stood apart from the pack. Elka raised his bow for a shot that no Indian ought to miss. His arrow went wide. The pig stood still, baring its ugly teeth. Elka stepped closer. He shot again. This time he hit a tree. He shot once more. The long arrow sped for the pig's face. In flight it suddenly leaped, passing clean over the pig's head. The pig ran away.

Others shot pigs, several pigs. Elka was deeply troubled. Not because he hadn't killed the pig for its meat, or because others might think him a poor shot. He was troubled because the incident boded so much ill. The pig in the flesh had looked just like the one in his dream. In his dream he wouldn't shoot. Today, he couldn't shoot. It was as if the pig of his dream were holding him to his word.

What claim did the spirit of the wild pigs have on him?

"Why couldn't I shoot him?" he asked Kurum, walking homeward in the path behind the old fellow. Kurum, who had heard

Elka sing spirit songs in the cane at Big Rocks, preferred not to get involved with Kworokyam.

"Hnnnn," he replied, shaking his head from side to side, "I don't know."

Walking silently now, Elka knew in his mind the answer to his question. This question, all his questions, were simply attempts to make things what he knew they were not, to escape his future. He knew he had committed himself to the pigs' spirit and through them to Kworokyam. Maybe singing the songs deliberately had done it. He did not want to be a witchdoctor. Yet, he did. There was only one question remaining: How long before he would become Kworokyam's? He was to know the answer by the time of the next full moon.

The old granny of Big Falls, who had prophesied Elka's future as a witchdoctor, now lived at Baking Plate. Elka told her how he had not been able to kill the pig.

"Fool him next time," she said in her husky whisper. "Hide your looks behind palm leaves."

He listened to the old crone. He tied leaves on his arms and legs. In this disguise he killed two pigs. His success gave him boldness, and he threw off the leaves. Again his arrows went astray.

On the night of the second strange hunting experience his rest was disturbed by the fat pig which he now knew quite intimately, both in the flesh and in his dreams.

"Little Brother," began the pig. Elka fought the mesh of his hammock trying to escape him—but there was no escape. Whichever way Elka turned, there was the pig looking directly at him.

"Why are you coming after us to kill us?" the pig continued. "You should be knocking palm fruit from the trees for us to eat."

As Elka dreamed, the fat pig offered him a flute.

"Play the song of the vulture," he commanded. Elka took the slender wooden flute and blew softly on it, *ku ku wi, ku ku wi*. As he played the plaintive tune the pig's face changed into that of a man. His bristles became long, black hair, like a man's after he had combed it out.

"I want you to be a witchdoctor," the creature, now part pig, part man, said to him. "When you are one, you will not eat me, except for a tiny piece along my back. If you eat more of me than this, I will eat your spirit. If you neglect me, you will also die."

Elka was shaking when he woke up. He ran to Mapari's hammock and roused him.

"Uncle, the pigs have talked to me again!"

As he spoke, his whole body tingled, as it had from the first prick of the ant belts. His uncle sat up and by the light of his night fire could see that Elka was trembling from head to toe.

"Hnnnn. It was Kworokyam you saw."

Then it *was* Kworokyam. Mafolio had said Kworokyam would appear as a pig to Elka.

"Uncle, I'm scared!" was all Elka could say.

"I'm one who knows Kworokyam somewhat," his uncle said with satisfaction. "I blow to cure when no greater one is around. I will make you a witchdoctor. Now go to sleep until dawn. We'll attend to it then."

Go to sleep—how utterly foolish! The pulse beat strong and fast in Elka's stomach. It was not of his dream that he thought now. It was of the frightening experience of being made a witchdoctor, which he knew at last was coming with the dawn of another day.

5

To the Sky and Back

Morning came. Elka helped his uncle build a witchdoctor's house.

"We'll use it when we go to the sky," his uncle explained. This meant that the two of them would enter the small doorless, windowless shelter, and after singing the necessary songs to transport them in ecstasy, would enter that strange land where humans were interlopers and the spirits relaxed in comfort. It was where witchdoctors learned in what spot the hurt resided in a sick body and how it could be got out.

Before going to the sky, however, there were to be preliminaries in the open clearing where all the villagers could take them in.

"We must impress them with your closeness to Kworokyam," Uncle Mapari said.

In front of the big house in the full glare of the blazing sun the old man and Elka sat on their stools. The village granny from Big Falls was going to assist; she knew about such things. She sat on a mat made from the bark of a Brazil nut tree. The people sat or squatted around them in no particular order. Elka and the granny brought nothing to the ceremony, but his uncle bore a bulging basket of paraphernalia. All grew quiet. Even in the bright light of day there was no inclination to treat the spirits with frivolity. Except for the usual yapping of dogs and whining of a few children, the only sound was the intoning of Elka's uncle.

"Let your mind be filled with many spirits," Mapari enjoined Elka. "Not with just the bush hog, but with the anaconda, the vampire bat, the vulture, the *haimara*." The more pets he possessed in the spirit world, the more pleased Kworokyam would be with him. The more songs he learned—one for each spirit—the more situations he could meet successfully.

Elka nodded. He would make friends with all the spirits. He would watch in the path and along the river's edge for the little smooth stones, some no bigger than a bead, that represented the spirits. If he ever went over the high mountains and saw Mafolio, he would ask if he had one to spare. Mafolio could give him many stones that would benefit his people. No doubt he could get stones from Muyuwa, too, though they might be corrupt, coming from him.

Still, there was much he could learn from that old steel-eye. Who could tell when a curse might come in handy?

Elka caught himself up short for such an evil thought. He was glad that those watching him could not tell what he was thinking. He turned his attention again to Mapari. What was his uncle saying?

"Take my tobacco." The old man was talking to the people, not Elka. He had brought out a dried leaf from his basket. Breaking it into small pieces, he passed it among the spectators.

"Crush it in your hand," he instructed. "Suck it in. Enjoy a tiny touch of Kworokyam."

All of them snuffed their crumbled tobacco, even the children. As they inhaled it, enjoying its exhilaration, the old man took from his basket two rolls of tobacco. Lighting the ends of these cheroots, he gave one to the granny and puffed on the other one himself. The two smokers leaned toward Elka. They blew smoke into his nostrils.

Elka gagged. He turned his head away to catch his breath.

"Don't sneeze," Mapari said sternly. "Swallow the breath of the spirits."

Elka tried to swallow the smoke. It burned his mouth and throat. It seemed to reach clear to his stomach. His eyes watered. He choked. Instinctively he raised his hand to his nose to ward off more smoke. And in spite of all his efforts not to, he sneezed.

He was frightened as he sneezed again. What would his uncle do, now that he had disobeyed his command? The old man seemed undisturbed by this most human reaction which had interrupted the supernatural atmosphere. Maybe it had happened before, in other such ceremonies—maybe to his uncle himself when he had been made a witchdoctor. Elka liked his uncle better for not scolding him.

"To be a true one of Kworokyam," Mapari was now saying, "you must know him as well as you know people."

Wouldn't Elka know Kworokyam well! The two old servants had breathed into Elka the spirits of as many pets as Elka had fingers. What a good start for one so young!

The sun reached the middle of the sky and turned the corner downward; Mapari and Elka entered the witchdoctor's dark hut. There the old man gave his protégé the tiny stones that corresponded to the pets he had bestowed by the smoke-blowing. From his basket he withdrew headdresses that in the dark Elka could feel were made from the feathers of the wild crane and chestbands made of pig bristles. After putting them on, the two men took more tobacco, Elka smoking a cheroot himself this time. He did not choke again on the smoke.

Mapari asked Elka if he knew any spirit songs. He did. Of course he did. He could teach his uncle. They sang and smoked, smoked and sang, without end it seemed to Elka. The end came, all too soon. Too soon because his uncle announced that they were ready to go to the sky.

Elka shivered with fear. Since he first learned that Mafolio had gone to the sky when he occupied a *shurifana,* he had wanted to go. He had wanted to see this otherworldly land of little people. He had wanted to enter this place to which admittance came by complete abandonment to the will of Kworokyam. But now that the time had come, he was afraid.

"Uncle," he said, trying to postpone the experience, "you never taught me how to go to the sky. Maybe you should teach me today, and tomorrow we'll go."

"No, Little Body," his uncle replied. "We'll sing more songs of Kworokyam. We'll sing to the hummingbird, that most gracious of spirits, and she will come down and transport us both to the sky."

Fear gnawed in the pit of Elka's stomach. His fingers tingled, as his body had tingled after his latest dream. His arms hung loose and numb. His head was spinning crazily. He was giddy. He felt as he had when he wrestled with the drink and the drink had thrown him. The light in the shelter was dim, seeping through tiny cracks in the leaf walls. For Elka it was growing dimmer, dimmer.

At last it went out.

Elka did not know how it had happened. He just knew that he went to the sky. The sun had already started to sink behind the tall trees of the forest when he came out of the *shurifana.* The old granny cornered him by the sugar-cane press in the work-house. She asked him what he had seen.

He could tell her. It was fresh and vivid, not like an ordinary dream that fled with the dawn or even like the dreams about the wild pigs, which he knew were dreams. *He could tell her because he had been there.*

"We saw people there, little people," he said.

She nodded knowingly, her toothless face gleeful. She had been to the sky once, only once, and here was someone who had shared her rare experience.

"Some had red skins, some black, some white," Elka continued. "Some wore loincloths like ours. The bodies of others were hidden by clothes. I saw the anaconda and many bush hogs. The old snake and the pigs, my uncle said, would be my special pets."

While his own spirit was gone in blissful, yet rather terrifying close company with the spirits, Kworokyam had taken over his body. Kworokyam had dwelt in his throat, Elka knew. People who had been outside the witchdoctor's house now told him they had heard him speak. But the words they had heard were words Elka had never used, words he neither understood nor controlled.

"Oh, Little Body," said the grinning old soothsayer, "you *are* one of Kworokyam's. He has great things in store for you."

Her prophecy was confirmed by his dream that night. In it, Elka walked the trail to where he smelled the bush hogs. All he found was a pile of bones. He sang the song of the vulture. This breathed life into the dead bones. The reborn pigs grunted in appreciation.

"Old Elka is one of ours now," the wild rascals sang.

Elka awoke refreshed as morning came.

"I'm a real witchdoctor now," he said aloud, no longer caring who heard. And with his mind clear at the start of a new day he thought of the counsel of old Mafolio: "Be a good witchdoctor. Don't be one to harm people."

He jumped from his hammock. He would be a good witchdoctor. Let Muyuwa keep his infamous reputation. Elka would start to help people today.

6

Changes for Elka

Elka had been to the sky. He could breathe life into dead bones. Momentous things were happening to him, but most of the villagers just went on with their feasting and gaiety. Muyuwa's *yamo* dance—the dance of the anaconda—was still going on after two full cycles of the moon.

Before the dance ended, the white invaders came.

Elka had been right. They came in the wake of those who had gone out to the savannas. But by the time they reached Old Baking Plate the white men no longer followed the returning Wai Wai; they traveled with them.

Elka heard the knocking of canoe paddles and ran down the steep path to the river.

"Whoever in the world is coming?" he called to a party just rounding the river bend into sight.

"It's us!" they shouted.

In front and back paddled two of the Wai Wai men who had gone to the savannas. Between them sat a pair of tall thin figures with white skin, though Elka could see little of it; clothes and what looked like bowls on their heads nearly covered them.

Elka shouted a warning up the path. It was relayed to the

village. One woman gathered up her precious dogs and ran into the woods. Some villagers scattered into the thickly forested hillside where they could look without being seen. Muyuwa walked down the path to the river, and the braver ones followed him.

Elka was uneasy but tried to hide his fear as the heavily loaded dugout emptied its human cargo at the landing. He was amazed that the two Indians traveled with the white men and that they seemed unafraid.

One of the paddlers spoke to Muyuwa. Then the chief, stately and smiling graciously, welcomed the white pair. What gave him his confidence? Did he know that his black magic was as great as any the white men could produce? But Muyuwa did not seem to be thinking about casting spells. Had he been reassured about the white men? He was already accepting fishhooks from them!

"*Oklee!* Great, great!"

The old chief was actually laughing. It was evident that he thought the newcomers were harmless. Now he was leading them up the path to the big house in the clearing. More puzzled than alarmed, Elka fell into the line filing up the hill. Once they reached the village one Wai Wai after another emerged from hiding. Women produced food and drink. The white men inspected hammocks and other household items with interest.

Then without warning two gyrating strawstacks spiraled into the big house. Interest in the *yamo* dance had waned; Elka's initiation as a witchdoctor was one event that eclipsed it. Now rivaled by the newcomers, two costumed dancers chose this time to stage the most vigorous exhibition of their skill. But who wanted to look at *yamo* dancers when they could look at men with white skins? Admitting defeat, the dancers retired peevishly.

Elka fixed his eyes on the strange visitors. If they had come to kill, where were their weapons? They had neither clubs nor axes. He had noticed a gun in the canoe, like those the Wapishana used in hunting wild pigs, but they had not bothered to bring it up the hill.

The newcomers, he could see, were trying hard to please. They smiled and said Wai Wai words like *kiriwanhi,* "wonderful." Why should they want to please the Wai Wai? Why, being killers, had they not struck fear into the ones who brought them?

Elka edged toward one of the paddlers and put the questions to him.

"We *were* afraid, at first," came the answer. "Our spirits almost left us."

The paddler then told Elka an amazing story that he had once thought would end only in death for all.

The Wai Wai, he said, cut short their stay on the savannas after hearing fresh news that white killers were coming. The little group pulled hard on the paddles as they raced to get home —they would rather die in their own village. But they sensed they were losing out to the pursuers. The Indian's travel-day was short, for he had to hunt before he could eat. The white man, however, carried his food. He could paddle both early and late.

On the day of doom the Wai Wai camped behind a big rock jutting into the river. Before the sun fell they heard canoe paddles knocking. That would be the white men's Wapishana guides. The young leader who had taken his people to the savannas paced the rock nervously. Going to its edge to investigate, he spied two canoes approaching.

"They're coming!" he called back to the others.

He felt like running, but curiosity made him stay. He touched the knife tucked in his waistband. With his toes he reached out to the bow and arrows laid close beside him.

"Two tall ones sit in the front canoe," he reported to his people cowering in the bushes. "I can see now that their skins are white. They look like smiling ones. But whoever in the world can tell?"

Before going to the rock he had painted and preened. If he were to die he wanted to die handsome. Cold sweat now stood out on his painted cheeks. He folded his arms to keep them from shaking and stood frightened but unmoving while the on-coming party reached the rock and beached its canoes.

The two white men, each a head taller than the Wapishana guides, stepped out onto the rock. Accompanied by a Wapishana, they approached the young Wai Wai leader. First one, then the other, took his hand and shook it.

How would they kill him? he wondered. Were they going to throw him first, as the Wai Wai threw an opponent in wrestling? Then one of the Wapishana spoke to him.

"You speak our tongue. I've seen you on the savannas." He went on to say that the white men they brought were good men. It was not the spirits of the Wai Wai they wanted to catch, but their talk.

If to catch talk meant to make scratch marks, the young leader thought, the white men were already doing it. They had produced little papers from somewhere, and peering intently at his lips they made marks on the papers every time he spoke.

The Wai Wai back among the trees now came forward to meet the white men, fearfully and with great suspicion. Gifts were exchanged, and the Wai Wai learned that the men had names: Neill Hawkins was one; Bob the other. Whoever could steer his tongue around to say such names? Neill they would call Mistokin, reasonably close to one Wapishana's "Mistah Haw-kin'." Bob would be known as Bahm. Mistokin and Bahm were brothers; a third brother, Rader—Mlayla—was coming later.

The two groups camped just out of each other's sight that night. Excitement and uncertainty reigned in the Wai Wai camp. They went through no more than the motions of an evening meal.

"Did you see how they came wrapped in cloth, the way knives come?" one person asked.

"Maybe we should call them knives," replied a wizened old man, laughing nervously at his joke.

"Why do they come?" another asked.

"To tell us about God," said the one who understood Wapi-shana. "That's what I was told. But who is God?"

"Is God coming in their trail?"

"Does He have a wife?"

"Maybe they will kill us when we drop our guard."

The Wai Wai had little sleep that night. The adults found many excuses to get up often—just to make sure they were still alive. Not in a long time had a night fire been fed so frequently and willingly; many restless men gladly got up to perform this woman's chore.

They lived through the night unscathed—and through the next day, and then through the several nights and days it took to paddle up the river to their village. But the white men wanted to move on.

"We finally said we would help them," explained the paddler as he came to the end of his tale.

This recital lessened Elka's dread. Still, he was not going to drop long-harbored fears simply because of a few smiles and gifts. Muyuwa might offer his friendship for fishhooks and maybe someday a knife, and Yukuma might exert himself to make a good impression. But not Elka.

Almost in spite of himself, however, he found in the days following that he was strangely drawn to the brothers. He helped them catch Wai Wai words, an activity they pursued re-lentlessly day after day. From morning till night they kept at it, patiently, unswervingly, taking time out only to cook and eat the meat that hunters brought them, to make their many papers talk back to them, and to turn their faces to the sky or ground and with closed eyes speak to someone the Wai Wai could not see.

Each day, Mistokin and Bahm asked one or another of the villagers to help them catch words. Muyuwa and Yukuma did it frequently, Elka not quite so often. From time to time every-body tried to help, crowding into the open-sided house the brothers slept in at the river landing. The two made an effort to speak in the Wai Wai tongue at such times, but when the confusion became too great they would throw up their hands or cover their ears.

They took an interest in everything the Wai Wai did. One day Mistokin went with a group into the forest to where a canoe had been hollowed from a tree trunk and shaped, and helped drag it to the river. How surprised he was when they neared the village and women ran out of the house carrying fiery palm fronds and wiped the dugout with the flames.

"It is to keep the canoe from causing our children to fall sick," one explained.

One day Bahm brought out a box from which he took something shiny and as sharp as a palm thorn, and gently stuck it into the arm of a sick man. The man screamed, but in a day or so he seemed to be well. What next would these strange ones produce?

Mlayla, the third brother, finally arrived. Immediately he and Bahm said they were going over the high mountains and down the Mapuera. It seemed so important to them that they catch sight of many Wai Wai. When they called for mountain pack-carriers, Elka volunteered, but only reluctantly; he knew the trail was hard. On the trip he got sick. He flushed with fever, then shook with a chill. He would have unpacked his charms and blown his breath over his stones on himself—maybe even tobacco smoke—but Bahm happened to come by first.

"I've got medicine for you," Bahm said.

He did not insist that Elka take the small white pebbles he drew from his pack; but as Elka looked up from his hammock at the tall figure bending over him, he saw one whom he had come to trust despite his fears. This quiet, careful, patient, thorough man carried a persuasiveness that somehow made Elka obey.

Bahm explained how to swallow the pebbles. Elka did as he was told.

"If it doesn't work, I'll stick you tomorrow," Bahm said.

The next day Elka was well. Bahm's charms had worked. But never would he let Bahm stick him, he vowed. He'd rather die first.

After taking Bahm and Mlayla to the Mapuera headwaters, Elka returned to Old Baking Plate. Back home, he again helped Mistokin with his words. Bahm was quiet and serious, Mlayla talkative and good-homored. In Mistokin was something of both qualities. In addition, he was their leader.

One day Mistokin asked the people to gather together. He said he had caught enough Wai Wai words to tell them that God had made them and that in the world were two ways—one leading to God, one away from Him.

Elka was still puzzling over Mistokin's words when Bahm and Mlayla returned. The two who had traveled down the Mapuera said they had seen other Wai Wai, and had told them, haltingly, about God. Then one day all three said goodby to Elka and his people. Mapari and other paddlers waited in canoes to take them out of the jungle. Elka wished the Wai Wai men would not go. But they went—carrying the three white brothers with them.

The visit now provided endless days of talk in the village.

"Muyuwa is happy they came," said one.

For favors performed the old witchdoctor had gained more beads, a red-handled knife, and a new hoe to till his ground.

Yukuma called them his friends. And rightly so. Never before had anyone held him in such high esteem—as a hunter, as a guide, as one who could provide the desired word in the Wai Wai tongue.

Others, however, were not so certain in their judgments. What was the purpose of the white men's coming? Of their catching Wai Wai words? What were they trying to teach?

Elka, sitting in his hammock, asked a perplexing question.

"They talked about God. Who is God?"

The young downriver leader, his quarrel now forgotten, thought he knew the answer. Because he had ears for Wapishana, a language which seemed to help bridge the gap between the white men's own and Wai Wai, he felt closer than the rest to an understanding.

"God is not Mawalee," he said, speaking of a legendary figure who had sprung from cohabitation of the anaconda with the turtle and who, as his first act, had created the Wai Wai. "I heard them say that God made everything. And He doesn't forget the ones He made."

"Mawalee went away after he made the Wai Wai and we haven't seen him since," Kurum commented. It seemed to him that God had qualities Mawalee didn't have.

"I suppose my old husband is one to tell us about Mawalee," snapped Tochi in a mocking tone. She gave a vigorous twirl to the little clay spindle on which she was spinning a cotton thread.

"When Bahm and Mlayla came back from over the mountains why did they go with Mistokin into the forest one day and sit on their knees and close their eyes and talk to Someone above them?" asked another.

"They talked to God."

"Is He in the treetops?"

The Wai Wai had asked Mistokin about God's family.

"He has no mother or father," one recalled. "Just a Son— *Chisusu*, Jesus."

"I remember they said that men drove spikes through the Son's hands; spikes like those of the pimpler palm," said the bilinguist. The others shuddered. "They said that Jesus died missing us," he continued. "He died because He wouldn't stop loving us."

"How ever in the world could that be?" asked Tochi, looking up from her spindle. "What kind of love is that? Not Wai Wai love."

She was right. The Wai Wai loved a child because someday he would grow up to hunt meat for a parent, or to cook it. They loved for what love could give them. Other pressures sometimes equaled the force of such love; it was easy then for love to be swept away.

"I laughed when they tried to talk our talk," cut in one, preferring a lighter vein.

"When they asked our words, for 'fish' and 'monkey' and 'rock' and 'bread,' what were the marks they made on their papers?"

"Hnnnn. What were they?" asked another. "They talked back."

Those who had heard the men read what they put on their papers had doubled over in laughter. It seemed funny for their ears to catch familiar words and phrases.

"Gicha!" spat old Kurum. "We just talked for nothing. I said to old Bahm, 'You come,' and all old Bahm said was, 'You come.' My words just bounced back at me."

"I know," added Elka. "I told him how to talk our talk and he just stayed quiet and said 'Hnnnn.' "

"The strange ones talked like flies buzzing," Tochi said. "B-b-b-b-b-b-b——" At this they all laughed.

"We asked them something," said Fehwe, "and they just shrugged their shoulders like the silly trumpet-bird."

"Did you see them drink water?" asked one who thought water unfit for consumption if cassava drink or palm juice were on hand. "I called them alligators."

"On our trip over the mountains Bahm slipped in the mud. We called him a wild pig," Elka laughed. "He looked like a bush hog taking his bath."

This reminded the village granny that she had not bathed for a long time. Now that the strangers were gone, she said she could go to the river again.

"Bahm's spirit covered the path and I dared not walk in it," the old woman muttered.

One still suspicious Wai Wai was not so afraid of the white men's spirits as he was of their intentions.

"They came to spy out the path to our village," he cautioned. "Now they know. Will they come back and kill us?"

The circle of talkers fell quiet. This last word had sobered their thoughts.

Maybe it was this thought that prompted Elka some days later to ask Muyuwa, who was staying in Old Baking Plate a while, how he produced his black magic. He had gone to a field with the old sorcerer to entreat the spirits to make the field yield bountifully. Muyuwa, in a munificent mood, gave him a stone that he said was the spirit of the giant armadillo. If Elka wanted to make the cassava grow big, he now had the charm to invoke. Before they left the field Elka, hesitantly and a little ashamed, said there was one more thing he wanted from the old master.

"How do you send your spirit into the jaguar, Father?" No sooner had he asked than he looked around, afraid he had been heard by the tale-bearing wren. He knew that if one were around it would fly straight to the good Mafolio.

Muyuwa did not care who heard his answer. Without constraint he said,

"Point your lips toward the one you want to attack. Command the big cat to do your bidding. That's all." The jaguar could not be hurt even by the sharpest arrows while on such a mission, he pointed out.

"Hnnnn. Is that the way it is?" mused Elka.

Then emboldened to take one further step, he cautiously asked how *farawa* worked. Muyuwa explained by telling about a man named Wisho.

Wisho could calmly watch his own newborn twins being killed by a friend, but he became enraged at the death of his wife. Furious at losing one who satisfied his lust, he decided to perform the ritual of revenge under a *kechekere* tree. For the purpose he used a charred bone taken from the ashes after his wife's body had been burned.

"Revenge, big tree, the death of my little wife!" he chanted.

He went off to another village. Just after he arrived there a woman of his acquaintance was killed by a falling tree. At one time this woman and his wife had been like sisters. But they had quarreled when his wife denied the woman some bread. The woman, in anger, had blown a fatal curse on Wisho's wife. Then she moved away, only to be struck down by the tree.

The pattern was plain: Wisho's wife died because of the spell; her former friend, whose death came within the traditional six-day limit, by *farawa*.

"Do? What do you do?" said Muyuwa to Elka. "You bury the bone under the tree. The spirit of the tree does the rest."

Muyuwa told of another person who had been accused in a killing. *Farawa* in this instance was aimed directly at him. His name was pronounced under the giant tree. News of the ritual reached him, perhaps, by the jungle's rumor network. Believing in the inevitability of *farawa*, he may have been frightened to death. Or maybe it was the work of Kworokyam's demons. Muyuwa did not know how it happened. No man could be completely sure of the reason for these beliefs. They must simply be accepted.

And why not? *Farawa*, blowing, spirit-eating — all were effective. No one asked why the dawn came each morning. It just did. "That's the way it is" was the stock phrase to explain the inexplicable.

Just as Elka had feared, sickness now spread through Old Baking Plate. It came in from the savannas with the few adventurous men who had paddled the white brothers out of the jungle.

The paddlers came back hot; their stomachs pained; they

spat up blood. Elka's uncle was the first to die. Mapari had not wanted to make the trip, but Ahmuri insisted that her old husband earn a knife, so he went. No sooner had he returned than his germs spread through the village and his tortured old body perished.

The wailing began for Mapari. Before it ended, Fehwe the village headman died. With a dull ache in his stomach Elka buried him, the companion and teacher of his childhood days. But there was no time now for mourning, not even for their leader. Others were sick and had to be cared for.

Muyuwa and Elka sped from one hammock to another to blow on the sick. They had no time to build a witchdoctor's house. They just took their stones and tobacco to the side of anyone who writhed in his bed. Elka would smoke a cheroot, exhaling through an open fist so that the smoke billowed on the affected part of the sick body. At times he took his smooth stones from his mouth to rub them on his patient. Sometimes he inserted a small hollow stick in his mouth and sucked the evil from the critical spot. All the while he sang to the spirit of the tree frog or of the mosquito or of the bush hog—especially to the spirit of the bush hog.

Elka and Muyuwa, thrown together by the terrifying plague, blew until it seemed that they could blow no more. Still they must race to another. The quick spread of the disease left Elka little time to think about black magic as he had done that day when he was with Muyuwa in the field. He had more than he could do to try to make his people well. He and Muyuwa blew all day and all night on one young man, who did get well. But others died—old men, a few women, one little boy.

Elka longed for sleep. However, even in the brief periods when he lay in his hammock, sleep sometimes would not come. His mind would not rest. He thought of the nightmare they were living. He used all his fingers to count the dead. *Okwe,* how sad. . . . The count spilled over to his toes.

So it went for many months, sickness and dying. New people came over the mountains from time to time because they were curious about the plague or wanted to hear more about the white men. Life in the village went on as best it could, improving as the disease gradually abated.

Now that he was a witchdoctor Elka often saw the wild pigs in his dreams. It never failed: He would be told their location while sleeping; the next day he would lead the hunters to where they rooted. Because of his pledge, he left the killing to others. Increasingly the villagers would ask him:

"Where shall we hunt the old things, Little Brother?" And if he had been told in his dreams, he would inform them, to the benefit of the village meat supply.

Fishermen brought him their hooks or their traps before testing their luck on the river. Elka would blow his breath on them, a procedure certain to lure a delicious catch.

He traveled to other villages where death or sickness had struck. The people built him witchdoctor houses, in which he went to the sky to find the cures for their sufferings. He blew through long nights. He blew until his throat was dry and his body ached from fatigue. But his strength always returned. He seemed to be thriving. In both strength and physique, it was becoming increasingly clear, the stinging ants had worked with skill. His fame grew. His influence with the spirits became known far over the high mountains. Some said he rivaled Muyuwa.

"Give old Elka time and he'll be greater than . . ." They didn't like to finish it—the tale-bearing wren, of course.

The plague in the village brought three big changes in his life. In succession came a wife, new standing with Yukuma, and new regard by his people.

As the disease began to run its course, Elka found time to go with old Kurum to hunt toucans.

"Little Brother," Kurum said to Elka as they sat in a hunter's blind high in a tree waiting for the big-billed birds to come in range of their arrows, "your uncle, the husband of my daughter, has died. You wouldn't want Ahmuri for your wife, would you?"

Elka could have fallen out of the tree. Instead, he suppressed his excitement and quietly replied,

"I'd kind of like to have her."

His desire to take Ahmuri had run stronger than the growing admiration he had had for Mapari. He loved his uncle's buxom young wife. He was sure she liked him, at least more than she did her old husband. But even though he was dead, there was still Yukuma to think of. His cousin's desire to possess the women of Kurum's family had not ceased with the birth of his and Tochi's child. Yukuma intended to keep on sharing Kurum's wife while claiming their younger daughter, too. If he wanted Ahmuri, as Elka knew he did, this was enough to make Elka hesitate to take her.

Kurum and Yukuma were not the best of friends. They quarreled frequently as a result of their jealousies. Once Kurum had bounced his younger rival on the ground by cutting the cords on the hammock in which Yukuma slept. He preferred that Elka have Ahmuri. Now he pressed for a decision.

"Shall I be with you?" Elka asked Ahmuri in the communal house a short time later. As he sat by her fire, the reflection of the flames danced in her dark eyes like the whirling of the *yamo* dancers. She tossed her head to one side and smiled. Her hair fell lustrously to her shoulders this morning. Elka thought she had never been prettier. He hoped she would say yes.

She sucked her breath in quickly to show assent. Without another sound she rose, untied her hammock, walked to the other side of the house, and strung it below Elka's. This made them husband and wife.

But Yukuma was not one to give up easily.

"Old Elka has taken the woman I wanted for a wife," he complained. He went about muttering threats. He said he would put an arrow in Elka's stomach. One day when Elka came back from hunting, his brother, Yakuta, warned him not to lie in his hammock.

"Yukuma blew on it while you were gone," he said. The young lad trembled, for he was sure an evil spirit contaminated the hammock.

"The old thing wants to kill me," said Elka angrily.

His wrath rose to such height that he was about to break tribal custom. Because reprisal was easily touched off, the Wai Wai were seldom direct; one spoke disparagingly *about* his elders, not *to* them; gossip was aimed at someone absent; even in speech the obliqueness showed when one said, "I'd *kind of* like to have you help me." Maybe it was dangerous, but Elka decided to have it out with Yukuma. He stalked to the field where his cousin was burning trees.

The main burning having been completed, Yukuma was gathering up half-charred branches for a second fire. He did not see Elka. He stooped, half turned away, and fanned on a faggot with his breath. Elka picked his way around still smoldering logs. He felt as hot inside as he knew the timbers to be. Angrier than he'd ever been in his life, he strode to Yukuma.

"Why did you blow on my hammock?" Elka asked, standing over him. "Don't you like me? I like you. Why don't you like me?"

Startled by the sound of Elka's voice, Yukuma dropped the smoking brand as he stood up. He was shocked not only to see Elka but also to experience this head-on encounter.

"I didn't blow on you," he said. He displayed none of his superior airs.

Elka replied that people had seen him blowing on his—Elka's—possessions, and demanded to know if Yukuma had gone any further toward spirit-eating.

"It is bad to me that you blew," Elka said, his anger mounting. "Now I want to kill you."

He picked up a stick from Yukuma's pile. He gripped it tightly and a dark look came over his face. The stick was solid. With a well-aimed blow . . . Never before had he really wanted to kil anyone.

Yukuma took a step backward, speaking in genuine terror a he did so.

"Don't be trying to throw me. I didn't blow to make you die only to make you unattractive to women. But I don't want tha now. I want to like you, and you to like me."

It was not that Yukuma feared Elka could best him in a exchange of clubbing. But he knew that if anything happened t Elka he would have the tribe to face. There might even be thos who would perform *farawa* for Elka.

"We'd be missing each other if one of us were to die," Yukum said, attempting a smile. It was not the scornful sneer he usuall gave, but a smile of conciliation.

Elka relaxed his hold on the stick. His desire to kill, nearly all consuming, passed quickly. It was a relief to him that Yukum sought to heal their breach.

"*Taa,* all right," Elka said. He threw down his stick.

The two walked back to the village, taking different path Elka had gained new status with his familiar adversary. An now he knew that Ahmuri would belong to him.

The death of Fehwe had deprived Baking Plate of a villag leader. The pall of death hung over the place. Who could liv there with so many spirits crowding the air? Moving as a grou the villagers abandoned their fields and dwelling. They loade their canoes and paddled downstream. Briefly they settled o the bank of a branch creek. Then, restless and without leade ship, they moved to a spot above Muyuwa's village of Deep Eddy But soon they moved again. Up and down the river they roame stopping here at one's suggestion, there at another's. One plac no one wanted to settle at was Deep Eddy. Nobody wanted t stay near Muyuwa, who could smile so graciously to outside but be so sinister to those in his own tribe.

Nevertheless, Muyuwa, whatever people thought of him, was still chief of all the Wai Wai on the Essequibo. So one day when they had gone back to harvest an old garden field at Baking Plate, they listened to the chief's emissary, his adopted son, who had come to invite them to a party of drink and dance. He held Muyuwa's knotted *shim-shim* before Yukuma, as he had been instructed. Then he picked up two carved stools that had been left in the old house and carried them to an open spot where he sat on one and invited Yukuma to sit on the other.

"My father," he said, when they were seated opposite each other, "would kind of like to have you come drink some drink."

It was the start of a chanted palaver called the *oho*, or yes-saying. As a *shim-shim* changed hands, the two parties always cajoled with flattery and deceit. When a man wished to get help on a work project, to contract for a marriage, or to avoid an open break with an antagonist that could lead to spell-casting, he also resorted to the *oho*.

"I don't suppose you people will come to our poor old house," the emissary began, disparaging what he had to offer.

"*Oho*," came Yukuma's response as a scarcely audible beat to the rhythmic chanting.

"You people out-dance us."

"*Oho*."

"You make better drink than we do."

"*Oho*."

"But we want you to come."

An *oho* that was begun at sunup could go on past midday, if it took that long for the one who began it to get on the "good side" of the other. One time Muyuwa and an opponent sparred for more than a day and night, not budging from their stools until their differences were settled.

It was time now for Yukuma to begin the flattery. Instead, he spurned politeness by making short work of the palaver.

"We'll come," he said abruptly, and took the *shim-shim*.

To his fellow villagers Yukuma was an unripe one. He was hotheaded, boastful, a show-off. He could not rally his people. Only a handful went with him to answer to Muyuwa's call.

Then Muyuwa sent another invitation. This time his son approached a different man, the husband of Elka's sister. Despite the gay plumes he wore in his nose, Elka's brother-in-law was colorless, physically weak, unstable, one who had made them wander aimlessly—but the people went with him to Muyuwa's village. He led them for a while after that, too. Yet he was not one to talk with enthusiasm. He was a sad one and unsure of himself. If a tall palm needed to be cut down in order to obtain its fruit, he would send others to do it but would not go himself. Seldom did he propose that they cut a new field from the forest or make a canoe. A chief had to be leader in these activities. This man did not want to be a leader.

Sickness still took a life now and then. Because of this and the fact that they were leaderless, the people who had once called Old Baking Plate their home decided to go across the high mountains to live on the Mapuera. Some said they would like to see Mistokin and his brothers if the three decided to come back —but maybe they would never come, and the Wai Wai might all die while waiting. Furthermore, if the Baking Plate people went across the mountains, maybe those in other villages on this side would go also. Perhaps it would be a good thing after all to abandon the Essequibo. They laughed when they thought of Bahm and Mistokin coming back only to find the houses empty.

It was all set. At the dawning they would start on their journey. But that night Elka dreamed. Before him stood a white man like Bahm.

"Don't go over the high mountains. Stay here," the man told him.

Elka waked the people to tell them of his dream.

"So that's how you dreamed? Hnnnn," they said in amazement. "Then we'd better not go. We'd better obey and stay on this side of the mountains."

Plans for the exodus were scrapped before dawn ever came.

In a little while Muyuwa again sent a *shim-shim* to the wanderers of Baking Plate. This time the group was camped on the bank of another creek. The old chief's messenger threaded his way up the tree-clogged stream in search of Elka.

"Little Brother," he said, starting the *oho* on his arrival, "I don't suppose you could ever get your people to come drink some drink at our place."

Elka had never carried on the *oho* but was willing to try. He kept at it for a respectable time before saying rather timidly that he'd kind of like to say yes. He gathered the people at the creek's edge and asked if they would go.

"We'll go," they said. They were eager to go. He accepted the *shim-shim*. Each day at dawn he untied a knot. Finally, when the string was free of knots, they followed Elka to the canoes and set off for Deep Eddy.

"Where shall we make our costumes?" they asked him.

"We'll stop at the sand bar just before the village," he replied.

Elka was one who knew what to do. He had ready answers. At Deep Eddy it was to young Elka that Muyuwa handed the drink. The old chief showed by this that he recognized Elka's new position of leadership.

After the party Elka took his people to a site he had long thought suitable for a village. A half-day's paddling downstream from Deep Eddy, it was a level area with a pleasant rock landing and a swift-moving creek bordering one side.

"Here is where we will build our house and cut our fields next dry season," he said. They sucked in their breaths to show they approved. Their leaderless days were over. Elka was their village headman.

"First, though," he continued, "we'll go back to Baking Plate and gather the food growing there."

"The old house has fallen," someone in the group said.

"But the yams are good," Elka countered. "We'll go there and raise shelters for our hammocks."

"I'll build a house," Yukuma said, as if such a project would show his importance, which he alone thought he still possessed.

Elka's vision was with the future.

"Someday we'll come back here and build our village," he promised. "We'll call it Yaka Yaka." It was the name of his favorite banana.

7

Excuse for Failure

year after their first visit Mistokin and Bahm returned to
ld Baking Plate and found Elka and his people there, harvest-
g the fields they had abandoned earlier. Elka, for one, was glad
 see them. They helped him turn back the lingering sickness
ith their magic—soft white pebbles and juice squirted from a
iny thorn. It was good magic, Elka conceded. It was some
me since the thought had entered his head that they might be
illers. More and more he was drawn to the pair. Occasionally
e spent whole days helping them "catch words" in his language.
[e had been amazed at first that they could not talk Wai Wai, but
en he was amazed at how quickly these ignorant ones were
arning.

Elka was learning something, too. Bahm and Mistokin had a
undle of papers wrapped in black leather—a Bible—which they
ade talk back to them every day. God's Paper, they called it in
Vai Wai. They wanted Elka to help them put it into his lan-
uage, and as he helped he began to find out what it had to
y.

"The Paper talks about God," they said to him. "It tells how
od made the trees and the rocks and the sun."

Had God made the sun, Elka wondered. Old Muyuwa used
to offer gifts to the sun occasionally, when he wanted it to hide
behind a cloud so that rain would come and wash their garden
fields. But Elka had not known that anyone made the sun.

God's Paper said that the One who made all things had
breathed into the nostrils of the first man and he began to live.
How strange! Mawalee had never done that. It was the Wai Wai
who did the blowing here, to keep alive or to kill. Mawalee did
not care if one blew on another to cause his death. He had left
and never came back.

"God loves the creatures He made," Bahm explained.

"Hnnnn," replied Elka. "Is that the way it is?"

He was impressed with their teaching because of the way they
lived—he saw them as "different ones." They did not steal Wai
Wai women. He found this hard to understand, especially since
some of the women invited being stolen.

Their earnestness gripped him most. There was Chiriminoso
for instance. How they struggled to gain him for God!

Chiriminoso was a witchdoctor of sorts who led a small village
tucked away near a stream of the Mapuera. Although old, he
decorated himself like a young man, with feathers in his nose
and plumes in his armbands. He loved crowds. For this reason
he had answered a *shim-shim* to drink and dance at Baking Plate.
On arriving he found the white visitors, and their teaching nearly
made him forget to dance. Often after bathing in the river he
stopped off at the open-sided hut they and their Wapishana
paddlers occupied near the landing. When the brothers said it
was lesson time, Chiriminoso would bang on a rock with his
hoe and call the people into the village clearing to hear what
more God's Paper had to say. Once while waiting for the brothers
to climb the hill for a lesson, which they taught both in Wai Wai
and through Wapishana interpreters, Chiriminoso told Elka he
had heard about God "just a little bit" when Bahm and his
brother had stopped in his house on their trip down the Mapuera.

the year before. He liked the little he had heard. Now he wanted to hear much more.

While Chiriminoso was at Baking Plate one of his two wives died. He buried her with no great feeling of regret. After all, she was old and he still had a young wife. The incident hardly interrupted his thoughts as he kept on listening to the teaching; he was beginning to get ears for God's Paper. Then his young wife fell sick. Chiriminoso sat by her hammock and used on her all the charms in his limited collection. He asked Mistokin and Bahm to use theirs.

"If Bahm's medicine makes her well," he said to Elka, "I'll become a companion of Jesus." If it failed, he added, he would go back to his village over the high mountains and there strive to know Kworokyam better.

Sickness had spread widely in this on-again, off-again *shoriwiko* dance, as it always did when large groups of Wai Wai gathered. Bahm himself fell ill, and the old women of the village came round his hammock to tell him he would die. But Mistokin nursed his brother back to health. Then the two white men put out great effort for Chiriminoso's young wife. They reached deep into their box of medicines, until one day they used the last they had. But they still talked to God about her constantly. Elka saw Mistokin sit on his knees one day and heard him plead both in his own language and in Wai Wai.

"Heal her for your sake, Father."

There was no doubt that they were worried about the girl, even beyond the concern they had shown for the other sick. Here, Elka sensed, was something beyond their desire to heal the hurt in a body. Here was their chance to win Chiriminoso to God, and how earnest they were. God, it appeared, was in this battle Himself.

The young wife died. Bahm, who buried her, appeared so sad that it made Elka feel sad too. God had fought for her, but God had lost. Lonely old Chiriminoso, decked out in new feathers

D

as consolation in his grief, went back over the trail to home.

In the days and weeks that followed, Mistokin and Bahm did not appear to blame God. He knew, they said, why He had permitted her to die. They worked harder than ever to help the Wai Wai throw off their fear and become God's people. Elka knew his tribesmen were far from this, as an incident at Baking Plate soon revealed. One afternoon in the village on top of the hill someone began an impromptu dance. Many villagers were attracted—more by the drink than by the rhythm. At sundown an old woman puttering near the edge of the clearing suddenly streaked toward the house that Yukuma had built.

"Murderers! Murderers!" she cried.

The shuffling stopped instantly as the dancers, sluggish from half-intoxication, came to life and crowded around her. She had seen a strange man, she panted, hovering in the forest.

From her agitation they knew trouble lurked in the shadows. Where there was one man, surely there were more. They must be enemies; friends always came openly with loud announcement of their approach. Still terrified, she was able to calm down enough to confirm their fears. She had seen the man once, in one of their Mapuera villages. He was the brother of a man in their own village who had recently died, and probably he was blaming them for the death. He must have come for his revenge.

"Murderers!" they shouted, taking up her cry in panic.

Yukuma put his hands to his face and sobbed.

"I'm the one who will be killed," he moaned, insisting that he was the target. Maybe he had death on his mind. Elka had heard talk that Yukuma's baby, the one Tochi bore him, had died by the hand of its father. Maybe he had cursed an enemy, as he had once started to curse Elka, and was now afraid of reprisal.

Someone remembered that Mistokin and Bahm had in their house at the bottom of the hill a gun that could protect them. And the Wapishana who lived with them had guns also. Who first dashed down the path? Elka did not know; he knew only that he became part of the surging mass sweeping toward the house at the river's edge, crying,

"Murderers! Murderers!"

"Get your gun, Mistokin," pleaded Yukuma in the excited babble as they reached the house.

Mistokin did not move. Instead, he told them to be quiet and to speak one at a time. He wanted someone to explain what it was about; he wanted them to be reasonable.

How could they be reasonable at such a time? Weren't their very lives at stake? At this moment enemies might be pulling back the strings of their bows, their long arrows poised to bring instant death to all crowding into and spilling out of the little house.

If only Muyuwa were present with his witchcraft, thought Elka. If only he had listened more closely when Muyuwa explained the working of his black magic. Mistokin still did not move. Because he didn't, the Wapishana men didn't either. Mistokin said he and Bahm had not come to kill but to tell of God's love for all the Wai Wai, not just for those at Old Baking Plate.

How foolish, thought Elka, to let love interfere in the pursuit of an enemy.

Mistokin agreed to go with them in search of the invaders, but he refused to take his gun. He even said he thought they were wrong, that no men were lurking in the bush. After hours of searching, he convinced them. They finally admitted that their hysteria had come from the imaginings of an old woman. To reassure them he took his hammock to the top of the hill to sleep among them. The talk was slow to die, however, and once during the night panic broke out again. Mistokin got up and talked to them in a way that no one had talked to the Wai Wai before. In calm stern tones, speaking in their native tongue, he said to them,

"If you had God living in you, you wouldn't be so afraid."

The people looked at him in the glow of a dozen or more night fires. Peevishly they muttered,

"*Foleeto,* old bossy one!"

"It's bad for you to want to shoot people," he went on. "Your sour drink has caused you to see and hear people in the forest who are not there. Now you've carried on enough for one night. Let's get some sleep."

Why didn't they say something, Elka wondered, fuming inwardly. Sitting in his hammock he looked over to where Mistokin had lain down again. Why didn't he—Elka, their leader—speak out and tell the meddling foreigner that the Wai Wai did not like such talk?

He remembered hearing that God's Paper spoke of "the *fear* of the *wicked*." Mistokin had said they were afraid because a voice within them told them they were bad. It told them that every one of their evil deeds brought its due. The thought was enough to keep Elka silent and, while others tossed restlessly in their hammocks, to make him sit on his and ponder. Maybe they were afraid of the consequences of their deeds; no doubt some-one had killed and now was afraid of being killed. He remembered, too, that Bahm had said their badness would have to go before they could forget their fears. And only God could take the badness away.

The missionaries talked straight and emphatically—not like the Wai Wai, whose speech was filled with hints and veiled threats. They read from God's Paper to give their words authority. They spoke out against many things that nobody had ever challenged in the tribe before. They said God did not like people to kill innocent babies. And since the missionaries came the killings had stopped—except maybe for the death of Yukuma's child.

But Mistokin and Bahm spoke against more than killing. Why, they even stood up against begging and stealing! One day Elka saw Bahm take back some ax heads and knives that Yukuma had stolen. Bahm told him a man should work to earn such tools; it was not good to get them by whining or to take them when no one was looking.

Yukuma boiled over in anger.

"Why do you tell us what to do?" he demanded. "We aren't children. You be your way, we'll be our way."

To this Bahm said no; their lives were filled with badness.

Elka wondered how Bahm and Mistokin dared reproach Yukuma. Elka knew that he could never stand up against begging. And he knew that he could never insist on the return of something that had been stolen when begging had failed to obtain it. Didn't they know that an offended thief had only to turn to sorcery for retaliation?

Yukuma stood defiant, but Elka grinned. Bahm was so right. Yukuma was filled with badness. Like most people, Elka could readily see where the fault lay in others. Oh, how he could talk about his cousin's wicked deeds! Then suddenly he hung his head. Yukuma was bad, but wasn't he bad too? Hadn't he done many of the same things Yukuma did? Elka felt uncomfortable inside. For the first time a Wai Wai admitted personal guilt, even though at this point he saw "just a little" badness in himself.

A crowd had gathered at the sound of Yukuma's angry voice. Bahm now turned to them, saying,

"God's Paper talks about you people."

It did? Oh, yes, Elka remembered. It had said God made them. But didn't Bahm always smile when he told them that? He was very serious now.

"God made Himself known to you by these trees, this river, the sky," he said, turning to Elka, who was the most attentive. "You have turned your backs on Him. Instead of serving God, you have chosen to serve the things He made."

"Hnnnn," Elka responded, not quite understanding.

"You are not alone in turning away from God," Bahm continued. "People in my own country turn their backs on God, too."

They do! thought Elka in surprise. He wondered if people in

Bahm's country were like the Wai Wai.

"I was no different from you."

What? Bahm with a pigtail? The thought intrigued Elka.

"Someone told me that God loved me and wanted to take my badness away. I stopped turning my back on Him. That's all. Now I've come to tell you that God loves you, too. He wants to take away your badness so you can be His children."

"But *you* don't love us," said Yukuma, who had been mumbling under his breath, with an air of injury. "If you did, you wouldn't take back the things we took. You wouldn't make us work to get knives and beads. You'd give us all the things we want."

"We love you," Bahm said, "and so does God. But He—and we, too—want you to do what is right."

Some snickered as Yukuma turned away in disgust. Bahm shook his head sadly; he had tried to tell them what God's Paper said about envy and lust and malice and gossip, and it brought only resentment. Elka alone seemed to be getting ears. He was beginning to understand that while God loved them, He had a standard to maintain.

Some days later Yukuma told Elka he would not go when the missionaries called them together for a lesson. He was tired of listening to God's Paper. It said too many bad things about him.

Then came the terrible day when the men talked of killing their teachers. Bahm had hired a number of Wai Wai, including Elka, to go with him nearly a day's paddling downstream to turn a small natural clearing into an airstrip. Each morning they walked from their campsite on the river to the clearing, where they filled potholes to create the strip. In the evenings they walked through the forest to their camp again. Finally the holes were filled and a runway was smoothed; then they turned to cutting away trees at one end for a safer approach. The task was hardly begun when one morning the men in camp awoke in a grumbling mood.

"What are you going to pay us?" asked Muyuwa's adopted son, who always "walked sad" and now walked poutingly as well, up and down the riverbank.

"And when?" chimed in another.

Bahm admitted that his supply of beads, knives, axes, and hoes was low. He said there would be plenty for all when they had the field built and the first sky canoe came swooping down. Bahm thought nothing more of it and moved off toward the field. The men, however, stayed behind, complaining about their lot: "Why doesn't old Bahm give us knives and axes?"

"I don't like to hear him talk. He says there's badness inside me."

Then they got around to recalling the white rubber hunters who had been friendly at first to the Wai Wai and then had abused them.

"You wait," said one in a mark-my-words tone. "Bahm and Mistokin will stop giving us things someday and will eat our spirits."

Others agreed. Hadn't they heard a long time ago that the white men came into the forest to kill them?

"Hnnnn. I don't know about this," Elka said.

He had once been suspicious while others accepted the newcomers for the gifts they brought. But now he knew Bahm and Mistokin and knew why they came, and it was he who was ready to defend them against his tribesmen's threats. Conflicts existed between the white pair and the Wai Wai, true. But they were between their ways and the Indian ways. Bahm and Mistokin were not to be feared but to be listened to and observed. Shaking his head to indicate disapproval, Elka picked up his ax and headed for the path to the work area. The others fell in behind. He heard them talk as they walked.

"Our fathers fed fish poison to the rubber hunters," one said. "Mistokin and Bahm drink our juice, so maybe . . ." As they talked, a plan began to take shape. They had no fish poison, but their plan did not require it. They had agreed on the details when they reached the place where Bahm was marking out an area to be stripped of trees.

The Wai Wai were strangely cheerful as they went about their work—all, that is, except Elka. He was troubled, first that they should want to kill Bahm, and second that he would let them. They whistled and joked and laughed as they cut part-way through the smaller trees. One expert cutter moved to a big tree, the usual key to the cutting design. Its fall would tumble the lesser, partly cut trees to the ground. They maneuvered Bahm into a spot where the underbrush was thick and quick movement impossible, while they themselves found excuse to move to safer ground. Suddenly the laughing stopped and the men stood tense. One of them called to Bahm to distract him. He looked up.

"What'd you say?" he yelled.

But there was no reply. Behind Bahm the axman had made his final swing.

The giant tree wavered a second, then started its fateful plunge to the jungle floor. As it began to fall, Elka choked with alarm. He had been in on this plot to kill Bahm. He hadn't planned it, but he had known about it. He sickened.

"Bahm! Bahm!" he screamed.

Bahm did not hear him in the thunder of the fall. Or maybe Elka called too late. The giant tree lay prone. So did a dozen smaller trees around it, and torn branches covered the spot where Bahm had stood. All was deathly still.

"Guess we killed old Bahm," murmured one of the plotters coolly.

The silence was momentary. A jay, startled speechless by the sudden loss of its perch, recovered its voice and started scolding as it circled overhead. The whole forest then seemed to break into a jarring discord.

Through the din one welcome sound reached Elka's ears.

"It almost got me!"

It was Bahm's voice. He hadn't died. Unbelievable! Was this

Bahm's flesh they were seeing? Or was it his spirit?

He was picking his way toward them through the crowns of the trees. It was Bahm in the flesh. The plan had strangely failed. Bahm told how he had heard the tree trunk split and had dived behind a nearby stump. Two smaller trees, pushed by the big one, fell on either side. The tangled mass did not so much as scratch him. Believing he had been the near victim of an unavoidable accident, he asked them to be more careful next time.

The Wai Wai could not understand why they had failed. But it took no great reasoning to convince themselves that never again should they try to kill anyone with so charmed a life.

They finished the airstrip and soon afterward all gathered there to see the sky canoe bring in the wives of Mistokin and Bahm, and Mistokin's three young children. Wai Wai reaction to the strangeness of white men had been nothing to their amazement now over the first white women and children they had seen. Their curiosity was great, and it continued day after day in the villages or wherever they saw the brothers' families. Not only the light skin, the waves in the women's hair, and their clothing, but the ways of keeping house and cooking gave the gossip circles much to talk about. The white women plunged into the work, helping their husbands in treating the illnesses of the Wai Wai and with the teaching as soon as they had gained some knowledge of the language. It was something of a shock when Mistokin said one day that he must leave to work elsewhere for God; Mlayla had already left to work for God among other people.

Bahm and his wife, now alone with the Wai Wai, studied unending days with Elka so that they might speak the Wai Wai tongue as if it were their own. Their goal, too, was to write down the language on paper. Only when this was done, they said, could the Wai Wai make God's Paper talk back to them.

Muyuwa, so friendly because he was getting the tools and other items he wanted, had helped the missionaries pick out a permanent station-site an hour's paddling downriver from Baking Plate. It was high ground, out of the reach of floodwaters. The landing was marked by a steep white clay-bank just where the river took a sudden outward turn. The mouth of a small creek flanked the sharply sloping bank, its cut providing a more gradual access to the flat land that lay above. The soil was black, not like the ash gray of virgin jungle soil. A village of the extinct Taruma tribe had once flourished here, Muyuwa explained; for this reason the yams would grow bigger. The level area continued for several hundred paces back from the river, then lifted to a ridge, enveloped like the lower land in dense forest.

Elka was glad they had chosen this spot. It was only a short distance upstream from the site of the village he was starting.

"What will you call your place?" he asked Bahm.

"Kanashen," Bahm replied. "It means 'God loves you.' "

Kanashen became more than a place of homes built on "legs," of separate kitchen houses to cook and eat in, of small storage buildings. Adjacent to it arose a large Indian village, composed of temporary houses at first, followed later by permanent ones as more Wai Wai came to settle near the newcomers. The mile-long path through forest and field to Elka's Yaka Yaka was soon well worn. Before the newness of the houses faded, Kanashen's landing had become a magnet, pulling in every canoe on the river. At all hours of the day, craft from up or downstream could be seen lashed to the scrubby bushes on the clay-bank. At first curiosity and the chance to work for beads and knives brought them. Gradually people were attracted because Kanashen was becoming a center of Wai Wai life.

In the middle of the fenced yard, whose front, back, and side gates always stood open, the missionaries planted a mango tree. Under its deep green, growing foliage many events important to the Wai Wai were to take place through the years. In its shade, and in and under the nearby missionary houses on legs, the Wai Wai were to learn—to get ears for—God's Paper and reading.

The lessons about God they studied on a special day that the missionaries called Sunday. The people met after the sun had turned the corner and was starting its downward course.

Elka looked over the group one day and saw that nearly everyone had come. Yukuma, his peeve over the stealing episode long forgotten, sang loudly the songs he had learned. He might be off key or a beat behind the others, but he sang. As Bahm taught from a board with cut-out pictures, the women took their cue from Tochi, who sat and spat and talked to her neighbors. Her hard and bitter face reflected her ill temper. Old Kurum sighed; he guessed he'd *never* get ears for what the white ones were trying to tell them. As Bahm talked, however, Elka found he was getting good ears. So was his friend Mawasha, who had come across the mountains and now with Elka, Kirifaka, and a few others was beginning to understand.

Old Muyuwa came to listen. In reading he was slow but earnest. He was among those who came every morning before field work. Dressed in loincloth and a pair of old tennis shoes Mistokin had left behind, he carried a slate under his arm. He took his place on an improvised bench, just like Bahm's other pigtailed pupils.

Elka did more than try to make the strange scratches on paper talk back to him. He was not content until he knew what the scratches said—not just what they said out loud, but what they spoke to his mind. In the Sunday lessons, in the reading classes, and in the long language-informant periods with Bahm he learned about God and His Son, Jesus Christ.

Most of his people were slow to learn. But Elka had a yearning to know that made him awake each morning eager for another session with Bahm. He seemed able to learn where others stumbled and stopped in frustration.

Bahm had once thought he was presenting God to Elka in a spiritual vacuum. He was wrong. Elka believed in the spirit world with more conviction than he did in the physical. He believed that it was full of evil demons, that it trickled out a small amount of good only when pleaded with and appeased. It was not hard for him to believe that God was a spirit.

But how could a Wai Wai believe that peace and love, rather than injury and vengeance, flowed from a spirit? The missionary tried to show Elka that while the Devil was the prince of this world, marshaling his demons in the powers of wickedness, God was stronger still and held even the Devil's final destruction in his hand—that, though sin abounded, grace abounded even more.

Elka knew the evil side of life; he would have to become acquainted with the good. He could be won if he could be made to see that Jesus Christ was the one good Spirit, infinitely greater than any evil spirit.

Much of what he heard gripped him. The village granny lay dying; Elka decided not to blow on the old prophetess. Instead, he prayed that God would make her well, "if you want to, Father." The light of God's Paper was shining, like shafts of sunlight piercing the dark forest, so that when the granny died, Elka was able to bury her with peaceful mind, although he did not understand God's way. God's light was picking out aspects of his life that Elka saw as if for the first time, aspects he was beginning not to like. What did it mean, to love? The Wai Wai loved their puppies, and their babies, and their wives when they satisfied human desires. Was there more to love? The Paper told how God loved. His love caused Him to *give,* not to *get.*

For them, God had given His only Son. What could it mean?

Elka tried to talk about these things to his people. It was hard, though. No one wanted to listen.

"Come and drink," they would say to him. And because no Wai Wai stood aloof, Elka joined the eat-and-drink circle of an *onahariheh.* He took deep draughts of the sour *kurayi* pot and forgot about God and His Son and His love. At these times Bahm seemed an interfering outsider.

On one such day Bahm had tramped to Elka's village because he needed help on some translation. Elka was in no shape to assist in language study. With his friends he sat in filth, his stomach swollen into a huge round paunch, his thoughts keyed to nothing but taking in more drink. Bahm was shocked and saddened to see this usually alert Indian, so capable of understanding the deeper meaning of life, sit there in a stupor, looking up at him through glazed eyes.

The following day Elka was sober again, eager to give the help he had not been able to give the day before. His mind thirsted once more for the lessons Bahm could teach him.

"Soon friends will come to help me and my wife teach you and your people," Bahm told Elka. He spoke of Claude and Barbara Leavitt, also members of Unevangelized Fields Mission. "They will come in the sky canoe and will live here at Kanashen."

How was a Wai Wai to say "Claude" and "Barbara"? Trying to roll these strange names from their tongues, the closest they came were "Kron" and "Maramara." These were the names that were to stick.

One day the big flying canoe did swoop down from the sky to the small savanna. Kron, his wife, and two tow-headed youngsters stepped out. Elka and his people clustered around them to ask all sorts of questions.

"Why isn't the hair of your children black, like the hair of our children?" "Do you have a mother and father?" "What do you carry in your baskets?" "What have you got to give me?"

But soon the Wai Wai gave up in disgust. They walked from the airstrip to their canoes and paddled against the current to Kanashen. The newcomers, they muttered, were just as Bahm and Mistokin had been. When the Wai Wai talked to them, didn't they just smile and throw the same words back and make scratches on paper? Was everybody from outside so ignorant as not to know Wai Wai talk?

Kron wore glasses. He had had them on when he stepped from

the sky canoe. The next day Elka showed up at Kanashen with a new design on his face. He, too, wore glasses—scarlet circles painted with oily annatto seed and outlined in sooty black.

In Kron they were to find a husky outdoorsman with restless drive and initiative, one who easily took his place in their hunting parties and around their pots of peppered fish broth.

Florine, Bahm's wife—Ferochi as they called her—stood tall like her husband. Her hair was long and black like Wai Wai hair and her sparkling dark eyes matched theirs. Maramara was more their stature, but her hair reminded them of a puma's tawny coat. Ferochi helped them in their reading. She also wrote songs that taught them about God. It did not take Maramara long to find a home among the Wai Wai. It became easy for them, especially the women, to look to her in learning the ways of God.

Another white woman, Florence Riedle, came within the year. To the Wai Wai and her fellow missionaries she became Achi— Big Sister. She was a master of the magic of medicine. The tribe had learned something of the white man's potions from the others, but Achi lifted the healing art to new heights. She said that God had enabled men to cure sickness, and the Wai Wai should thank Him when they were successful. This brown-haired, brown-eyed woman of thirty, whose smile was broad and quick, was to become to the disease-ridden Wai Wai a symbol not only of health, but of sympathy toward them with her understanding of their ways.

Kron and Bahm added porches to their kitchen buildings. Here the Wai Wai gathered to watch the white families eat their meals. Elka often brought Ahmuri and their children, now numbering three. During his visits there, or at the medicine room Achi had set up under her house-on-legs, Elka heard much complaining by his people. They often came to tell of a grievance against a neighbor, or to beg, or to steal behind the missionary's back. Here he heard self-appointed informants keep the missionaries posted on the wild exploits of his younger brother. Yakuta, a bold, spoiled boy, had recently come into his armbands. Now he was a brash youth whom neither Elka nor anyone else could control.

Tattling, backbiting, and threats of blowing to cause misfortune were constant wherever the people gathered. Jokes and laughter usually resulted from someone's embarrassment or from a reference to sensual behavior.

More than once somebody among them would remind the missionaries that the Wai Wai were a dying people.

"Will you take your dishes with you when you leave after we are all dead?" one asked. The Wai Wai had no hope for the future.

Exposed, on the one hand, to a life centered on the Christ of God's Paper, and on the other, to the ways of his people, Elka was becoming seriously troubled. To have God was good, he said. But he was a Wai Wai. Could he live differently from his people? He was torn between the way of God and the way of his people. They were divergent paths.

Elka decided he would try to walk both of them.

One day a man who had come from a village on the Mapuera fell sick. A woman began the death wail. Others, more practical, thought to provide a leaf shelter for the sufferer on the edge of Kanashen. Three witchdoctors sought to pull him from the brink of death. Elka, Muyuwa, and a visiting chief of the Mawayana tribe from over the mountains blew tobacco smoke on the man and sang the songs of their spiritual pets.

Then Achi appeared with the shiny thorn that she called her medicine needle. She could just wait with her magic until they had tried theirs, Elka decided. She stood by, her needle poised; Elka sang rather uncertainly to the bush hog, the crested guan, and the spider monkey. Then, losing himself in his work, he sang to the otters, calling them from the Essequibo, the Kuyuwini, the Kassikaityu, from all the rivers of the area. His companions took up the chants. Patiently Achi waited. Finally one of them turned to her.

"Do you want to stick him?"

"Yes."

"Go ahead and stick the old thing."

She stuck him, prayed briefly, and withdrew. Elka started his chants and blowing again.

The man recovered. But who could tell to whom the credit was due?

Both God's way and the Indian way governed by Kworokyam held fascination for Elka. More and more he liked the merging of the two ways into his sorcery. God was good. And was not his brand of witchcraft good, too? Though he had been tempted on occasion to turn to black magic, he never had. He prided himself on his goodness.

But one day the time came when the two ways fought in the pit of his stomach. The inner battle started on the way to a dance.

Chiriminoso, the lover of gay crowds, had summoned all the Wai Wai to the village of Big Falls on the Mapuera. A messenger delivered his *shim-shim* to Deep Eddy. He started the *oho* with aging chief Muyuwa.

"We'd kind of like to have you people come."

Muyuwa, however, finally turned him down.

"I'm getting to be an old man," he said. He no longer had much spring in his step. His hammock called more strongly than field duties. "I don't walk the trail well any more. Maybe Elka will go. He's a younger fellow."

So the messenger paddled on to Yaka Yaka.

"This is news about the dance," he began when he reached the village.

Elka responded with an *"Oho."*

"Our drink won't be very good."

"Oho."

"But let those who want to come, come."

"Oho."

"And those who want to stay at home, stay."

In due time Elka sucked in his breath to show he accepted the *shim-shim*. He called the people together for a tribal council in his house. After obtaining reasonable quiet he stood up and addressed them.

"This is news about the drink over the high mountains," he began. "How do you hear it?" A buzz of excitement showed they were eager to go. He counted the knots of the *shim-shim* on his fingers.

"Start making your bread for the trip today." He ticked today off on his left little finger. "Hunt meat tomorrow." He ticked that day off on his next finger. Other jobs were assigned for days represented by the next two fingers.

"On this day," he said, grasping his thumb and pulling it toward them, "we'll leave."

"Oklee! Great!" they all shouted. A time of dancing and drinking was ahead and they were happy.

Elka led the gay travelers, a dozen or more men and their families from several villages. His selection by Muyuwa to receive the *shim-shim* indicated that the old chief considered Elka his successor. For this youthful chief and witchdoctor, the trip soon promised to be a test of his mettle.

A young wife fell sick just after they left the canoes for the high mountain trail. Two dawns came on the trail while Elka blew. She got well and they moved on. They reached the Mapuera landing, and there a small girl became sick. She could not travel, so they had to camp for several days.

"While you wait, make your dance costumes," Elka instructed. He himself made a *shurifana*. He took the girl—they called her Little Crab—into his witchdoctor's house. He prepared to go to the sky.

From his basket he took a leaf of tobacco, rolled it like a cigar, and smoked it. One by one he took out his little smooth stones and inserted them in his mouth. *Koosh koosh*, he blew the smoke

past them onto the fevered girl. *Pt-pt-pt* he spat. He took out a
stone and rubbed it on her hot cheeks. He sang his songs again
and again, calling on the bush hog, the anaconda, the otter, the
white-headed guan. Then he sang to the hummingbird. There in
the darkness of the stifling shelter his spirit ascended trancelike to
the celestial regions.

How long he was there, he didn't know. He never knew the
extent of these journeys. On his return he hastened out of the
shurifana to find the girl's father, for Kworokyam had revealed
that he would *not* heal her.

Elka himself was stunned and dismayed at this refusal. He felt
ashamed, even, that the spirits would spite such a little one. He
would have hidden this shocking discovery, as a faithful servant
protected the reputation of an erring master, but he did not want
the girl to die.

"Brother," Elka said, trembling, when he found the father in a
leaf shelter near the river. "Take the little thing back to Achi.
Take her without waiting for the dawn. Maybe Achi has medicine
to heal her."

Little Crab died before her father could start the trip.

The next morning all merriment was gone. Elka told them they
must move on to the dance, but his voice sounded as though the
journey were for the wailing of a chief. He ached deep in his
stomach. He tried to put the dead girl from his mind, but he could
not. *Why had Kworokyam let her die?*

If Bahm or Kron had been there they would have prayed.
Maybe he should have prayed. Maybe he should have said,
"Father in the Sky, this is old Elka. I am asking you to heal this
Little Body."

Did God ever let a little child die?

It was too late to talk to God. Little Crab was dead. He wondered what it was like to be dead. Did you burn in the fire if you
were not a companion of Jesus, as God's Paper said? Where was
the little girl now? He didn't know. He knew only that she was
not living and the Kworokyam had not kept her from dying.

The people loaded the canoes for the journey downstream. As usual, there was confusion in getting under way. But today it was quiet confusion. During the preparation another young father stepped from his place in one of the canoes. In his arms he held his small son. The boy had a fever.

"I cannot go to the dance," he said. "My son is sick. I will take him now to Achi."

To Achi? Why not to Elka's *shurifana*? It was still standing. Had this one lost confidence in Elka's ability? Had they all? As the man left to take his boy back over the trail, they all looked at Elka with querulous expressions. He was resentful at first. Then his resentment faded to despair. Maybe *he* had lost confidence in Kworokyam.

Once more they appeared ready to continue. A white-headed guan came to rest on a rock in the river. A young tribesman, proud of the gun he had earned at the mission, quickly loaded his piece and stood up to take aim. The gun blasted noisily. The bird flew off unharmed—it was the youth who was hurt. His gun had blown up from too much powder. Blood oozed from a nasty cut on his arm.

People pulled him from the canoe and laid him in the path. His usually big wide eyes were closed tight in pain and fear. Those who circled round him were afraid, too. What misfortunes had overtaken them on their journey! Suddenly all eyes seemed to turn to Elka. He stood in the circle, motionless, numbed. Before him seemed to lie, not the wounded young man, but Little Crab. It was not the stifling crowd around him that he felt, but the closeness of the dark *shurifana*. Little Crab was dying all over again. Kworokyam would not save her.

Someone was talking. Were they speaking to him? No. No, they weren't talking to him. They were calling the name of a local witchdoctor who lived near the river landing.

The local man came. From his basket he withdrew some tobacco, rolled it into a cheroot, smoked it, and blew smoke on the wound. The hot smoke bathed the powder burns, and the young victim winced. The witchdoctor sang a song, one just for the occasion. The bleeding stopped. The youth seemed to feel better; he decided he could go on.

Elka, the bystander, felt relieved. Kworokyam was still curing people. The other sorcerer had been successful; he knew a song that had stopped the bleeding. Then as the people got back into the canoes a terrible thought struck Elka. Maybe Kworokyam wasn't to blame for the little girl's death. The spirits, he realized, had *chosen* not to work through Elka. That was it. Kworokyam had not killed her; Elka had!

Of course, he had not clubbed her, as his stepfather used to club babies and as some of his people had killed their children. Nevertheless, her dying was his fault. He had pledged himself to good witchcraft. But if he failed to induce the spirits to work good for his people, were not the results the same as if he had intentionally worked for their harm? Because he had lost his powers with Kworokyam, because he could not persuade Kworokyam to overcome the evil with good, the little girl had died.

He was feeling unsure of himself when another thought struck him. The local witchdoctor had prevailed because he knew a song to use against the youth's bleeding. The song, not the witchdoctor, had made the blood stop.

That was it: knowing the proper song. It wasn't Kworokyam's fault that Little Crab had died. It had been the limitation of Elka's repertory. Elka felt better because this he could remedy. He would be diligent to learn new songs. He would keep a sharp lookout for new charms. His old confidence in Kworokyam and his own ability to intercede with him had returned when, still on the journey down the Mapuera, he was pressed into service again.

Old Kurum was sick this time. His stomach hurt badly. They stopped at the mouth of a stream. Without benefit of a *shurifana*, Elka started blowing.

"He will die," clucked Tochi. She seemed anxious to be rid of him.

Elka knew Kurum wouldn't die, not with the songs he was singing. By dawn the old man was well. Elka had been successful. He was elated. He had been right; it was all in knowing the necessary songs!

"On to the dance!" he shouted in glee, and on they went, arriving in the merriest of spirits.

Elka led in the dances. Stomp! Stomp! the men's line moved in one direction. Stamp! Stamp! the women moved in the opposite. Forward and back, forward and back. Rattles, flutes, whistles, and drums.

Their host Chiriminoso, Elka, and others knowledgeable in ways of the dance never let the singing stop.

"Drink, I dare you to throw me," the dancers sang. But it did again and again. They danced all night, dropping from the lines only for drink and for revelry carried on in the shadows. The sun came up and they turned to games. In fun they hit with sticks at an "anteater" and an "armadillo"—tribesmen in impromptu but comically realistic costumes; the animals fell over dead, and the dancers laughed uproariously. The sun reached the middle of the sky and was turning the corner as they stumbled to their hammocks, weary and drunk.

They slept the rest of that day and all night. The next day the men entered the forest to get more palm fruit for drink. That night only the women danced. Most of the men were tired from climbing the tall palms to cut the fruit.

Elka didn't dance the following night, either; he was sick. He tossed fretfully while the others danced. The next day he awoke with a burning fever. His head hurt; he was dizzy and weak; he was hot and yet he was cold. He blew on himself. He called for Mafolio, and the old master, just back from a healing trip, blew. But still Elka suffered.

One dawn after another came, and each time he was no better. Now it was her son-in-law for whom Tochi was predicting an early death. Elka was desperate; he thought he would die. He covered his eyes with his hands. In what may have sounded to others like a groan from a sick man's hammock he addressed himself to God.

"Father in the Sky, this is old Elka talking. Would You be the one to heal me?"

That day he started to mend. His fever broke. He knew he would get well. He was not sure whether to credit God or Kworokyam. By the time he was nearly well, the dance was over. Ahmuri, his wife, was baking the last of the bread to feed them on their homeward trip. But they could not go just yet, for others were now sick.

Mafolio had done much blowing and singing of witchcraft songs already. He was tired. He would welcome Elka's relief. Elka forgot his own sickness and threw himself into the task of exhorting the spirits to deal kindly with his suffering tribesmen. Day and night he blew and chanted, blotting out all thoughts except of the pains of the patient before him. His spirit pets responded to his songs. They carried away the hurt of everyone he treated. Once he even tried the songs he had sung for Little Crab. This time they worked.

All around him the people—Mafolio, too—were saying, "Elka, our Little Brother, has influence with Kworokyam that no one else possesses."

Deep inside himself, however, Elka doubted. He had had no power to cure Little Crab. And if he had failed then, might he not fail again?

He saw as a certainty now that the songs had not been the cause of failure with Little Crab, because he had sung them no differently today, and today they were working. Kworokyam could still heal people. Wasn't he doing it now? The thought that his lack of songs was at fault had been a comforting excuse for his failure. Now this was gone. He was back to believing that he himself must have been to blame—at least his relationship to Kworokyam was at the heart of the trouble.

This thought brought despondency. He was weak, helpless to help others, he told himself. His abilities were mere whims of the spirits over which he held no control. The people should have known this. But seeing his successes now, they forgot about his failures. (There had been other deaths before Little Crab's, he began to recall.) What was it the people were dinning into his ears? "Old Elka knows Kworokyam well. He can make the spirits take back their pain and fever."

Despite his own misgivings, it was true that he was having nothing but success now. Were the spirits choosing to lift him up today, only to let him fall tomorrow? Finally the last of the many sick persons he treated got well.

"I'm missing my house across the mountains," Elka said to his followers. "Let's go home."

Two days up the Mapuera sickness struck again. This time it was Tamalkuku, Elka's two-year-old daughter. She burned with fever, and Elka feared she would die. This time he talked to God.

"Make my little girl well, Father. I want to be trusting in You. If You make my girl well, then I'll receive You. My bad past I will let go, too, because of You."

He finished. He was surprised. He had talked to God before calling on the spirits of the forest. Why had he done this? He didn't know. But he used no charm on his girl, and she got better. He guessed that God had done it.

At the Mapuera landing, where the mountain path began, Tamalkuku was playing around an unattended campfire. She stumbled over a rock in the shadows and fell headlong into the fire. They pulled her out to find that her stomach and side were badly burned. The local witchdoctor who had prevailed in behalf of the wounded young man was on hand with a song again to reverse the action of the burning. Elka, however, thought the best hope for his daughter's recovery lay at Kanashen. Achi's medicine was what she needed and this, not charms, was what he said she should have.

Early the next morning the trip began again. He carried the fretful little victim for a while; then Ahmuri took her. Through the days and nights of the trip Elka alternately prayed and blew. The child was delirious when they came in sight of the steep white banks of Kanashen. Before the canoes were beached Elka called,

"I've come, Achi. My child is bad off."

Achi had heard them from her house, the nearest of the mission group to the river. Soon she had the girl in her medicine room. She treated the burns by shots from her needle and by ointments and drugs, and said that with care the child would live.

"Who kept your daughter from getting a worse burn?" Achi asked Elka. "Who kept her alive?"

"She lay in the fire a long time before anyone saw her," he said, looking down at the toes he was wriggling because he did not want to look at Achi.

"Who protected her when she might have died?" Achi asked.

There was a pause.

"God protected her," Elka sighed. "He is the one to make her well." And then he asked, "Why did God let my child get burned?"

"Maybe," said Ferochi, Bahm's wife, who stood near, "maybe it was because you pray and blow. Maybe He is trying to teach you that you can't do both."

Hnnnn. Maybe God was. Did it mean that Elka must choose between God and Kworokyam? He did not want to make such a choice. He was a witchdoctor. How could he choose God over Kworokyam? And yet, if he chose Kworokyam, what about the feverish, dying Little Crab? Elka's touch with Kworokyam was still in question. How long would the death of Little Crab torment him?

8

"Into the Pit of My Stomach"

The conflict between Christ and Kworokyam worried Elka constantly. He was puzzled, too, that the teaching of God's Paper, so disturbing in his life, had little effect on his people.

It seemed to have no impact; actually that was not quite true. Some who heard had their own version of the teaching. The sorcerer who had succeeded when Elka failed came down from his home on the high mountain trail to one of the Sunday lessons and heard that a man should be the head of his house. He went back home and beat his wife; he said he had God's Paper to justify him.

Yukuma knew what to do with the teaching: talk much about Jesus to impress others. He talked, but he did not waver from belief in the evil spirits. His second son, born of Tochi, was a child he wanted to have grow up. He carefully observed the taboos in order to preserve the boy's spirit. He refused to eat with Elka, because Elka had once sat high up in a toucan hunter's blind and Yukuma did not want the child's spirit to be carried up into the tree only to fall to the ground and be crushed. He would not dig a posthole for fear his child's spirit would fall into the hole and be covered with earth.

But one day Yukuma's son became hot; he seemed about to die. Frantically, Yukuma asked what he had done to make the child sick. Tochi reminded him that he had exerted himself in the child's first days by helping to carry a heavy box for the missionaries. To make amends, Yukuma took a heated axhead into the shed where the box, containing a small generator, had been placed. Pouring cold water on the ax, he bathed the generator in a cloud of steam. Then to offer further apologies for breaking the taboos of *foi*, he went to the airstrip, where he had done the carrying, and there steamed the field with cold water and hot rocks.

While he was gone his son died. Embittered on his return, Yukuma found no comfort in his old tribal beliefs, except to talk ill of Muyuwa, whose black magic he believed had killed his son. He found no comfort, either, in the Jesus whose name he so glibly spoke.

Others attended the lessons at which God's Paper was taught. They also learned to read the portions already translated. Yet what they encountered seemed merely to entertain. There was no reflection in their lives of the Paper's message. Maybe Elka was not wrong when he said the teaching seemed to have no effect on them.

His friend Kirifaka, an orphan, had sampled Christian doctrine and practice by living with the missionaries. One day he peeled off the clothes they gave him, put on his loincloth again, and went back to Deep Eddy, apparently willing to turn his back on all that they had taught him.

Elka's brother, Yakuta, now handsome as a copper statue, was given a girl his own age for a wife. She failed to satisfy him; older women attracted Yakuta. He took first one man's wife, then another's; he believed in sharing. In payment for meat from a hunter, he once loaned his current woman.

Yakuta and Kirifaka were among the quickest readers. They sang songs about Jesus. They knew many stories from God's Paper. But what did it all mean to them?

Yoshwi was a one-eyed woman whose sight Tochi boasted she had nearly destroyed by a spell. Yoshwi's tongue was as biting as her foe's. She heard that God said not to kill. But she vowed if her next child was a boy—she had had many boys—she would kill him.

A number of others now threatened killings and violence. Men said they would kill to get wives. Among them was Mawasha, Elka's friend of many years. He was muscular and taller now than any in the tribe, yet shy and gentle. His thick hair was like a black halo. Likable, quiet, unemotional Mawasha refused to let God's Paper deter him in announcing that he would kill, if necessary, to take another man's wife.

Rikaru, a hunter hired by the missionaries, did more than threaten. This Wai Wai youth in his late teens had spent at least half his years on the savannas as the foster son of a Wapishana. He seemed to belong to neither tribe. During a time when only Achi and Bahm's wife were at Kanashen, he became involved in a number of annoying escapades, put down by those around him to inborn meanness. One day he quarreled with a woman over a string of beads. Because she refused to give them to him he secretly followed her, her daughter-in-law, and the girl's three young children downstream; when the moon lit the path near midnight he crept from the river to their camp and bludgeoned them all in their hammocks.

His crime remained unknown for several days. In the meantime he returned to Kanashen, where he stole another man's wife. Elka, working on Achi's house, heard Ferochi scold him for his conduct.

"You should be ashamed," Bahm's wife told Rikaru. But his mood was one of defiance. He went upriver. In his absence someone discovered the five bloody, crumpled bodies floating in a quiet bend of the river. Somehow everyone knew that Rikaru had thrown them there. What should be done if he came back? When Ferochi suggested that they catch and tie him, the Wai Wai melted away, for they feared the consequences of direct action.

A group of Wapishana arrived just then. They had heard that the mission women were alone. Maybe there was work that needed doing? Was there? Indeed there was—capturing a murderer.

Ferochi had to take the lead in Rikaru's capture. When he was finally caught, she sat down at the radio in a futile gesture to call Georgetown to ask for police. At least she presumed it was futile. The transmitter had been dead for weeks. Achi had said to pretend to call. Maybe if Rikaru thought they were in touch with the outside world he would give them less trouble. Ferochi leaned over the set, twisting dials and speaking to it. Unexpectedly, the receiver crackled an answer:

"Come in, Kanashen. Please repeat what you said about five killings." Ferochi did; whereupon the radio promptly went dead.

The police were more afraid of the Wai Wai than Rikaru was of them. The representatives of civilized law were sure that these nearly naked Indians must be savage cannibals. Before they arrived, there were some anxious nights at Kanashen. Rikaru, imprisoned in an old kitchen, boasted he would get loose and kill the white women next. Elka nailed chicken wire across their bedroom windows and fastened slats to form a protective ceiling. Finally, within a few hours of one another, the police flew in from Georgetown, Bahm and Kron returned from the Mapuera, and Rader Hawkins and his wife, Ann, en route by canoe for several weeks, arrived with a new radio transmitter. In the hubbub Rikaru escaped. He was recaptured and, as if to show his contempt for his captors, easily escaped them again. Taken prisoner once more, he was flown out to a Georgetown jail. For a year he awaited a trial that never took place. No one knew just how Her Majesty's Government ought to handle a case of murder among savages. In the end, to prevent further embarrassment, he was freed.

Rikaru was the first Wai Wai killer to face the white man's

judgment. Elka was more concerned with God's judgment of badness: not just murder, but greed and gluttony, malice and hate, including his own. He had tried to be a good witchdoctor. But what had he done for his people? Were they better off than they had been before the spirits of the forest were blown into his nostrils? They were better off, he reasoned. But were they better off for his blowing or, as Bahm and Kron had said, for God's breath of blessing?

Christ or Kworokyam? He wondered . . .

No sooner had the horror of the multiple murders slipped a little from memory than the people were stirred by events that set God in direct opposition to the world of spirits. And the pit of Elka's stomach was the place of battle.

Ekufa, a tiny baby, was brought by his parents to Elka for treatment. He suffered from convulsive fits. Achi had said that God and her medicine could cure them. But Elka's ability to manipulate the spirits drew the parents to him.

"Will you blow on this little thing?" the father asked Elka, bringing his son into Elka's house at Yaka Yaka. Elka sat in his hammock, silent. Now and then he turned a parrot roasting on a spit over the fire. The father held the baby toward Elka as if to plead for his intervention.

"Why doesn't your wife's father blow on him?" Elka asked, referring to Chiriminoso, the child's grandfather, who had once more come across the mountains.

"The old father of my wife cannot find a cure," said the young man. "He told us to take the boy to one who is more of a witch-doctor than he is."

"Why don't you take him to Muyuwa?" Elka asked. He did not want to accept responsibility for the child's life. He gave no explanation for his reluctance; to himself he repeated the name "Little Crab . . . Little Crab." Why couldn't he forget the girl? Why couldn't he think of all his successes?

He could still see no difference in her case from the others.

He'd used those same songs to advantage before. New songs were not what he needed. Was his relationship to Kworokyam at fault? Or was it Kworokyam himself?

The sun was in the middle of the sky. Light streamed through the doorway into the dark house. Then without warning, a cloud covered the sun. The shadow nearly blotted the youngster from Elka's sight. Death was a shadow. It was moving in on this sad family. In pity for the young pair, he took the baby from the father's arms.

"I will blow. Ask the men if they'd kind of like to help you build a *shurifana*."

He laid the baby in his hammock and bent over him to blow. He kept on blowing and sucking at the hurt. After the witchdoctor's house was finished, he took the child there to continue working his charms. He blew and sang. With the coming of night he called all the spirits he knew to come. He especially appealed to his favorite pets, the wild pigs. Mafolio had said to work all night, and this he was doing. He went to the sky, not once but many times. He communed with the spirits on this high plane. The dawn came. Elka squeezed out through the leafy sides of the hut. He handed the hot, nearly lifeless package of bones and skin to the distraught parents.

He would blow again later in the day, he promised.

He did; that day and the next and the next. Deep down in the pit of his stomach he knew it was no use. The child would not live. He knew because the smoke he had blown on the fevered brow did not stick as it did when Kworokyam was to grant relief. It left the child's head the instant it touched his skin.

The boy died the morning after Elka's third day of blowing. The mother wept; the father sat silent and staring; the villagers began their wailing. None was more disturbed than Elka.

Why don't my charms work?

Bahm came by one day as Elka was helping build an addition

to Achi's house. He asked Bahm about healing.

"The spirits used to honor my blowing," he said. "Why don't they now?"

"The evil spirits heal sometimes," Bahm said, "but just to fool us. Kworokyam is the Devil's servant. It is his way of getting us to worship him instead of God."

"Hnnnn. Is that the way it is?" he observed, reluctantly. Again it was God against the spirits. Why did it have to be? Why couldn't a man both blow and pray if he wanted to? Couldn't he give his worship to God and his service to Kworokyam?

"God's Paper tells us we can't be followers of Jesus if we serve another," Bahm said.

In his usual thoughtful way Elka called Bahm's words to mind again and again. He knew that to serve Jesus Christ instead of the spirits would bring changes in his life. He did not want to face changes now. They could wait. He would consider them and decide about them at another time. For the present he would sweep aside Christ, God's Paper, his puzzlement over Kworokyam. He was turning to his old love, dancing.

He asked everyone from the villages around to come to his house to dance. More than a hundred came. They were the ones who on Sundays assembled at Kanashen to learn the ways of Jesus. But their thoughts were not of Jesus this evening. Much drink had been prepared. Their costumes were ready, and the people were anxious to start the dance. Elka had installed a door to keep them out until he was ready.

Inside the house, he lay in his hammock. Ahmuri also relaxed. How calm they were, and soon they would be hosts to a hundred painted, feathered, and thirsting Indians who clamored outside to get in! It might have been the calm before a storm. Elka lay there until he was rested. Then he said to his wife,

"I'd kind of like to have them come in now."

The party got under way noisily. The sour drink spawned

drunkenness. Hilarity gave way to violence. With no malice toward the door, but simply because it was in the way, the revelers tore it from the house.

Intoxication continued in some of the villages to which the guests returned the next day. But for those who lived at Yaka Yaka there was a quick sobering, and for Elka a return to the soul-searching that neither drink nor revelry could suspend for very long.

Malu, the third son of Yukuma and Tochi, was missing.

At dusk, Tochi became aware that the toddler was neither in the house nor in the village clearing. She stepped to the doorway and called. There was no answer. She called again, loud and shrilly, with the anger of a jay. Still no answer. She remembered where she had seen him last. Quickly, with a clutch of fear in her throat, she ran to the river. She called again, this time rather weakly. She went back to the village, and continued calling.

Yukuma, away for the day, sensed something wrong on his return.

"Where is my son?" he demanded.

"I don't know," Tochi said in a meekness unnatural to her.

"Why did you not look after him?"

The people of the village were now disturbed over Malu's disappearance. Some hurried along the path to Kanashen to see if he were there. Yukuma ran to the river. He jumped and skipped down the slippery banks to the rocks below and dived into the water. A mighty swimmer, he was everywhere—in and out among the rocks, on the bottom of the river. But he did not find the boy.

Yukuma approached Elka. Angry, frightened, and saddened all at once he said,

"Kworokyam has carried away my boy. Two of my children are dead. I want this one to live. I would kind of like to have you go to the sky and look for him."

In times past, Elka would have been quick to comply. Now he wished he could tell Yukuma that he would talk to God. He was feeling that God, not Kworokyam, would be their help. He said nothing, merely looked at the distraught Yukuma. Elka seemed unable to talk. He couldn't open his jaws. It was like the time when the young man who had wounded himself needed his help, and he could do nothing.

The villagers were now gathered around the two. They wondered why Elka said nothing, why he stood and stared at Yukuma.

"You *are* a witchdoctor, aren't you?" Yukuma shot at him, with some of his old arrogance. "You do have a basket of charms?"

"Um-hum," Elka said weakly. The spell was broken. "I am a witchdoctor."

"Go to the sky," the people demanded, almost in a single voice.

Elka had no choice. A *shurifana* was quickly built. Elka put on his animal chestbands and feathered headpiece. Clutching his basket of charms he entered the little hut alone. Just afterward Bahm came by, for Kanashen had been alerted to the boy's disappearance.

"Elka, where are you?" Bahm called.

"I'm in here, Bahm," Elka answered. "I'm going off to see Kworokyam." Bahm went away to look for Malu. Elka began his singing, but he merely mouthed the words. For Bahm's voice had started a different train of thought. His mind dwelt not on going to the sky but on his talk with Bahm that recent day at Achi's house.

"Jesus came to do away with the evil spirits," Bahm had said. "He came to release us from their power. If you receive Jesus, He will set you free from the spirits' binding cord. But you must choose either Jesus or Kworokyam."

"I'm a witchdoctor," Elka had replied, raising an issue he felt was worth special consideration. "I talk to the spirits for my people. What am I to do?"

Bahm thought that his position as a witchdoctor made no difference. But he said that Elka himself would have to make the choice; he would not urge him to throw over his charms before receiving Christ. When Jesus comes in, Bahm had said, Kworokyam must go.

In the *shurifana* Elka sang to the bush hogs. But it was not his pets he thought of. Instead, he remembered what God's Paper said about the time when the evil spirits obeyed Jesus' masterful command and forsook the tortured man who lived where the dead were buried. Elka had been impressed by the story while helping Bahm to translate the Gospel according to Mark.

Where did the spirits go? Into a pack of wild pigs feeding in the mountains. The pigs became violent and ran down a steep bank and drowned in the water. How scary it was! Were they like his pets, these wild pigs to whom the spirits fled?

Elka went on singing his old familiar songs. But when he sang to the hummingbird it did not come down to carry him to the region of the spirits.

From inside the big house, where they had taken to their hammocks, the people called into the *shurifana*. They supposed that the spirits had come down to occupy Elka's body. In their usual manner they started chatting with them while Elka, they thought, was sojourning in the sky.

"Where is Malu?" they asked.

"We don't know," answered Elka, imitating the falsetto he had heard the spirits speak in when they used a witchdoctor's voice.

"Did Kworokyam carry him away?" asked one in the big house.

"No," Elka replied. "We don't know where he is."

"Do you think he sank?"

"He probably sank."

Elka tried again and again to contact the spirits. But Bahm's words kept coming back. He could not concentrate on Kworokyam. All the while he felt as if Bahm—or maybe it was God—were there in the dark hut with him. Maybe for this reason the spirits refused to come down.

Greatly disturbed by his failure to lure the spirit of his pets, Elka left the *shurifana* in dejection. Yukuma was there waiting.

"What did the spirits tell you in the sky?" he asked anxiously.

Elka thought it best to say nothing of his failure, or that his thoughts had been of God. Turning away from Yukuma's pleading eyes he said,

"I did not hear them clearly."

Yukuma started to turn away, hope nearly lost. Then thinking suddenly of one last resource, he turned back to Elka to suggest,

"Maybe you can go to sleep and dream." There was no bravado now. Yukuma was entirely servile toward his cousin. "Maybe Kworokyam will reveal to you in a dream where my son is."

Elka tried, though it was no use. Elka did not dream that night. He hardly slept.

Malu was found three days later, his body floating in a backwater of the river. If Elka needed proof, here it was, in the sad sight of Yukuma's third dead son: While thinking thoughts of God, Elka could never exercise Kworokyam's power.

That was it. That explained his failures. Stuck fully onto Kworokyam, Elka could call and Kworokyam would answer. Stuck just a little and wavering toward God, Kworokyam held him in disdain.

God's paper said he could not serve both God and Kworokyam. Well, Kworokyam felt that way, too.

He was surely going to have to choose between the two.

Not long after Malu's drowning, Bahm and Ferochi left the land of the Wai Wai for a short rest. Before going, Ferochi taught the Sunday lesson. She said God had created all things. Elka was to think of this many times in the coming cycle of the moon.

In this and other lessons he had learned of the nature of God— of His holiness, justice, mercy, love. He heard the stories of Adam, Abraham, Moses, Samuel, David, Elijah, Isaiah. The Gospel accounts of Christ's ministry, His life, death, and resurrection, and the Acts of the Apostles—these, too, were materials for his thought.

In the continuing work of translating God's Paper, Elka still was the key informant. He continued to receive an insight into scriptural truths as his keen mind dug deeply into them. The first epistle of John was one of the books opened to him.

"... *Beloved, believe not every spirit, but try the spirits whether they are of God: because many false prophets are gone out into the world. Hereby know ye the Spirit of God: Every spirit that confesseth that Jesus Christ is come in the flesh is of God: And every spirit that confesseth not that Jesus Christ is come in the flesh is not of God. ...*"

Thus began the fourth chapter. It was something to think about in this world of spirits.

"*Ye are of God, little children, and have overcome them: because greater is he that is in you, than he that is in the world.*"

Maybe this explained why God's children did not fear the spirits of the forest.

"*He that loveth not knoweth not God: for God is love. In this was manifested the love of God toward us, because that God sent his only begotten Son into the world, that we might live through him.*"

They could learn something about love. Was there not a better love than that which the Wai Wai knew?

"Whosoever shall confess that Jesus is the Son of God, God dwelleth in him, and he in God."

Hnnnn. So that's the way to become a child of God, a companion of Jesus.

"There is no fear in love; but perfect love casteth out fear. . . . We love him, because he first loved us."

No fear. This seemed to fit his need, a need that Kworokyam with all his frightening power had never met. Maybe this gave meaning and hope to life. There was badness and fear, yes; but there was a release from this trap after all.

It was Elka's decision to make. Which should it be?

Kworokyam, the world of spirits, mostly evilly disposed toward man, who, without appeasement, rained fear, hate, pain, and death?

Or Christ, who came so far to bring love, peace, and life?

Kworokyam, whose power for evil would someday be destroyed by Christ?

Or Christ, eternal God?

Elka began to speak to the people in his house about God.

"Hnnnn. Maybe Jesus Christ is the one we should believe in," he said.

"Huh!" they said to one another. "Old Elka is just talking talk."

One Monday, with Ferochi's lesson fresh in his mind, Elka went hunting with his brother Yakuta. The trail gave onto a big rock.

"Who made this?" Elka asked suddenly, his question catching Yakuta by surprise.

"Who made that rock?" repeated Yakuta. "Why, I don't know who made it." He was more interested in bringing down a fat-bellied spider monkey than in discussing who made what.

"It was Jesus," Elka said, ignoring his brother's lack of interest. He climbed the rock and sat down. "This is of God's making."

"Is that so?" Yakuta grunted with a toss of his bronzed shoulders. Yakuta went on hunting while Elka sat and thought. Jesus, not Kworokyam, was the one he wanted to serve, Elka said to himself. Maybe he should ask Jesus to come into the pit of his stomach right now. "But," came the challenge of doubt, "maybe I'm not a true one. If I do receive Jesus, I will receive Him forever."

No, he was not ready yet.

On Thursday of that week he went fishing with Kirifaka. They followed the stream that bounded Kanashen under the sunset and emptied into the Essequibo at one side of the village landing. Threading their way up the creek, they shot many fish with their arrows.

"Why have we caught so much meat, Little Brother?" Elka asked Kirifaka. "Who is giving us so much food?"

"God," Elka continued, answering his own question. Kirifaka looked bewildered. And then Elka bewildered him even more: "I think I'd kind of like to receive Jesus."

"Why do you want to receive Jesus?" Kirifaka said with some scorn.

"Be quiet, Little Brother," commanded Elka. "Bow your head and close your eyes. I'm going to pray."

Kirifaka did as he was told, partly in obedience and partly in fear of the strange things that Elka was saying.

"Father in the Sky, this is old Elka. You are good, Father. Look, You have given us our meat. We didn't have any before and we haven't had to go far to get it. You showed it to us. You are good, Father."

He had meant to ask Jesus to enter his life. Somehow this was the prayer that came out. That night he dreamed he was teaching God's Paper to the people at Yaka Yaka. The next day he told his wife about it.

"*Kofi!* How scary!" exclaimed Ahmuri. "Why are you like this? Why don't you work your charms any more? You're a witchdoctor, but you don't sing your songs. How do you suppose Kworokyam likes that?"

Elka said nothing, but he noted Ahmuri's deep frown. He had noticed that she often frowned. Her hair might string down from the knot in back, but it didn't have the happy snap as when she used to swing her head about so saucily. He didn't think of her long, though, for other thoughts filled his mind.

The night before lesson time, Elka again dreamed that one like Bahm appeared before him and said,

"Let go of your sins. Say to Jesus, 'Come in.' If you do, He will come in."

Elka got up early on Sunday. He told his dream to his wife.

"Maybe that was God's spirit," she commented, not knowing what else to say.

It was time for Elka to come to a decision.

Here he was, a chief, a witchdoctor, a handsome young man, his body and limbs well filled out, his features clean-cut and pleasing. He was one to whom not only his own villagers were looking for leadership, but others as well; one ripe in the ways of forest and field, in weaving hammocks, in many other skills.

And he was torn by indecision.

Before others began to stir in their hammocks he left the big house. He strode across the clearing and entered an abandoned field which was being rapidly overtaken by jungle growth again.

"Father in the Sky," he said aloud on reaching the middle of the field and looking up as if he saw God sitting in His heaven, "Father, I want to know You. So make Yourself known to me forever. What do You think about that? Old Elka wants You to come into the pit of his stomach, Father, and make his spirit strong."

He sat on a charred log, still intact after the burning so many seasons before. He no longer looked up. He spoke as if the One he talked to sat next to him on the log.

"Here I am, Father. I'm a witchdoctor. This is what I am. I'm a bad person, too. I get angry. I scold my wife. And I'm sad about those things. But this is the way I don't want to be. So my old being, take it out, Father. You can because your Son died for my badness, in order to take it away. Fix me to be another kind of person. I want to be like You."

In contrition the young Indian bowed his black-crowned head, which even at this early hour was decorated with the downy white feathers of an eagle. One by one he named his sins: hatred, lust, envy, foolish pride.

"This is the way I am, Father," he prayed quietly and sincerely. "Fix me to be like Jesus. That's all I have to say this time, Father."

That afternoon Elka went with his family to the lesson at Kanashen. As he sat in the main room of Kron's house he drank in the teaching of God's Paper.

"I'm really beginning to hear it with good ears," he said to himself, smiling at the happy thought. Things were beginning to fit together. He saw now why the missionaries could live as they did. It wasn't they who were good. It was Jesus living in them. He understood, at least a little bit, the peace they possessed. If they let God into them, they were good and had peace. If they didn't let Him in they weren't good and were miserable. This was the way it fitted together for him.

"Hnnnn. So that's the way it is." Why hadn't he been able to know this long ago?

A few days later Elka faced the issue at an *onhariheh*. The eat-and-drink session took place in a hut at the edge of the clearing at Kanashen. A sick child was there, and a number of villagers had congregated in the shelter to find out how he was doing. Someone had brought a pot of fish broth. They were about to dip their cassava bread when Elka told them to wait.

"I am a companion of Jesus now," he said. "I want to tell

you that. So let us talk to God. Let us all be telling him it is He who gives us our food. Bow your heads and close your eyes."

Mawasha would not bend that towering head of his. Neither would others bow their heads or close their eyes. Alone, Elka closed his eyes. He did not see Achi approach the little circle with a hypodermic in her hand for the child.

"We will now talk to God," he said.

Achi, believing he had called for prayer because she had come, started to pray.

"Dear Father . . ."

It was as far as she got. Another voice was addressing the God of heaven. She opened her eyes to look, though she knew the voice. Elka was leading a group of his people in prayer!

"Father in the Sky," he prayed, "You give us our food. You are good to us. Jesus is the good one. Fix the ones here to know You. That's all I'm saying now."

He was slow in opening his eyes so did not see Achi run from the hut toward Kron's house.

"Claude!" she cried, running up the stairs to the gallery off the kitchen. "I just heard Elka pray. Do you suppose it can mean he has received the Lord?"

Kron learned of Elka's faith in a talk they had about a forthcoming dance.

"The people want to lift up drink," Elka reported to Kron. "They told me, 'We'd like to make strong drink and catch women. We want you to call a dance.'"

"What did you say?"

"I said, 'Hnnnn. I don't know about that. I have received Jesus.' But they just said, 'Gicha! You've received Jesus. That's bad to us. We like strong drink. That's the way we are.'"

Elka related how he had told them then that if they made strong drink he would not drink it. If they asked him to dance and take women, he would refuse.

"Hnnnn," they had said, "why are you like that? We're surprised at you."

Only Kirifaka, Elka went on, had said that maybe Elka was a good one.

In talking about the people's desire to have a *yamo* dance, Kron and Elka decided that a time of games, with sweet drink and much meat, would be a good su stitute. Elka left Kron to talk about it to his people. Kron went to the radio to report to Bahm in Georgetown that Elka had become a Christian.

Elka, witchdoctor without equal and witchdoctor still, but now Christ's witchdoctor!

9

Go Ahead and Die

Elka became a companion of Jesus as an earnest act of faith. He started his walk with God by carrying the burden of his witchcraft.

From a rafter in the big house, within reach as he lay in his hammock, hung his basket of charms. Since his momentous decision the smooth little stones, the leaf tobacco, the sucking tube, the headdress, and the chestbands had not been touched. Elka was still a witchdoctor, but he no longer practiced his art.

"I'll ask our Father in the Sky if He would kind of like to make you well," he would say to one who came with burning cheeks and aching head.

"But I want you to blow the breath of the spirits on my aching old head," the sufferer would reply. "We don't know God, but we do know the spirits."

"Hnnnn," Elka would say, puzzling a moment.

Maybe he could blow just this once; then again, maybe he ought to pray instead. Hoping to resolve the matter to everyone's satisfaction, he would look at the supplicant and gently advise,

"Go ask Muyuwa to blow on you."

Inactive, but still a witchdoctor. He would remain one as long as he held onto his basket of charms. Often he lay in his hammock, thinking about God. And always, it seemed, that basket of charms hanging above him came between him and his Father in the Sky. He wished he could get rid of it, maybe throw it in the fire or give it to Kron to carry away. But he was afraid to take the step.

Witchdoctors parted from their witchcraft die. This was fact; just as it was fact that people died from spirit-eating and *farawa*. He was a companion of Jesus now; still, he knew these things happened. He knew the spirits of evil were real.

"Jesus Christ is greater than any spirit," Bahm had said. "God is the only good spirit."

And God's Paper had said it, too: "Greater is he that is in you, than he that is in the world." If Jesus was in him now, could Kworokyam, though savagely angry at being abandoned, kill him and eat him as Elka had once thought?

Of course he could not, Elka reasoned. Jesus was in him. Kworokyam couldn't touch him. But just as he began to feel more confident, old Machere met his awful death and Elka's fear returned.

Machere was village headman at Yawara upriver from Deep Eddy, and a witchdoctor, too—not of Elka's power or fame, but still one who blew long and hard over the sick. One day his wife fell terribly ill. He worried that if she died he would have no one to lift up drink for him and his guests, and for a headman this was important. He blew on her; so did her old father, a murderous chief of the Mawayana tribe. But their powers were not enough to save her life. Machere's charms were useless. After she died he carried his open basket into the forest one day and threw it as far as he could from the path into the brush.

"I've thrown the old things away. I've scattered them so they can never be found," he said aloud, to no one in particular. He told himself, "If my charms could not save my wife from dying, they cannot harm me now."

But the belief by which Machere had lived was firmly ingrained in him. Twice during the night he woke up trembling. He admitted the next day that maybe he had been hasty. Before the sun sank he was almost certain that in tossing his basket into the undergrowth he had thrown away his life. Some days later, harassed and shaken, he came to Elka at Yaka Yaka.

"What about this, Brother?" he asked. "My charms are scattered all over the floor of the forest. Am I going to die?"

"Hnnnn," Elka said, glancing up at his own basket overhead. "I don't know if you will die. I just know that after receiving Jesus I want to give up my charms. You should receive Jesus."

But Machere turned away, fearful and sad, and went home. Some said he wasted away there, languishing a little each day, unable or unwilling to eat. His villagers brought him to Kanashen, thinking that if anyone could save him the missionaries could. They strung his hammock in a leaf shelter and from it he called for Elka.

"This is how I am," Machere said weakly when Elka arrived. "I'm dreaming. In my dreams I am singing the songs of Kworokyam."

"Why are you doing that?" asked Elka. "That's bad."

"I see my dead wife. She says, 'Come to me.' "

"*Okwe,* how sad."

"The spirit of the *haimara* fish is calling me."

Machere thrashed in his hammock. His breath came hard. He sweated and had chills. He groaned and sobbed. Just before he died he gave a blood-curdling scream. Those standing by said it was the cry of *farawa*. They recalled that Machere had recently eaten a woman's spirit. The woman's husband had taken one of her bones to the hills of the Mawayana people with the intention of performing the dread ceremony of revenge. Machere's frightful cry was confirmation that the rite had taken effect.

Talking over the event with Elka, Kron suggested that if Machere had died of *farawa*, it couldn't be because he had thrown away his witchcraft, so Elka could take courage. No, he couldn't,

Elka had replied. A Wai Wai could die from more than one cause. Machere might have died from violating the sorcerer's code as well as from *farawa*. If he had, which Elka thought probable, the horror of his passing would be explained.

Continuing to learn more about God, Elka prayed for guidance and strengthening in his new life. He wrestled within himself and one day decided, despite his fear over Machere's death, to give up his witchcraft fully and with finality. As he and Kron talked over the games they planned to hold at Kanashen they agreed that then, when all the people were present, would be a good time for him publicly to hand over his charms to Kron.

Soon the word was out and spread through the tribe—"Old Elka is going to give up his spirit pets!" Elka, whom they regarded as their greatest contact with the spiritual world, even above Muyuwa and Mafolio, was throwing over Kworokyam! Unbelieving, they came to him with their questions, but his only reply was,

"Come to the games. When they're finished, you will see."

Individually and in groups they begged him to reconsider.

"Who will blow on our sick? Who will go to the sky for us?" they asked. When they felt they could not persuade him for their own sakes, they pointed out the danger to which he was subjecting himself.

"Remember Kirifaka's grandfather?" they asked. "He was traveling the Mapuera one day and lost his charms in a cataract. Within a few days the old man died."

He understood their point: The fellow hadn't meant to lose them, and yet he died. And here Elka was deliberately giving his up. But to all their arguments he shook his head. Again and again he tried to explain that now with Jesus in his life, Kworokyam could not live there, too. Sometimes he despaired of their ever understanding. So to give them something more within their grasp he would say,

"As a witchdoctor I don't get to eat bananas and pineapples

and things roasted. And I am denied the meat of my chief pets, the bush hogs. I can eat just a small poor part along the pig's backbone, and this only after it has been hung over the fire for days to be smoked." Then, lest any should think his decision had come because he was tired of self-denial, he would add, "Because of God I am giving up my charms."

The people asked Muyuwa to exert his influence. The old sorcerer and Elka met on the far side of the creek at Kanashen, where some of the tribe was now living. Muyuwa had asked Elka to join him in blowing on Chiriminoso, who lived there and was ailing. Elka came, but he refused to blow. Muyuwa was dumfounded. He asked if it were true that Elka was giving up his charms.

"Um-hum, Father," Elka said.

"Why are you going to be doing that?"

"Because I want to."

"That is bad to me if you do. A witchdoctor never stops being a witchdoctor. Unless he wants to be dying."

"But I have received Jesus," Elka said. "I have received Him in truth. For this reason I want to throw away my charms."

"*I* am not one who will give up *my* pets," Muyuwa said emphatically. "I don't want to and I won't."

"I won't die, Father," Elka said respectfully, but in a confident tone. "God will protect me."

"Save one charm, just one—to protect yourself."

"If I hold even one back it will be bad to God. So I want to give them all up, and all my sin."

Muyuwa sat down on a rock in the shade of a tree. Elka squatted alongside him.

"It's like this, Father," he said, trying to explain to the old, hardened mind. "I'm going to try God to know if He is true. If I die, don't you be receiving Jesus. If I don't die, then you become His companion."

"*Gicha!*" the old man swore, getting up and walking in the direction of Chiriminoso's house. "I see I'll have to call on

Kworokyam alone." Looking back at Elka, he muttered, "I'm the one who must do all the blowing around here."

When Muyuwa failed to dissuade Elka, the people looked to Yakuta as their one last hope in changing their leader's mind. "He will listen to his brother," some of them told Yakuta. "Didn't he make your spiteful old father lift you up instead of killing you at birth? Elka loves you. You talk to him."

Yakuta found his chance to speak up one Sunday afternoon as he walked behind Elka along the narrow trail from Yaka Yaka to Kanashen, where they were going to hear God's Paper. They came to a creek bridged by a fallen tree. As they crossed, Yakuta spoke to his brother.

"Why are you giving up your witchcraft, Big Brother?"

"Because I have received Jesus."

"Hnnnn." Yakuta lapsed into silence.

Farther on they reached a new field of cassava. The path led over and around the charred timbers of the recent burning. Yakuta pressed his point again.

"Why don't you want to be a witchdoctor when you are with Jesus? I love you, Big Brother. We all love you. But you don't love us. If you did you wouldn't be giving up your charms and dying like Machère."

Elka stopped and turned around.

"It's like this, Little Brother," he said. "I'm trying Jesus so I can know if God is true. And I have to give up my charms to try Jesus. Don't be afraid. I'm not afraid. I won't die—maybe."

"Save just one charm."

"No."

"Save the charm of the wild pigs, your pets."

"No."

"They'll carry you away and eat you."

"I don't think they will."

"*Taa,* all right," said Yakuta, giving up. "It's up to you. Do what you want."

Elka, despite his trust in God, was not altogether sure of his fate. Maybe, just maybe, his old pets would eat him. He was a little afraid. Yet his faith was stronger—at least a little stronger—than his fears. He had put himself in God's hands. What was to happen to him was up to God.

The day appointed for the start of the games—near the end of the rainy season in 1954—dawned clear. The hot time of year was coming, and this day soon became a sweltering one. Visiting villagers from outside Kanashen built leaf shelters to protect their hammocks and night fires. The shelters were scattered on all sides of the mission yard. Elka and his family occupied a hut above the high clay-banks of the landing, just off the main path to the river. From the many shelters came the men to try their strengths and skills. They wrestled. They shot arrows at an old mattress and at a deer made of banana stalks. They divided into sides of some twenty each and pulled on a hundred-foot rope in a tug-of-war. They hit a ball into the air with their fists or threw it with force to one another.

The rougher the game, the more they liked it; but the heat eventually became unbearable for such exertion. Then they ran through the gateway of the mission compound and down the path to the landing for a cooling swim in the river.

The women watched from their shelters or from under the shade of the big mango tree. Games had been planned for them, but this first time they preferred to sit on the sidelines and cheer their men on, which they did amidst much laughter. They also busied themselves in providing ample supplies of drink and food.

There was no sour drink at this party. The missionaries had taught the women a way to make good *kurayi* without fermenting it. Cane sugar was substituted for the chewed cassava that had produced the souring action. And a hunt before the games had brought in plenty of meat, including seventeen delicious monkey heads.

For Elka, the games were a time of new insight. He saw that

his people could be happy without drunkenness and gluttony and without paying homage to the evil spirits and their own wild lust. He was glad for this. He wanted his people to be happy. In the days of his Christian beginnings he had found that true happiness lay in serving God, and that revelry and passion brought only distress and misery.

After four days the drink was running low and the meat was nearly gone; the hard-played games were at an end. Some of the people had nearly forgotten what Elka intended to do, but now that the games were over they remembered. A few of them stopped in at Elka's shelter to see him and Ahmuri. They looked at the basket of charms hanging over his hammock. They shook their heads, fearfully.

An old chief of the Mawayana, some of whom now lived at Kanashen, came by to warn him. Elka's sister stopped and pleaded with him. Tochi came with her scolding tongue, complaining bitterly that he would die and leave her daughter husbandless.

"You're going to die," one after another said. "You're just a young fellow. After you die, we'll all go back across the high mountains to live. We're not going to believe any of that old talk of the missionaries. They'll say, 'Hnnnn. Stay here, stay here.' But we won't listen to them."

Elka assured them all that it was not the missionaries who had changed him, but God.

"I'm doing this by myself. But you go ahead and keep *your* charms if you want."

"All right," said a man of suspicious nature. "But don't give up your charms to the missionaries. Who knows what white men with their magic powers may do to us if they get your charms?"

He suggested that Elka bury his stones under a *kechekere* tree. Then if Elka changed his mind he could dig them up again.

"No," Elka said. "If I fixed them that way I would not be obeying God."

The sun sank behind the tall trees. Elka heard Kron call the people together in the mission yard. He himself did not go but stayed in the shelter with Ahmuri. From where he gently swayed in his hammock he could see them come from all directions. Gone were the stalwart wrestlers and the jumping, shouting, laughing rope-pullers. In their place he saw a sobered people. They knew what was coming. And he saw that they were frightened and sad.

Nearly every Indian he knew was there, including visitors from the Mapuera. They probably numbered more than a hundred, but no one bothered to count them. This was not the colorful assemblage of Sunday lesson-time. The roughness of the games had been hard on decorative feathers; body and face paint, if still on, was streaked and indistinct.

Kron was sweaty, too. He had played hard with the Indians, but he looked as though he could go on for days without giving in to fatigue. His clothes, of course, made him stand out in the group. But it was the expression on his face that was striking. There was no fright in Kron's eyes. He was quiet and serious, but there was no look as if the end of all things were at hand.

The disheveled Indians squatted on the ground, or sat on their stools or mats. All faced the mango tree where Kron stood. He said nothing; he was waiting along with the others, waiting for Elka to come.

Elka, in his hammock, reached up and pulled his basket down from overhead. He opened it and looked at the charms for the last time. He would give them to Kron, and Kron would dispose of them in a place unknown to Elka. He closed the basket, tucked it under his arm, and then bowed his head.

"Father in the Sky, this is old Elka. Because of You I am doing this. Make my brothers and sisters and my mothers and fathers and uncles all to see that You are strong and that because I am obeying You, You will fix me fine. That is all, Father."

His wife busied herself with a household chore to show that she wasn't interested in what was about to happen in the mission yard.

"I'm going, *chuya,* my dear," he said to Ahmuri. "I'm going to give up my charms right now."

At first she said nothing, which was a way of showing disagreement. Then she spoke, in anger but through tears,

"Carry your old charms away. Lose the old things. Go ahead and die if you want."

Abruptly her mood switched to sorrow.

"I'm going to kind of miss you. I don't want you to give them up."

Then, on a note of helpless resignation,

"You won't obey me. So go ahead and die!"

Elka moved toward the waiting crowd. Ahmuri knew that he would not turn back. With a sob, she cried out to him as he departed,

"I don't like you any more!"

He walked as a sad one. He had hoped she would see it differently. But the path to the yard was short and he had little time to think of Ahmuri. As he approached his fellow tribesmen in the gathering dusk there was enough light to see that all eyes were on him.

There was a pair of steel-hard eyes—Muyuwa's. The single eye of the half-blind Yoshwi was fastened on him. Far back in the group a nervous voice burst out, breaking the tense silence,

"We're going to watch you die now." Was it Yukuma's voice? That would be like him.

"Hnnnn," said Elka quietly in reply.

He had passed through the gateway and was inside the yard. He spoke aloud as he drew near to the upturned faces.

"Whether I die, that's up to God. If God is not a true one, I will die. If He is true, I will not die."

"Why are you talking that way?" This came from Tochi. "You are talking like somebody who is not a Wai Wai, and we don't like that. *Gicha!*"

Elka, now standing with Kron beneath the tree, took the basket from under his arm and held it firmly in both hands. He looked first at it, then at the people. The tiny stones inside that oblong woven container had meant much to him, and through him to the people, during the past few years. As long as he kept them he held a power over the people, and over the spirits. Now he was relinquishing it to the One to whom it belonged.

From the people his eyes turned to Kron. No word was spoken, but he knew Kron's thoughts. Kron had told him when they planned the games that if Elka gave up his charms it would be the most thrilling moment a missionary could have.

Kron's lips parted in a half-smile. Elka started to return it. Just then a young man broke from the group and rushed forward. His eyes wide with fright, he grabbed Elka by the shoulder and shook him, pleading,

"Brother, you're going to die. Don't do it!"

Elka drew away. His time had come. He spoke to his people, firmly but not too loudly. He told them what they all knew but wished were otherwise, that he was giving up his charms.

"I'm trusting in God. I don't want to be taken up with Kworo-kyam any more."

Not a single person sounded an approving *taa*. The young man groaned and sank to his knees. Elka handed his basket to Kron. It was all over in that one motion.

Elka sighed inwardly. His first thought was not that the pulse still beat in his breast, not that Kworokyam had failed to strike him, but that he had obeyed God, and for this he was thankful and glad. And then in the briefest of pondering he wondered about the future. The people, for instance, and the spirits he had abandoned—what was this turning point in his life going to mean in his relationships to them?

He saw that Kron had put the basket under his arm and was turning to speak to the hushed group.

"Elka is no longer a witchdoctor," Kron said. "Don't ask him to come and blow on you. Ask him to come and pray to God for you."

Kron said he would take the basket with him to America, "but not so I can become a witchdoctor," he added with a laugh. No one else laughed; they believed he might. No, he said earnestly, he would take Elka's charms to his country as a testimony to the Christians there that one former witchdoctor in the jungle had become a faithful companion of Jesus.

He prayed, thanking God for His power to save this person who had been a servant of the evil spirits. He asked God to throw His protection around Elka.

The people waited for Kron to finish praying. Then they melted away silently, still filled with fear and sadness. Some went to the landing to paddle home, others with flares took the path for Yaka Yaka, and many turned to build their night fires at Kanashen. In the shade of early darkness, two stayed behind to have a word with Elka. They were his brother, Yakuta, and Kirifaka. In measured tones Kirifaka spoke for them both.

"Big Brother, if you see it get light and get dark again," he said, referring to the coming dry season, followed by the wet one, "if you live to see these, then we, too, will receive Jesus."

While Kirifaka spoke, Yoshwi, starting down the path to the river, paused for a moment. Through the dusk she strained her good eye to look across the yard at Elka. She had known him as a boy on the Mapuera. She had seen him grow to manhood. She had watched his career as a servant of Kworokyam. And now she had seen him renounce the evil spirits.

What this action would mean in Elka's life she did not know —or whether his turning from Kworokyam to God held meaning for her own life or for the lives of the Wai Wai. As she stepped down the footholds in the bank to her canoe she told herself that she would keep watching through that one eye. She would see what the spirits, or God, or Elka would do next.

10

Blowing without Stones

The scene under the mango tree stayed fresh in the minds of all the people. Elka did not fall into the river and drown on his way home to Yaka Yaka that night. When he walked the forest trails no jaguar leaped from overhead to tear him to shreds. But this in no way lessened his people's belief that he was doomed to an early death.

"Maybe Kworokyam is having fun with old Elka," someone said during a gossip period. All such sessions now started and ended with Elka's repudiation of the world of spirits. Maybe Kworokyam was going to let Elka hope for awhile, they said, but just when the infidel seemed to have a firm grasp on life Kworokyam would snatch it from him.

The rains gave way to the *tali-tali's* song, and still with the new dry season Elka did not die. His people saw him as strong and hearty as ever—in fact, robust of shoulder, arm, and chest, a handsome one, still expert with the bow, still skilled in all the ways of Indian life. Yet, they said, these enviable traits would not save him from paying with his life for rejecting the tribal beliefs.

He was not afraid. He might have wondered about the outcome of his step of faith, but fear had vanished. The struggle within him between God and the spirits had been fierce, but God had won; and since he was the child of God he was filled with the confidence of victory.

His children, now numbering four including the daughter of Uncle Mapari, believed he would die. "I'm going to be missing father," the older girl had once said to her half-brother Kulanow and his small sisters.

His wife, something of a scold like Tochi her mother, became almost more than a man could bear. Ahmuri was hospitable, a good housekeeper, probably the best in the tribe, and she looked after her family well. But believing that her children's safety lay in strict obedience to the taboos, she reproached Elka bitterly for his abandonment of Kworokyam.

"Why did you give up your charms?" she asked one morning as they bathed in the river, enjoying the water's warmth in the chill, misty air. "When our children get sick, how are you going to blow on them without your charms?"

"If they get sick, I'll talk to God."

"God doesn't heal us," she said, splashing water over the baby so hard that it cried.

"Huh! Being a witchdoctor doesn't bring them healing. I know." Elka thought of Little Crab and the baby boy, failures of his witchcraft. He had healed some—many, in fact—but he wondered now if they hadn't mended because God was merciful in spite of their not knowing Him.

After they had returned to the house Ahmuri stirred the pot of fish broth with a knife. They sat around the fire, warming themselves and dipping huge chunks of cassava bread into the grayish soup. She spoke her mind even more plainly:

"If our children die, I will not be your wife."

Elka knew he was losing his wife, but fear for the children was not the cause of it; his brother Yakuta was. Yakuta, who had stolen many women in other villages, had recently come back

to Yaka Yaka. Living under Elka's roof, he had thrown his enticing smile toward Ahmuri who, bitter toward her husband, was
attracted to the comely, carefree brother. Soon she was responding to Yakuta's wiles.

Elka had heard the village gossip. "God's Paper says it is not
right for a woman to be like this with a man who is not her husband," he told her. She met his gentle reproof with anger. But it
was nothing compared with the outburst of her mother.

"What are you doing, scolding my daughter!" snapped Tochi.
She spat contemptuously into the fire. She always took her
daughter's part against Elka. And now that he had forsaken their
tribal beliefs, her wrath was doubly kindled. "My grandchildren
have a snake for their father."

"You go alone to the teaching of God's Paper. I'll burn in hell
all by myself," Ahmuri burst out rashly, hoping to provoke her
husband.

Brazenly, Yakuta expressed brotherly love for Elka while trying to steal his wife. "I'll be missing you when you die," he said
when they hunted together or went to inspect fish traps or just
swung in their hammocks during the heat of the day. "Won't
you ask Kron for just one of your old charms? Get back the
stone of the bush hogs."

This was not merely a passing thought for Yakuta, nor was he
as concerned over his brother's life as he appeared to be. The
whole tribe had been amazed that immediately after Elka gave
up his witchcraft the bush hogs, so common in the forest, had
disappeared. No hunter had shot one. None had even seen or
smelled one. The pigs had vanished, mysteriously and completely.

"The old things don't come in Little Brother's dreams any
more," Kurum had grumbled.

"They don't even appear when we call them to their favorite
feeding places," Yukuma had added, speaking with his old scorn.

Elka knew their talk, but Yakuta repeated it to him anyway.
" 'It's because of old Elka that the bush hogs, our meat, have run

away.' That's what the people are saying. They want you to get back your charm that controls them," Yakuta said. He was a powerful persuader with a convincing tongue. But when he talked like this, Elka felt his words merely glanced off and buried themselves in the ground.

In turning from witchcraft Elka appeared resolute. He saw sorcery as evil and something to leave alone, for witchcraft had stood between him and God. Now God was the one to stand between him and the power of evil spirits.

One day two white men came to Kanashen, not missionaries like Bahm and Kron; they said they came to study Indian ways. They watched the Wai Wai bake their bread and make dance costumes. They wrote it all down in their notebooks. They asked Elka to sing a song that called a pet from the sky. He refused. He did not want to step over God to go back to witchcraft, or to give his people occasion to think that he had.

Elka stood firm, but he stood alone among his people in faith in Christ. His stand for God—and the very fact that so far he was still alive and able to take such a stand—was an endless source of wonder for his people. They themselves would not believe as he believed; they reacted to the new teaching in many different ways.

One practice of the new belief was shared by nearly all: They attended the Sunday lessons at Kanashen. With varying degrees of verve they entered into the singing of hymns in their own tongue. Some closed their eyes during prayer—though most felt it safer to keep them open when heaven was being called on. They had a willingness to be taught—not necessarily to *learn*, if to learn meant to receive and embrace. They would listen to the teaching and take into their minds, without applying it to their lives, the lessons from God's Paper.

They found no problem in thinking of God as a spirit. The evil spirits lived within them and ruled; so could God's spirit, if they so chose. In fact, Jesus became to them another spirit, added to the unlimited number around them. Once during the Sunday lesson the wind blew oddly in the clouds overhead. Tochi called out that the buzzing sound was Jesus stinging people. Another suggested that Jesus had with delight cut open the nest of the big wasps and these were stinging to a second death the souls of those who had died.

The reaction of most was to talk about Jesus, to make Him a household name, to sing about Him on river and trail. But no one was willing to take the step that Elka had taken, to put Jesus Christ in place of Kworokyam.

God's Paper was like a new charm. One sick woman, afraid she would die, resorted to the singing of hymns, not for the doctrine they taught or the comfort they might bring, but because to her they were magic songs.

Bahm's teaching emphasized the contrasts in the spiritual world. "Jesus died and rose again to destroy the evil spirits," he said. "He sacrificed Himself to break the hold of the bad spirits. He cut the binding vines of the taboos. If He did that, how could He live alongside the evil spirits within you? It must be Jesus or the spirits. If He comes in, the evil one must go."

Little by little some effect could be seen. There were no child killings, despite occasional threats. A few persons were beginning to feel uneasy in their old ways—at least, at times. Typical was Tochi. Sometimes it seemed that the love of God was getting under that old brown skin. Almost in spite of herself, now and then, she let a pleasant side of her nature show through. Elka had seen her weep when Malu was drowned. Once in a while she looked at Ahmuri and at Rataru, her other daughter whom Yukuma had claimed, wishing for them a better life than she had known. Some days she even told Yukuma that maybe she ought not be his wife, that he should cling to Rataru and she to Kurum. Perhaps she meant it, perhaps she didn't.

For some the reaction to the teaching and Elka's witness was to become even more fearful about the retribution of the spirits.

One father sat faithfully listening to the stories of God's power. But all the time he worried that the spirit of the dead Little Crab was slowly pulling his own child down the slippery path to death. Witchcraft, he believed, was his only hope to ward off the disaster.

The conflict within the tribe between the new ways and the old had grown sharper in the days after Elka threw away his charms. The people readily accepted the little acts of kindness, the interest, and the love of the missionaries and now of their young Christian leader. It was the message of sin and salvation that disturbed. It was disrupting to their ways of vengeance, gossip, sensuality—ways in which they preferred to live. For this reason opposition to the message mounted, though little of this was in the open.

Some of the resistance took the form of a continuation—perhaps an intensifying—of the old practices. The lure of the sour drink and dance orgies seemed not to abate in the slightest. And Muyuwa, friendly as ever to their faces, worked behind the missionaries' backs. For him medicine was the divider. His cures were a part of his belief in spirits; the missionaries had made it plain that their medicine was an instrument in the hand of God. The two medicines were rivals, Muyuwa saw, because the two systems they represented were rivals. He urged people to avoid Achi's pills and to hide when she came with her shiny needle.

Reading was something new that all who took part in enjoyed. They thought very pretty the alphabet letters that Ferochi painted on wood chips and strung on a wire hanger, and were delighted with the pictures she drew of familiar objects in their primers and simple books. Bahm taught the men, one by one or in small groups, up to five classes a day. Whenever he was gone, Kron took over. Achi taught the women. Ferochi was pressed to keep Yakuta and Kirifaka in new material, for they learned quickly. Mawasha was slower, but he plugged away steadily. Let him learn something and he knew it thoroughly. He was not one to forget.

Elka was impressed with words and letters. One morning he showed up for class with the respect he felt for reading plainly visible on his face. Instead of the usual symmetrical design decorating his cheeks and forehead, he had painted letters of the alphabet. Because he looked in his piece of broken mirror to put them on, he had of course printed them backward.

But with Elka, there was a deeper appreciation of his new learning. The day came when he decided he should help teach his people.

In the big communal house at Yaka Yaka he built a study desk, just high enough off the dirt floor so that he could sit at it on his little carved stool. Here he studied and also taught his wife to make the letters talk back to her. And here, using a blackboard he had obtained from the missionaries and hung over the desk, he taught his people Wai Wai letters, and not content to let his teaching stop there, the truths of God's Paper. Before calling them together he was careful to ask God to cause them to get ears, or understanding.

"Will you come?" he would ask them.

"Um-hum," they would reply.

They gathered either in the big house in front of his board or in the communal workhouse. The men sat on their stools, the women on woven mats. They would not close their eyes—the majority wouldn't, at least—when he prayed. They listened as he taught, but when he had gone through the alphabet and started on God's Paper they refused to act on his words that admonished them to become companions of Jesus.

"I'm not a witchdoctor any more," he would say. "All my badness, I don't want now. I want to be a talker to God." He often started his lessons by speaking of the world of nature with which they were all so familiar.

"Look, the ground is what God made," he would say. All eyes

followed his gaze as his face dipped toward the earth floor. He spoke also of the sun, the stars, the sky, the rocks, and the big mountains. In imagination they let him take them to each of these handiworks of God.

Yoshwi listened carefully to the talk of earth and sky. Holding a squirming four-year-old boy and a baby girl in her lap, she nevertheless focused her good eye on Elka; if she spoke crossly to the boy or guided the baby's mouth to her breast, she did it absently. Her mind was completely taken up with the words Elka spoke.

From the world around them he would go on to talk about Jesus, the life He lived and His death on the cross. "Jesus' hands and feet were pierced," he said. Yukuma was impressed with this vivid detail of the story, though his mind could not grasp the deeper meaning. Later, Yukuma was helping build an addition onto Bahm's house. He put nails to his palms and insteps and wondered how it must have felt.

Sometimes Elka spoke of the badness in the Wai Wai people and the trouble it caused. "If a snake gets in your house, do you keep looking at it or pick it up and play with it? No, you kill it or fly out of the house. Sin is like a snake. But Jesus can help you overcome sin. Let Him lift you out of it."

He knew they still thought he was to be the victim of Kworokyam's retribution. For this reason he often said, "You think I am one to be dying. But I am not going to die because of Kworokyam." All doubt was now settled in his own mind, and with a new confidence he thrust out the challenge he had spoken before: "If I die, don't you become a companion of Jesus. If I don't die, answer to God in the pit of your stomach. Let Him turn you around."

"How will He fix us?" asked Mawasha in the first indication that he was interested.

"Jesus will fix you fine," Elka answered.

"Maybe that's the way it will be," someone said.

After this faintest of assents Elka would dismiss them with, "That's all I want to tell you today."

Usually the people were silent as they left these sessions, lest their buzzing talk give Elka the idea that they approved of what he told them. Occasionally someone would ask Elka if, being a companion of Jesus now, he were still a headman.

"Um-hum," he would answer, "I'm still a headman. I am a headman if that is the way God wants me to be."

Sometimes a person would say he was seeing Elka as "another one." Why, he wanted to know, were people obeying him? Before, Elka was not always obeyed. Now, however, he spoke with authority. He said, "This is right" or "This is wrong." He did not change his stand on right and wrong according to the desires of the person asking him.

Elka knew why. He no longer had to fear that his spirit would be eaten. He did not have to ward off a dire fate by appeasing someone who did not like his reproving words.

Elka was saying these days, "God's Paper tells us how we should live." The people had thought he would die, and nobody obeyed a dying one. Yet they were obeying him. Indeed, Elka was now more of a leader than he had ever been in all his life.

Elka knew the secret: He was changed—he was "another one."

Much of his time was spent with the missionaries. He was still an informant for language study and for scriptural translation. They were a sort of Paul, he a Timothy. But in frequenting the missionaries' homes and seeing the tools of a white man's culture, he developed an appetite for the things they had. He liked the high chairs in which Bahm sat the baby son who had been born to him and Ferochi and which Kron had for his third child. Elka made one like them, out of materials at hand, but serviceable for his baby. He wanted to keep the infant off the ground and away from the eggs of the roundworm. His desire for things, however, did not stop with those he could copy. One day after learning to operate an outboard motor the missionaries had attached to their canoe he told Bahm, "I'd kind of like to have a motor for my canoe." As headman of Yaka Yaka, he said, "I ought to have a lamp to light my house at night."

He wanted to exchange his loincloth for shorts. A couple of years earlier he had had a pair but never wore them. He used them instead to cushion the seat of his canoe. The missionaries were struck by this voluntary request for clothing—until he insisted on red shorts. Then they knew that he wanted them for display, not modesty.

Bahm and Kron tried to explain that they did not want to make the Wai Wai dependent on the white man's world. If they should have to leave, how would the Indians continue to get goods they had come to depend on? And if they could get them, how would they pay for them?

They did help the men get guns for hunting. But they limited ammunition to six shells per man each month. This compelled him to keep up his skill as a bowman and allowed him to save his meager income for more essential things. They sold metal plates to his wife. She had no such handy item in her little stack of utensils. But they provided no cooking pots. These could be made; the people who no longer knew how could learn the skill again.

Elka had an answer as to how to pay for the things he wanted. All the tribe, he said, should give him part of the goods received in trading their grater boards to the Wapishana.

The matter of his position as the ascending chief seemed to swell him with pride. Learning that the land he lived in was governed, in the last analysis, by a woman in a far-off land, he asked one day if the Queen of England would not say, "I am going to go visit old Elka."

How deflated he felt when Bahm replied that the Queen had never heard of Elka.

He would pout for a time if his demands were not granted. But this mood did not dominate his life. Rather, in general he de-

voured the spiritual food of God's Paper, showing unusual insight for one who had had Christ in his life for so short a time. He read and reread until they were memorized the stories and scattered portions of God's Paper that Bahm and he had translated. He spent hours writing in his manuscript books. He became addicted to letter writing, turning out missives on his little desk to others of his people who could read, to the missionaries at Kanashen, and even to Achi, who had gone home to the States on furlough.

He lost no occasion, either, to be a witness for Christ. One day some visitors to Kanashen took their notebooks and accompanied the Wai Wai to Deep Eddy to see a *shoriwiko* dance. At one point the hilarity subsided. Elka stepped out from the shelter where he had been sitting and led the people in a song the visitors had also heard at the mission, "Jesus Loves Me, God's Paper Says So to Me." Then, before they ate, the people followed him in reciting a verse from the Paper. He prayed; some closed their eyes, some did not. But whether they understood the meaning of the song or not, all had sung as if they did.

Muyuwa's opposition to the gospel was becoming more apparent each day. Though he still ruled his village of Deep Eddy with a firm hand because most of the people there were related to him, he was losing his grip on the Wai Wai in other settlements. People looked on him as an old man, one who had had power in his day but whose day was fast dying.

A series of calamities brought the conflict into the open. First, his wife and her sister fell sick. He tried to blow their sickness away, but even the spirits seemed to have left him. Because he had chosen to pit his witchcraft against the missionary medicine, he would not let the sufferers be taken to Kanashen, and this did not put him in good favor with the people. Most of them had come to see the value of the shots and pills and other treatments their beloved Achi gave them. The two old women died on the

F

same day. The loss of his wife cost him prestige, for what was a chief without a wife?

He desperately wanted another wife. Picking out a young girl, he tried to take her by force. When she and her family protested, he threatened to eat the spirit of her brother. The tribe met one day in the yard at Kanashen and in the safety of numbers scolded him. Remaining wifeless, he went back home to nurse in the pit of his stomach this mortifying wound.

Soon afterward his grandson became deathly sick. In this illness the old sorcerer saw a way to regain what he had lost and to assure that Kworokyam's position, challenged by the missionaries and Elka, would never be challenged again. Slowly, the way opened for Muyuwa's one bold stroke. It was to involve severe testing for Elka.

The sick boy's mother was the one-eyed Yoshwi, his father the adopted son of Muyuwa. Yoshwi had come over the mountains with another husband, but he gave her up when Muyuwa's son said he wanted her. With the threats of the old sorcerer backing up the demands of his rival, how could the man hold onto his wife? Her first husband had been weak-willed, and the one she had now was not much better, hiding as he did behind the power of his foster father.

The son of this union was now four years of age. Yoshwi found him hot and delirious one morning. She untied his hammock and prepared to carry him from Deep Eddy to the mission for medicine. Muyuwa, seeing that she was about to leave, stopped her.

"Where are you going?"

"I'm going to take the boy to Achi. He's hot."

Muyuwa saw the chance to work his charms to good advantage.

"Why do you want to take him there?" he queried.

"Achi has medicine to heal him."

"Her medicine is no good. I took some and it didn't help me."

"Look at Elka," his daughter-in-law said. "He takes it. He's strong."

Uttering an oath, Muyuwa refused to let the boy go.

"I can blow on him and make him well." He believed he could. His old wife and her sister were one thing, this boy was another. He knew just the song to cool a boy's brow and bring the sparkle back to his eyes. Besides, he had to do something to redeem himself and he knew of nothing else to do.

For days he blew and invoked the spirits to come down, confidently at first and then in desperation. The boy was no better. Yoshwi, picking up the child from his hammock, felt his burning forehead and pleaded with Muyuwa. Before this sickness she would have scolded and insisted on having her way, even with her obstinate father-in-law. But she had given in on that first day of his illness and now after days of worry she was, like her son, limp and nearly lifeless. Her husband sided with his father, of course, and she had no will to oppose them both. So Muyuwa continued to treat the infant.

One day the boy appeared to be dying in his mother's arms. Finally, after exhausting all the techniques at his command, Muyuwa said he would go for help. At last! thought Yoshwi. If only it were not too late!

The sun had started its downward course when Muyuwa shoved off from the landing and nosed his canoe downstream. He had failed to pull the child through himself, but Kworokyam had not failed—not yet. There were songs that caused the spirits to smile that he did not know, he admitted. And there was one who would know the songs that were needed now. There was only one such person among all the Wai Wai: Elka.

Muyuwa paddled swiftly and silently past the abandoned landing of Baking Plate and then swept on past the high clay-banks of Kanashen. As he neared the landing of Elka's village he stopped paddling for just a moment. He nodded his head. Things were turning out well, better than he had expected at the start. If he could persuade Elka to go back with him and work the witchcraft in which he had once been so skillful, not only would Kworokyam prevail; in the process Muyuwa would tear Elka

from the God he had chosen. And what sweeter victory could
the spirits desire? Then wouldn't those who had turned against
Muyuwa come crawling back and say how wrong they'd been to
choose the missionary medicine over Kworokyam's!

It was nearly dark when he pulled up at the landing and
walked the path to Yaka Yaka. He met Elka just outside the
doorway of the big house and quickly told him that he wanted
him to blow on the boy.

"Oh, I don't know, Father," Elka said. He had been cleaning
the old rusty shotgun he once had earned and was on his way
into the house to hang it over his hammock. "I don't want to be
blowing on people any more. It's bad to me."

"Don't be saying that," Muyuwa said. "I came to get you.
Come do it just this once. I won't ask you to do it again."

"It's kind of bad to me to blow," said Elka. "I'll come and
pray over the boy."

"Hnnnn," said Muyuwa, "I don't see that as good for cures.
You threw away your charms. You abandoned your pets. Why
did you do that? You didn't obey me."

"Um-hum, I gave them away," Elka replied, "and because I
did, I don't want to blow."

"You'd better come, Little Brother." Muyuwa flushed with
anger. His whole plan hinged on Elka's coming. "Come and satisfy me. If you don't come and my grandchild dies, I'll talk bad
about you."

Ahmuri had stood silently in the doorway, listening to the
talk. She spoke to her husband now.

"Go ahead. Go with him. He'll eat your spirit if you don't."

Elka shrugged off her warning. No one could eat the spirit of
a companion of Jesus. Muyuwa tried again to persuade him, first
by coaxing, then by threats. Ahmuri, fearful that old Muyuwa
still had power to harm them, urged him to go. So did Yakuta
when he came in from the field.

"All right," Elka finally said, reluctantly. "I'll go and blow on
him."

"Will you?" Muyuwa asked. He wanted to make sure of it.

Elka sucked in his breath quickly, indicating he would. "Um-hum, I'll blow."

He asked Yakuta to go along. His brother could talk with Muyuwa because he didn't feel like doing so. With only the three of them in the large dugout, it cut through the current with ease. As they drew abreast of the white clay-bank of Kanashen, Elka asked why Muyuwa hadn't stopped at the mission for help.

Muyuwa cursed.

"They can't make him well."

Elka said little else during the trip to Deep Eddy. He was tired. He had spent a long day in the forest and had carried two big turkeys back to his village. And Muyuwa had chosen to come at a time when he was feeling a bit discouraged over his people's attitude toward God. He had held out as long as he could against the three who argued with him. But the weight of their words seemed to crush him. He had given in, and now the world seemed to be confusion.

Once he prayed:

"Father in the Sky, this is old Elka. It is bad to sing the songs of Kworokyam, I know. I said I would sing, so maybe I'll die if I sing his songs, and You know I don't want to be doing that."

Muyuwa heard him pray, but did not hear the words distinctly. The old man said in a tone of plaintive begging,

"Oh, I've brought you for no reason."

But Elka had given his word that he would blow on the boy.

Yoshwi had waited long for Muyuwa to return. The sun sank behind the tall trees and the tree frogs started their nightly croaking. Still he did not come. She shifted the boy in her arms, and her tears dropped on his hot body. Then she heard a knocking at the river. Muyuwa was back, bringing Kron maybe, with a little bag of medicine. Yes, now she remembered that Achi was away, so it would be Kron. Her boy would soon be all right.

When Muyuwa entered the house she was startled to see not Kron but Elka and Yakuta. This was real disappointment, for she had counted on the medicine. Elka must have come to pray as she had seen him pray over others. Well, if there was to be no medicine she at least would welcome his prayers.

Elka said nothing. Avoiding Yoshwi's good eye, he took the boy from her aching arms. He laid him in a hammock, drew up a stool, sat down. Muyuwa reached up for his basket of charms. He fished for a particular stone and held it out to Elka.

"No," said Elka. "Just tobacco. I will sing Kworokyam's songs and blow without the stones." He had given his word to blow and would not go back on it, but to ease his conscience he refused the use of a stone. It was his method of not going back all the way, all the way that he had come since that day under the mango when he had given up his stones.

Yoshwi could not believe what she was seeing and hearing. What was Elka doing? Maybe it was her poor sight and throbbing head. No, her faculties had not lied. This was Elka—Elka who had handed his basket of charms to Kron under the tree, Elka whom she had watched so closely, who had taught them in his own house that Jesus and the spirits could not live side by side. This was Elka, and he was blowing and singing the songs of the evil spirits.

Elka blew, *koosh koosh*, and sang his old incantations through most of the night. One after another the songs came back that once he had used with such success.

> Dear little agouti, creature of the forest,
> Come with your grizzled coat
> And lie in the bosom of this child;
> Spirit of the agouti, hide your evil,
> Bring healing, bring health.

He sang to this rabbitlike rodent and to the squirrels and fat-bellied spider monkeys. He sang to all the pets he once knew— except the wild pig. For some reason he did not feel like calling on it. Neither did he sing to the hummingbird. He could not bring himself to ask that spirit to come and transport him to the sky.

As he sat by the child, conflicting emotions surged through him. He found he was singing the songs he had once used so often, and it seemed as though he had never abandoned them. Yet once a song was sung, he was filled with guilt and shame. He wanted to pray for the child; but he felt he could not both pray and sing Kworokyam's songs, and he had promised to sing and blow.

He blew until the dawning. Then he stood up. "Come, Brother," he said to the sleeping Yakuta. "It's time to go."

Muyawa stirred from his napping. He looked at the boy and then at Elka.

"That's all the blowing, Father," Elka said. "Now maybe he won't die."

"Are you sure he won't?" Muyawa asked.

"I don't think so," Elka said. Yoshwi had the boy in her arms again. He was still hot. He stirred a little; he was asleep, yet he wasn't. "No, I don't think he will die."

Muyuwa was grateful. If the boy lived, it would be to Kworokyam's credit. And people would say that old Muyuwa wasn't so bad after all, refusing the missionary medicine and not praying to Jesus. And they would know that Elka had *blown* on the boy, not prayed over him. Yes, they would know. Muyuwa would see to that.

Relieved and joyful, the old man looked around for something to offer as payment. Seeing a stalk of bananas hanging near the doorway, he cut it down and pressed the fruit into Elka's arms.

"Come, I'll take you back to your village," he said.

Elka replied that he did not want to go back by the river. He and Yakuta would walk the trail through the forest. He was so insistent that Muyuwa finally let them go.

The trail was long and hard, and Elka had had no sleep. He was nearly exhausted when they reached the edge of the Kanashen clearing. A draught of starch drink would be most welcome.

"Wait," Elka said, putting out a hand to hold Yakuta back. If they entered from Deep Eddy, Kron would ask why they came from that direction. He had already declined to travel by river because he did not want Kron to know how he had spent the night. So they circled around Kanashen and entered it from the path that came up from Yaka Yaka.

"You came?" hailed Kron as he saw the brothers walk the path to his house. "Where did you come from?" Both were standard greetings.

"We came to see you," Elka said. He did not want to lie by saying they had come from Yaka Yaka.

"What do you have?" Kron asked, in the Wai Wai way of talking about the obvious.

"Oh, just some old bananas," Elka replied.

"Where did you get them?" Kron enjoyed this exchange of small talk, and he was becoming proficient in the language. Elka hesitated. To say Yaka Yaka would be a lie. To say Deep Eddy would reveal an act Elka felt to be even more despicable than lying. He started to tell the truth. But he could not form his lips to say "Deep Eddy."

"Yaka Yaka," he finally said, choosing the lie.

In the big house at Yaka Yaka, Ahmuri asked her husband if he had blown on the sick boy.

"Um-hum," he said, and sucked in his breath, almost choking on it. "Oh, how bad! I see it now."

Tears welled in his eyes. "Now I guess others will come and ask me to blow on their children when they get sick."

He turned aside. In a dark edge of the house he poured out his broken spirit to God. "Father, cease to frown on me," he pleaded in asking for forgiveness. "Make me one to be strong, one who will obey You, not people, whatever they may ask me to do. People out-talk me. Make me out-talk them."

He wept bitter tears that streaked the designs on his face. After hours of weeping he dried them and painted his face again. He now felt his Father in the Sky had cleansed him. Once again he prayed. He thanked his Father for pardoning him.

At Deep Eddy the boy did not get better. Muyuwa had nothing to boast of, so he said nothing. Bahm saw the boy's father on the river one day and asked about the child.

"He doesn't get well," the father said.

"Do you want him to die?" Bahm knew of Muyuwa's determination not to let the boy have medicine. Usually the missionaries did not try to persuade the people to take medicine unless they submitted willingly. This time, however, Bahm was sure that if left unattended the boy would die.

"If you want your boy to live," he said to the father, "bring him to Kanashen."

The lad was seriously ill with malaria. The missionary medicine broke the fever and the boy began to gain strength. Muyuwa's plan had failed, and his place with the people was further eroded. They criticized him more than ever for keeping the child from the medicine for so long. The old sorcerer was broken; the people seemed content that finally he was.

Elka recovered from this setback. Gradually his pride and lust for material things were supplanted by a growing love for God and for his own people. He was to make steady strides. In a few days the attention of the Wai Wai was to turn swiftly from the faltering old one to Elka.

Kurum hobbled back to the house from the Yaka Yaka river landing. Breathlessly he called to Elka:

"Little Brother! One of your old pets, the anaconda, is on his way to kill you!"

Kurum had been whiling away the afternoon, bathing leisurely in the cooling water. He saw something stir a distance from the rocky bank.

"Whoever is that coming?" he had asked himself aloud. "Maybe it's a tapir."

The creature then lifted its head and Kurum saw it was a giant serpent. He saw it swim back and forth, each time getting a little closer to the riverbank. Kurum scrambled from the water. Trembling, he paused only long enough to tie on his loincloth. Then he hurried as fast as a sickly old man could along the path to the village.

"Little Brother," he said, gasping in excitement. "I saw a different anaconda. It had a white head. Like the ones that are pets of witchdoctors."

"Hnnñn," said Elka, his mind going back to former days.

"Was that the one that used to be with you?"

"I don't know. Maybe so."

"What if you'd been down there? He might have eaten you."

"An anaconda might have eaten me," Elka said, smiling a little, to Kurum's amazement. "But his spirit couldn't. I'll be careful when I bathe that he doesn't wrap his coils around me."

The incident was forgotten for a time. But three days later, while women of the village were bathing at the landing, the snake showed itself again. They scrambled out quickly, and at a safe distance tied on their bead aprons. As they raced to the house they wondered if this were not Elka's old pet. Over their cooking fires that night they talked about what they had seen. It delighted Kurum that even Tochi confirmed his story, which she had not the slightest inclination to believe earlier. Hearing them tell of its whitish head, he said with enjoyment,

"What I saw, now you've seen."

They talked of burning hot peppers at the landing, a charm sometimes used to drive away the spirit of the anaconda. Elka, however, said he thought they shouldn't.

"I don't know what you saw, whether it was just a snake or Kworokyam," he said. "But let's not be afraid. I have received Jesus. I'm not afraid of the anaconda spirit. If you receive Him you won't be afraid, either." Then he prayed before them that

God would make Himself known to them so they would not have to fear.

The following Sunday, Elka and his people were on the river, paddling to Kanashen for the afternoon lesson. Suddenly the snake appeared again; it lifted its head in the water just below the Kanashen landing. It thrashed its long body just the way Kron's outboard motor did. The people, frightened and excited, warned Elka that the pet he had spurned would surely get him now.

The canoe was already riding the waves kicked up by the monster. They knew it was a big one. Stretched out, it would probably be the length of four or five Wai Wai men. Elka was frightened a little by the physical danger of being so near the creature. There seemed a good chance that in their agitation the people would upset their heavily loaded craft. But the greater danger of spirit-eating that so terrified his people he did not feel at all. He silently prayed that God would quiet the little fear that he did have, and then with assurance he calmed them and steadied the rocking canoe. Paddling swiftly, they reached the landing unharmed. They never saw the snake again.

Elka should have died. Yet this disdainer of Kworokyam still lived. But for how long? The spirits were sure to descend on him some day with all their fury. Maybe the time was not far off. Scarcely had the anaconda been brushed into memory than one morning someone at the river shouted,

"Wild pigs!"

The bush hogs, gone for so long, had come back. Not since Elka gave them up—these, his chief pets—had they been sighted. Now they were swimming across the river, a large pack of the sharp-toothed swine. They were headed for the Yaka Yaka landing.

Hearing the call from the river, the people took up the cry: "Wild pigs! They're coming to kill Elka, their old master! Brother, they're coming to eat you!"

At last, they were sure, his time had come.

II

Shoot First, Then Eat

Elka dropped the fiber he was rolling into string. Dashing from the workhouse to the main building, he reached into the rafters for his old shotgun and a basket of personal belongings. With dexterous fingers he quickly opened the basket, pawed through it, and drew out two shells. He bounded to the doorway, picking up a canoe paddle as he rushed on, and sprinted toward the river.

Others in the village who had not bothered to gather their weapons were already hurrying to the landing.

"Wild pigs! Wild pigs!" they shouted.

The person who sounded the first alarm had been giving his dogs an early morning walk by the river. At the smell of the pigs the dogs went nearly wild, straining against their leashes. Dogs tied to their shelves in the house soon picked up the scent. Wild pigs! And no one to turn them loose!

Elka heard neither dogs nor people. His ears were only for the grunting of the hogs. To kill one and eat it, that was all that mattered. How like old times the sound was! *Wuh wuh!* the pig in his dreams used to say. *Wuh wuh!* not one but many were now grunting. And the smell. It had been nearly a year, yet this morning it seemed as if their odor had always been in his nostrils.

He sprang past the slower runners in the path, and reaching the landing, ducked around the villagers already clustered there. He jumped from a rock into the nearest canoe. Drawing a knife from his waistcord, he slashed the mooring vine. The shells were tucked safely in his waistband, his gun was propped against a seat. He used the paddle to shove off from the bank and, kneeling, cut swiftly through the water.

At the landing and on the path people were still shouting. Some cried, "Wild pigs! The pigs have come back!" Others were calling warnings to Elka.

"Brother, don't go." . . . "Come back! They'll kill you!" . . . "They were your pets, Little Brother. You left them. They've come back for revenge!"

Any who had half-believed that Elka might escape Kworokyam's destructive vengeance now saw that notion swept away. Once it had seemed that he might escape, but now he would not; finally he was to die. Here was a direct encounter with powerful spirits, and no man was strong enough to come through such a test unscathed.

Elka's dog had been chasing squirrels in a field. He too sniffed the old familiar smell and raced to the river. Too late to ride with his master, he jumped into the water, swimming with almost the speed of Elka's paddling. Elka was nearing the middle of the river. The strong current carried both him and the approaching pigs downstream. He was close enough, he thought. He threw down his paddle and picked up his gun. But suddenly the pigs turned and started swimming back toward the far bank, frightened by the yelling and barking on the landing at Yaka Yaka.

Elka exchanged his gun for his paddle. Because he was more in the main current, he fell behind in what was now a pursuit. With quick short strokes he chopped at the river. Only once did he look back. Then he heard his people's warning again:

"They're Kworokyam's. They'll kill you!"

Hadn't the pigs relented and, turning back and fleeing, given him a reprieve? they asked each other. Why did he insist on chasing them? Did he deliberately want to die?

In his quick glance back at shore Elka had seen a tough-hided old man who bore the ugly scars of a near-fatal scuffle with wild pigs. There flashed through his mind, too, a picture of the dogs he had seen torn apart by the teeth of the angry beasts. All this had been done by very ordinary pigs, not spirit-driven pigs as his people were insisting these were. Yet to him these were ordinary pigs. Whether Kworokyam's or not, they had no power to harm him. Jesus Christ had broken that. As he pushed on toward them, how he longed to taste the flesh of hogs again! It had been years. But there was more in his quest than the satisfying of an appetite. By killing and eating he would prove to his people, once and for all, that the spirits could not harm one protected by God.

Had he looked back again he would have seen old Kurum move to follow him. Kurum reasoned that he himself had no quarrel with the spirit of the bush hogs, they were not his pets and for him there were no taboos, so he snatched a bow and bamboo-tipped arrows from someone who had thought to bring them. Kurum had been missing his favorite meat. He decided he'd try to get a pig.

He let himself down the rocky bank and stepped gingerly into a canoe. Some of the others must have been shamed when they saw the sickly old man setting out to trail Elka and the pigs; by the time the canoe pushed free of the bank Yakuta, Ahmuri, and a couple of others had jumped in. Two worn paddles lying across the bottom were quickly put into action. Those who had no paddles used their hands.

The pigs by now had reached the opposite bank and were scrambling with some effort up the slippery side. They got away only because tangled vines trailed to the water's edge and afforded them footholds. Moments later Elka grasped the same vines to pull himself up to the floor of the forest. His dog reached the bank with him and struggled up the slope.

"Don't go into the forest alone," those at the landing and in the trailing canoe called. Elka disappeared with the dog behind the bush curtain that lined the river.

Kululululu . . . Elka heard the rumble of the pigs as they made their way through the thick forest. They were keeping on a line parallel to the river. He reckoned that they were heading for the *ite* palms behind the abandoned village of Old Baking Plate. The pigs knew, he said to himself, that a meal of rich orange fruit awaited them there.

What was it they had told him long ago in a dream? "You should be knocking palm fruit from the trees for us to eat." He feed the pigs? Today they would feed him!

He hurried on. With his knife he slashed away vines and stringy air-plants, following a straight course for the most part. When the brush was too thick or a tree blocked his way he ran around it and sped on.

He knew the *ite* palm area well. Many times in years gone by he had dreamed of pigs feeding there. Waking, he had led hunters to the spot and they enjoyed a plenteous kill. Before becoming at once the pigs' master and the servant of their spirits, he himself had shot pigs there. It would be such a delight to shoot them once more. If he hurried he might get his prize before they reached the palms. Then he would have less distance to carry it.

"Why are you coming after us to kill us?" the pigs had asked him once in a dream. He had had no answer, for then his spirit was bound to theirs. But today he did. He was free, and it was in order to prove to his people that he was free that he pushed on harder and faster. Sharp, jagged-edged leaves scratched his legs and body, sometimes even drawing blood, but he did not notice. He was concerned only with killing and eating wild pigs.

He was gaining on the beasts. Their rumbling racket was more distinct, drowning out all other noises of the forest but the barking of his dog which had plunged ahead through the underbrush. Elka knew from its agitated tone that the pack was surrounding the dog. The pigs would leap and catch the animal by the throat if Elka did not get there in time to shoot.

He came on them sooner than he expected. Just as he had thought, they were closing in on the dog, ready to lunge and tear at him with their terrible eyeteeth. For their attack, the pigs had chosen a part of the forest not quite so dense as the rest. The sun was now above the trees and gave light enough for Elka to see that there were more pigs than he had fingers and toes.

One of the pigs turned from the dog to Elka. Sniffing the air, he eyed this new opponent. Elka, in turn, kept his eye steadily on the pig. He felt in his waistband for a shell.

What a big fellow he was! Was this the pig who had talked to him in his dreams? Was this the one who had pulled at his hammock and then swished by his face to stand in the sky?

"Hee hai yoko," the pig of his dream had said. *"Hee hai yoko,"* this one seemed to be saying now. He hadn't understood the words then and he didn't now. There was a time when he and the pigs had been in perfect harmony, but that seemed long ago. Now it was a dream that couldn't be recalled. It was almost funny, this parallel, and Elka would have laughed, but there was no time for laughing. The vicious old pig was poised to spring at him.

They've come back to kill you, Little Brother!

Quickly and quietly he placed the shell in the chamber. He raised the gun to sight at his straining enemy. The big fellow sprang. Elka squeezed the trigger.

The explosion reverberated through the forest. The pigs turned tail and ran—all but Elka's big fellow. In the midst of his lunge he had uttered a quick agonized grunt and had fallen short. He lay dead in front of Elka.

But Elka had time only to glance at the dead one. What a good meal he would make! With his dog, which had bounded forward as soon as the pack retreated, Elka chased the fleeing pigs. He got a chance to use his remaining shell just opposite the white clay-bank of Kanashen. Two of the fleeing pigs had turned back there, seemingly determined to settle their score with the dog. Elka quickly reloaded, took careful aim, and fired.

He tallied his morning's effort: two shells, two shots, two dead pigs.

The hunters from the second canoe appeared shortly. The remaining pig, separated from its fellows, was confused, first running in circles and then cowering among the roots of a tree. Panting and wheezing, Kurum summoned almost his last strength to draw his borrowed bow. His arrow went into the cheek of the animal. It was an easy and fatal shot.

Kurum shouldered his pig, and Yakuta reached for the second of Elka's kill. Elka, however, said he would carry it, something that as a witchdoctor he had not been allowed to do. They retraced their steps to the first pig. Ahmuri picked this one up. Yakuta's chivalry did not extend to her.

Ahmuri was rather proud of her husband. She had been afraid, like the others, that the hogs would kill him and the vultures pick away his flesh. He had been a brave one, she now said to herself, and it pleased her. He had been braver to taunt Kworokyam, even, than to run after the bush hogs alone.

The sun had climbed high by the time the hunters returned with their burden. Soon Bahm came by the house at Yaka Yaka, saying he had heard that Elka had killed some bush hogs. Sucking in his breath and smiling from ear to ear, Elka said he had shot this many, holding up two fingers. Opening all his fingers, he added that he would have shot that many if he had had that many shells.

"You shot two," said Bahm. "God gave them to you. That's enough for your meat."

Elka then butchered the hogs, another chore no witchdoctor ever performed. He divided the meat among the villagers, who accepted it fearfully, astonished at the inexplicable turn of fate that had allowed him to kill the pigs and live. He told Ahmuri he was hungry, that he'd kind of like to have her cook him up some meat.

Ahmuri was again frightened as she prepared her husband's meat. He had lived through the killing, but surely he wouldn't live through the eating! Nevertheless, she was filled with admiration, too. Maybe God *had* protected Elka from the hogs. And maybe, *just* maybe, He would protect him still.

Tochi came to her as she placed a potful of the meat on her cooking fire in the communal house.

"Is he really going to eat the meat?" Tochi asked her daughter.

"Um-hum," she replied. "He will eat it."

"Now he *will* die, *okwe*, how sad."

"Hnnnn. I don't know," Ahmuri said. She had reached the point of not being sure of either his dying or his living. "He gave up his pets and then he shot them, and he didn't die."

Tochi clucked knowingly as she went to her own fireside. She knew, as they all knew, that for Elka to eat this meat was really going too far.

Yakuta approached Elka's hammock, where he was resting from the chase.

"You shot the pigs, Brother," he said, "but are you going to eat their meat?"

Elka said he was.

"You are one who never used to eat that kind of meat."

"That's what I was. I have God now."

Elka had given most of the meat to the other men in his house, after first saving out a ham for Bahm, but in a kill like this there was plenty, and his own family had more than they could eat in a day. While Ahmuri was cooking he got up, took a stick from a woodpile, sharpened each end with his knife, and pushed the stick into the ground, slanting it over the fire. On the free end he stuck some of the extra meat, including the succulent ribs.

Yukuma approached the fire and sat in his cousin's hammock to watch. After some silence he said,

"Why are you roasting that? As a witchdoctor you couldn't. You'll get weak."

"No, I won't," replied Elka. "I'll eat this tomorrow, after I eat the meat in my pot today." Yukuma knew that Elka had renounced his charms, but like the rest of them he could not understand that the constricting holds of his sorcery had been broken.

Ahmuri mixed the juice from a palm fruit with cassava starch. She poured it into a pot for her husband. The boiled meat was done. She carried the meat pot to the small open-sided shelter where the villagers often ate, and came back to tell her husband his meat was ready. Elka broke off half a disk of bread from a rack above the fire before he walked out to the waiting pot.

Some in the house had been napping, others were feathering arrows or just sitting idly by, others spinning cotton thread while they gossiped. But all eyes were on Elka surreptitiously. As he moved, every man, woman, and child jumped up to follow him.

"He killed his former pets and now he's going to eat them," one said in a whispered shock.

"He's lived only to die at this time," said another.

"My spirit is about to leave me!" still another, utterly afraid, gasped.

Elka squatted before the pot. Balancing his bread on a bare knee, he cut off a slab from the pork in the pot—not the skimpy part he used to get as a witchdoctor, the part along the back, but a luscious lean morsel.

"If you eat more of me than along my backbone, I will eat your spirit." Huh! The pig in his dream had said that. But he had also warned that if Elka neglected him, Elka would die. Well, he'd neglected him, all right. Through a dry season and most of a wet one. And he was alive. Oh, wasn't he alive! Alive because God lived in him.

Elka looked at the people gathered around him. Some squatted
as he did; some clung to the poles that supported the leafy roof,
leaning over the heads of those on the ground in front of them.
All were striving for the best position to see. He noted that their
faces were drawn. Some stared blankly, as if almost in a stupor.
For these, fear had reached the point of numbness.

And why should they not be afraid? He knew what caused
their fear. He knew, because he himself had once been gripped
by it. It was the fear of death. Their leader, their relative, their
friend was actually going to eat the meat of his old pets, a meat
that by all the laws of Kworokyam was forbidden to one who was
master of the wild pigs! Death, maybe a sudden and agonizing
death, was the retribution for such an act of defiance.

He knew what they were thinking, but they told him anyway.

"Little Brother, the master of the pigs will die if he eats
their meat."

Old Kurum was speaking. No doubt he remembered the day
several years earlier, when Elka, young and innocent, had sung
the songs of Kworokyam. He remembered how he had warned
the boy that those songs were reserved for the servants of
Kworokyam. Elka had become a witchdoctor, and now he was
not one, and because he was not and was flouting all that
witchcraft stood for, he was doomed to die.

"My Little Body," Kurum went on, "I am an old man and
have seen many witchdoctors die when they were parted from
their charms. You gave up yours. Will your dying come by eating
the meat of your pets?"

He was sure it would, as were they all.

"I'm not a witchdoctor any more, and I won't die eating this
meat," Elka said, with full confidence. "I want you all to close
your eyes while I talk to our Father in the Sky."

He was the only one to close his eyes. He prayed that God
would give his people ears, that they would understand. He
prayed; they watched. They looked at the piece of meat on the

end of his knife. They looked at him. Any moment now Elka would roll over on the ground, dead. They knew it. Their fascination for things macabre would not permit them to close their eyes and miss seeing this awful happening.

Elka finished his prayer. He dipped his bread into the peppery hot broth to soften it. Then he tore off a piece of the bread to eat with his slab of meat. He took a bite of meat, then one of bread.

It was good, this wild pig, *oklee!*

He chewed with delight. He took another bite, and still another. Soon he was cutting a second piece and then a third. The people watched him silently. They followed the movement of his hand from pot to mouth. In quiet terror they observed every motion of his jaws. He smiled and joked, saying how good it was.

None laughed or even smiled with him.

12

"Greater Is He That Is In You..."

"You should have been there," Elka said to Yukuma between bites of juicy pork. *"You* would have shot lots of pigs." Turning to Yakuta he continued cheerfully, "Little Brother, next time take your arrows. Or maybe you want old Elka to do all your hunting?"

He laughed, but no one else broke the silence. It was as if the others were in a spell that held them motionless while the spirits of fear and frustration gnawed at their souls. *He* was the one supposed to be in danger, not they; but he was laughing. He was happy. They were the ones whose faces reflected a life-time of fear—a fear that was sometimes lost in a froth of gaiety but that came back again and again to haunt and to hurt.

Elka stood up, full and satisfied. He raised his hand to his mouth and shouted,

"Onhariheh!"

It was unnecessary to call them to eat and drink; they were all there. But his call shattered the air of brooding and stirred the others back to life.

Ahmuri broke from the circle to bring out the pot of palm-fruit drink. Other women brought stacks of cassava bread.

Elka stabbed into the meat pot and drew forth big chunks of flesh which he placed on the mat his wife handed him. This was for the women; when he had filled it, they withdrew into the house for their own feast. The men then gathered close to the pot, waiting for Elka to parcel out the meat.

"Let's sing 'Everything Is Good at My Father's Place,' " he said. It was the first gospel song they had learned in their own tongue; all knew its words, if not its meaning. Softly at first, then with more gusto, they raised their voices. After this they sang 'Jesus the Strong One Wants to Take You Along." Elka said he wished they would see Jesus as the strong one.

"He's stronger than any evil spirit," he said. "He's stronger in me than Kworokyam is in you. Jesus is in me now. That's why I am living." He told them to close their eyes while he prayed. This time not one eye remained open. . . .

"God fixes us fine," Elka said as they ate their meat and dipped their bread in its spicy juice.

"It's true that you have received Jesus," said a young fellow looking intently into Elka's jubilant face. "He does protect you. If it weren't so, you would have surely died."

"Um-hum," Elka said. "I want to obey all that God says. I don't want to obey Him partly. I wanted to drop off my old fear, and I have. God has fixed me fine."

They ate until the meat was gone. Then before the group broke up, the bowl of drink was passed around. One man paused on the way back to his hammock to observe,

"Old Elka is telling us the truth."

"I guess Kworokyam was thrown today," another said.

The others nodded. Truer words had never been spoken in all Wai Wai history. By killing and then eating the forbidden pig meat, Elka dealt Kworokyam a blow from which he was never to recover. Until that moment the people had listened to the teaching of God's Paper, but fear and indifference kept them from believing. Now they saw that God was greater than the evil spirits, that Christ had conquered Kworokyam. Elka's brave exercise of faith provided the proof.

"Look at Elka," his people often said in the months that followed. "He lifts up fish where the anaconda sleeps. He killed his former pets, the bush hogs, and the old things never hurt him. He ate them and they did not rise up to choke his throat. God is the one we should be choosing."

The patient teaching of the missionaries through the years, and the example of their way of life, had begun to take hold, imperceptibly at first, but firmly. And now the love and life of Elka and his growing leadership were having their effect. The tribe was first irritated, then impressed by his new and different behavior. He was quick to see a need—perhaps the cutting of a new field—and moved swiftly to accomplish it. His concern for his people sometimes was expressed in sympathetic mourning over one who had died. He showed more tenderness toward Ahmuri. He no longer looked upon her as a servant; through the eyes of his new faith he saw her as a loved one. When she was sick he did not berate her as other men berated their wives for such an annoyance. He cut across custom by assisting her in chopping and carrying wood and by minding the children when she was busy.

It was God's Paper that most helped Elka to grow as a companion of Jesus. The words it spoke were now penetrating to his tribesmen, too. Several Old Testament narratives had been put into Wai Wai idiom, and the people were beginning to comprehend them. They found new meaning in the lives and beliefs, the follies and foibles of the Hebrew people. God's Paper was becoming a mirror in which they could see themselves as Elka had already seen himself.

"My sin is bad to me," one and then another would say.

Ahmuri was one of the first to confess Christ. Fearfully and resentfully she had long watched the change in her husband. Slowly and almost against her will she saw him as strong and kind—kind as he had never been before he received Jesus. Had he not been patient, most of the time, while she flirted with Yakuta?

Ahmuri had heard Elka's earnest prayers replace the witch-craft songs. She could not quite give up her own belief in *foi*, the taboos governing children, but more than once she stood on the brink of exchanging superstition for faith. Though always busy, she occasionally made time to go with her husband to the Sunday lesson. Often she sat with him as he read from his Wai Wai Scriptures, and she took new interest in learning to read them herself.

Elka encouraged her to pray. He advised her not to hide her new-found faith within herself, but to speak of it to others. One day she had an opportunity in front of her mother. Ahmuri was baking cassava bread and Tochi was spinning cotton in the big communal house when Ahmuri said casually that she had "taken Jesus . . . just a little bit."

"*Gicha!*" her mother swore at this hesitant but sincere testimony. "Are you one to be talking this nonsense?" Tochi turned her spindle with a faster twirl. Yet even Tochi could not help noticing in Ahmuri, the once harried and resentful wife, a new trace of gentleness and sweetness.

Elka's younger brother, Yakuta, began to bring his carved stool more often to Elka's desk. So did Mawasha, his friend from Big Falls. For a half day or more they would sit at his side and listen to him read and study portions of God's Paper. Yakuta, a quick student, soon learned to make the Paper talk back to him. But when it talked about David's adultery he seemed to close his ears. He was proud that the wives of many men, including his own brother's, had succumbed to his entice-ments. Yet for all his self-satisfaction he was troubled by fear. He was frightened by the whistle of the toucan and other noises in the forest—not the noises themselves but what they stood for. They were spirits that boded ill. Sometimes in an effort to cast

off his fear he would sing with Elka a song the missionaries
had taught:

> Wherever I may be, Jesus protects me, . . .
> When I am in the forest,
> If I should still be in the house,
> Wherever I may be, Jesus protects me.

Still he was afraid. Only Elka, of all the Wai Wai, seemed to
have no fear. Why, wondered Yakuta, couldn't he be like Elka?
His brother had explained again and again that he was a different
one because now he had God's spirit in his life. Kron and Bahm,
too, talked to Yakuta, pointing out that the sin he seemed so
proud of was displeasing to God.

"When are you going to turn your life over to God?" they
asked.

"I know Him a little bit," Yakuta said, meaning that his
conscience had been pricked by the spirit of God. His lust and
his fear, these were two things he believed separated him from
God. On the trail from Kanashen to Yaka Yaka one day this
handsome, poised, self-satisfied young gallant sat down on a
charred log in a cassava field and looked up to the clouds.

"Father in the Sky," he began, for this was the way he had
heard Elka start a prayer, "I am Yakuta. Why am I the way I
am? I am very afraid. I would like you to take away my fear, and
maybe my badness—if I have any. That is all, Father."

He continued on home, relieved. He knew that Elka prayed
and was happy. Now he had prayed; he would be happy, too.
But his relief lasted only until nightfall when the flutter of bat
wings told him that the spirits hovered near, and the urge
welled within him to satisfy fleshly desires.

"You are wicked," Elka said to him one day. "Don't be
like that. Be receiving Jesus. He is the one who can make you
good."

Yakuta replied that he had prayed.

"I said the words you say."

"Saying words is not enough," Elka answered, explaining that if Yakuta had come as one sorry for his sins God would have changed him. Kindly, Elka helped his brother to see that it was mostly his sin which kept him from God. "Let God take away your sin and He will take away your fear, too."

Shedding tears as he bowed his head, Yakuta prayed, this time in contrition,

"Come into the pit of my stomach, Jesus. Take away the badness that is there."

The rest of that week the people of Yaka Yaka encountered a Yakuta they had never seen before. On Sunday morning at a gathering in the village workhouse they were astounded to hear his testimony.

"You know me as one who takes the wives of others," he said as he stood before them, next to Elka. "That's the way I was until I received Jesus a few days ago."

And that's the way he would be again, a number of his fellow villagers, said to themselves. But their amazement was to continue as the days came and went and the moon repeated its cycle over and over. Here was another person who had become a different one. No longer was he irresponsible. No longer did he cast alluring glances at the women of his tribe. Instead, he joined Elka in urging that the people make God's Paper a part of their lives.

"Why are you different?" those from other villages would ask as they realized that Yakuta had truly changed.

"Because I have let God make me different," he would explain.

Yakuta continued to sit on one side of Elka to learn, and now Mawasha sat on the other. The tall, serious youth would look at Elka and say,

"It's so hard, but I want to learn to make the Paper talk back, the way it does for you."

"Good," Elka would reply. "You learn to make the Paper talk. You also receive Jesus."

Mawasha had taken a girl of the Mawayana tribe as his wife. She had longed for many days to go back over the high mountains and up the small streams to the Mawayana hill country to see her people. Reluctantly Mawasha finally gave in and tore himself from Elka's teaching. He and his young wife, who was pregnant, set out on the arduous journey. When they finally reached her village they found sickness and death rampant among the Mawayana. So great was the air of fear and despondency that the young couple wished they had not come. They cut short their visit and started back over the trail. Mawasha's father-in-law, and others who were glad to escape the plagued village, accompanied them back to Yaka Yaka.

Mawasha led the procession over a trail in the Mawayana hills, scanning the forest before him for signs of animals and birds on which the party depended to supplement the baskets of bread they carried on their backs. Behind him trudged his wife, struggling to keep pace despite the burden of her unborn child. She knew her time was near, and it did not help to think that birth might come on a forest trail. From time to time Mawasha turned to look at her and at the others behind her, and urged them on; he wanted to get home.

Elka and the missionaries had tried hard to give Mawasha ears about God, and this tall, quiet, serious one had got them slowly, painfully, with real struggle. God, Mawasha knew, had made this forest, the streams through which they waded, the sharp rocks, the eagles that soared overhead. God had made him and his wife. It was good, what they had said about God and His love for the Wai Wai and the Mawayana and the other people in the forest. It was good that Jesus, God's Son, had given His life to pay for their badness so that it could be forgotten by God once they confessed it. He had seen Elka give up his basket of charms under the big mango. He had seen Elka live and not die. He knew by these things that Jesus Christ was stronger than Kworokyam.

He was close to becoming a companion of Jesus—close, but not quite there. What kept him from it was what Elka had said about children being gifts from God.

Mawasha's ears had closed at this point. He was not ready to accept this. Some children, yes. But if his firstborn were a girl when he wanted a boy . . . ?

A man of the forest, an expert with bow and arrow, one who knew well the lair of the alligator and the smell of wild pigs, Mawasha wanted a son to roam the forest with, one who, if he himself fell sick, would bring in meat and work his field until he was well again. But he was afraid his wife might bear a girl. What good would a girl be? Why keep a girl when he wanted a boy? Why shouldn't he kill a girl baby?

To receive Jesus, to become His companion, meant that all his ways would have to be yielded to Jesus. And Jesus, he knew, would not want him to kill a baby daughter. Elka had been very definite about this. So Mawasha would not answer to Jesus—yet. Instead, if his wife bore a girl child, he would kill the old young thing.

Finally the group reached the Mapuera and then, having ascended as far as their canoes would take them, left it for the trail over the high mountains. Late one day as the sun sank and the darkness fell quickly on the forest, Mawasha's wife knew her time had come. She cried out once from pain. A woman relative sympathetic to the girl told Mawasha that he should build a birth hut; the child would come in the night. It was a makeshift hut he put up with the help of his father-in-law, who usually aborted his wives before they reached this stage. The hut was a mere roof of palm leaves laid on long sticks fastened to tree trunks. In it they tied two parallel poles, one just off the ground for her to stand on, the other overhead for her to grasp during labor. Because there were no banana leaves, the woman relative quickly wove a simple leaf mat on which to receive the newborn child.

The night was wet and chill. Mawasha squatted in a corner

of the hut. Sullenly he watched as his wife lay in her hammock panting and in deep pain. He followed the movements of the older woman as she stirred up the fire to dispel some of the chill and placed a pot of water near it to warm. He was surly because he had a feeling the child would be a girl. Reaching into a pile of freshly cut firewood, he withdrew a short but heavy limb, which he laid at his feet. Then he settled back again to watch his suffering wife and her helper.

Much of the night passed. His wife now stood on the lower pole and pulled on the one overhead. Outside, the chilling mist had turned to rain. Thunder clapped noisily overhead and the echoes through the forest were long in dying out. Mawasha kept to his corner. Once in a while he fingered the heavy stick. He looked at his wife and from the pain and fright in her eyes knew his waiting was finally at an end.

A terrifying burst of thunder crashed above them and took moments to roll to silence over the expanse of forest. When it passed the cry of a newborn child was heard. Beneath his wife a baby lay on the leaf mat. Mawasha stood up to look. He had been right all along—it was a girl. He stooped to pick up his club. Just as he straightened up and took one step toward the child, his father-in-law ducked into the shelter out of the rain.

"Lift up your child," the man said sternly.

"Yes, lift her up," said the woman relative now attending the new mother.

"It's a girl child, but one you should save," his wife's father continued. In surprise Mawasha halted and turned to confront the man. Lift her up, he said to himself incredulously—this from one who had killed not only babies but wives! Oh yes, now when it was someone else's child his father-in-law wanted to save it.

He turned back to face the baby. For several moments he stood hesitating. He had wanted a boy, and his wife had given him a girl. He had sworn he would kill a girl. Yet now he wasn't sure . . . He tightened, then loosed his grip on the club. Finally he let it slide through his fingers to the ground.

It was not the admonitions of his wife's people that restrained him, but an unsounding Voice that told him how wrong it was to kill a child and an unseen Hand that steered him to the baby and made him bend over and pick up the tiny thing and hand it to his wife.

"We'll save the child," he said, turning his scowling face away from them all.

After they had rested there for a number of days Mawasha brought his family back to Yaka Yaka. Once again he was drawing up his carved stool alongside Elka's. He went faithfully to the lessons at Kanashen. The same unseen One who had whispered in his ear and guided his motions in the birth hut would not let him be. In time, Wawasha—the tall one, the plodder, the thinker of deep thoughts, the one who could not be rushed but who, when once convinced, was completely convinced—became a companion of Jesus.

No one had heard the gospel more often than Kirifaka. No one knew the missionaries or their songs and prayers better than this friendly and outgoing young man. But it took an attractive girl with a strong will to make him stand up for Christ.

Orphaned at the age of nine, Kirifaka had attached himself to the missionaries on their first trip into Wai Wai country. Twice he left the jungle when Mistokin and Bahm left, to live with them among savanna Indians until they returned to Wai Wai country. He became a member of Bahm's household and took to its ways. He was quick to learn reading; he memorized the songs Ferochi wrote; he knew how to pray. He put on the clothes Bahm offered and even allowed Bahm to cut his hair. But Kirifaka was sensitive to this break from tribal ways, and the ridicule of his people became hard to endure.

"We'll call him a buzzard," taunted some. "His hair is cut short like the feathers of that balding bird."

"Kirifaka is not a Wai Wai any more," others gossiped.

The day came when the pressures were too great and Kirifaka ran away, back to his mother's people at Deep Eddy. He peeled off his clothes for a loincloth, and when his hair grew a little he bound it with cord and hid its shortness in a bamboo tube. Life for him then became quite like that of the other youths, until he reached marriageable age. Pairing off the tribe's young men and women was a matter of negotiation by their elders, and the orphaned youth had no one to look out for him. While others his age were taking wives, he could not.

There was a particular girl whom he wanted above all others for his wife. She was Feya, whose people had once lived at the last village downstream but were now located at the edge of the airstrip. Feya was very short, and except for her full breasts could be mistaken for a child. Her eyes, big and round, said "I like you" every time she looked his way. Her mouth spread wide whenever she smiled. But besides the fact that Kirifaka had no one to bargain for him with her father, he despaired of winning her because she was promised to another.

Kirifaka often went to Bahm to talk about his longing for Feya. In giving up hope of gaining her, he was also losing hope of finding any wife.

"I will never get a wife," he said glumly one day.

"Have you asked God for one?" Bahm countered.

"It would be no use. There's no girl for me."

"Don't tell God there is none for you," Bahm said. "Ask Him for a wife and see what happens."

Kirifaka did, but felt his prayers were useless—until Feya herself took a hand in the matter. The girl was the only child of a doting, widowed father, and she was stubborn. She usually got what she wanted, and what she wanted now was Kirifaka. Though promised to another, Feya was determined to have Kirifaka for her husband.

One day a dance brought many Indians together at Yaka

Yaka. Before going back to their villages they paddled to Kanashen for a Sunday lesson. Kirifaka was there from Deep Eddy, and Feya had come from her village with her father. After the lesson the two met alone by chance—at least, Kirifaka thought it was by chance—in a small house on the edge of the clearing. Kirifaka sat inside, binding his hair into a queue. He looked up to see Feya in the doorway.

"Are you going back to your village?" she asked.

He sucked in his breath as a sign that he was.

"I'm going with you," she announced.

"You can't go with me," said Kirifaka, struggling to hide his emotion.

"But I'm going," she insisted.

"Why do you want to go with me?"

"I am going to bring my hammock and hang it under yours." And by this simple act she meant to become his bride.

"You are promised to another," he said.

There was a further reason why she could not go with him. Custom decreed that a man must go to the girl's house for marriage. Having had enough of running counter to tribal tradition as a lad, Kirifaka did not intend to violate it today. He tied the cord at the end of his pigtail. Standing up, he slipped his hair tube into place, and picking up his basket of paint and feathers, he left the house, saying no more.

He would ignore her bold ways. He wanted her but dared not let himself think about her. He should forget her. Her people had chosen another for her. That settled the matter for him.

For her, too, the matter was settled: she intended to be his wife before the day was over.

Kirifaka moved about the village, gathering together various belongings for the trip home, and then walked to the river landing to load his canoe. Feya, determined to do as she wished, sat silent and unmoving in the prow. Kirifaka, defeated in his efforts to keep her away, and inwardly happy that he had failed, jumped in

G

without a word and shoved off. Neither spoke.

They were well along on their way to Deep Eddy before Kirifaka broke the silence.

"What are we going to tell people? No one asked your father for you to be my wife. What are we going to do?"

With the instinctive innocence of a woman who has trapped her man against his better judgment, the young girl rolled her big eyes and grinned from ear to ear. She said softly and sweetly, with a slight shrug of her bare shoulders,

"I don't know. You will tell me."

Neither said anything to the villagers at Deep Eddy. No explanation was needed. Their standing in the doorway hand in hand, hammocks tucked under their arms, told plainly why they had come. Kirifaka's aunt, the tart-tongued Yoshwi, spoke as kindly as she had ever done. She told him to hang his hammock up higher than usual. Then she took the girl's and fastened it under his.

Thus was accomplished the first elopement among the Wai Wai.

The girl's father, enraged at the disappearance of his only child, soon learned where they had gone and followed them. He reached Deep Eddy at dawn. Entering the big house, he swept his eyes over the family groupings until he spotted his daughter and Kirifaka. She was coaxing a flame from her breakfast fire while her young husband sat watching from his hammock. The old man crossed to their place.

"So you came up here like this?" he said angrily.

Yes, she had. It was no use to deny that. The father turned away and stalked toward the door, calling back over his shoulder,

"Come with me."

The marriage was a fact; this he could not undo. But he could restore some respect for custom by taking the girl and her husband away from the youth's home and to his own.

Down the path from the village to the river the angry fellow trode, followed at a long distance by two meek youngsters. When he pair reached the landing, he was already seated in the prow of his canoe. Kirifaka threw in their hammocks and motioned for his bride to sit in the middle. He took a seat in the rear. He wanted to be as far as possible from the testy old man.

It was a strangely quiet crew that rode the downstream current that day. As they came to the white clay-bank at Kanashen they continued without stopping. The embarrassed Kirifaka, timid because of having again upset tribal tradition, was afraid of being seen, maybe even called to, by his friends there. So he picked out an ant's nest high in a tree opposite the landing, and kept his eyes on it until they were safely past and on their way to Feya's village, which now would be his also.

In the months to come Kirifaka's natural friendliness won over his father-in-law. It was unnecessary for Bahm to remind Kirifaka that God had heard his reluctant prayer for a wife. Nor was it necessary to point out that no great disaster had resulted from breaking tradition. Kirifaka resolved to learn more about the God who had answered his prayer. The faith that had been in bud for many years gradually blossomed. One day he was sure he was God's own when he fell from a tree and after lying under it unconscious for a time regained his senses and knew he was not badly hurt.

"It was God who kept me from dying," he said.

Soon he was helping his wife receive Jesus, too, and their Christian faith came to mean much to them. Sometimes Kirifaka teased his wife, but when one saw the deep admiration he had for this girl God had given him, there was no doubt that in the pit of his stomach was the tenderest affection for her.

Feya was an able person. To Kirifaka she gave a certain confidence that he had lacked without her. Together they were destined for leadership, a destiny they competently fulfilled in the years that followed. They became a blessing to Elka in his ministry. Not a little credit was due to the way they—or was it he?—had broken with ancient custom in marriage.

Kirifaka and Yakuta—the two who had promised to receive Elka's God if he survived the next dry and wet seasons—were now companions of Jesus. Before the *tali-tali* locust arrived to herald another dry season, still others chose Jesus Christ over Kworokyam.

Among them was Yoshwi, who had squinted carefully at Elka on that evening when he gave away his witchdoctor charms. She had sat enraptured under his teaching, only to be thoroughly puzzled when he went back to the songs of his old pets and blew on her sick son. It almost made her think he had not been serious in turning from Kworokyam to Christ.

But Elka told her very honestly that he had done wrong. He told her he had confessed his sin to God and that God had forgiven him.

One day Yoshwi was walking the path to the river to fill her gourds. She again thought about Elka's teaching—especially about God and forgiveness. Thinking back over her life she felt that she needed to be forgiven. She looked into the clear sky with her one good eye and began praying aloud.

"Father, what am I like? What will I be like later, after I die? I've heard, Father. But I don't have good enough ears yet."

What was she like? She thought of the time she would have killed her newborn had it been another boy, for she already had three boys and wanted no more. It was a girl, and she did not kill, but didn't her readiness make her a killer? She thought of her nagging and gossipy tongue, and the grief it had caused so many. Then, passing a giant tree whose limbs pierced the sky, she shifted her thoughts to the world about her. Who made all this? Who made the Wai Wai? If Mawalee, that child of the turtle and the anaconda, had made everything, why did he let them suffer and fear and die all alone while he wandered off untouched by their wretchedness?

Elka taught that they would wake up after they died. Either they would be with Jesus, and it would be pleasant and life with

Him would never end, or they would burn with the Devil—
Foleeto, old bossy master of their Kworokyam.

Jesus, Yoshwi had learned from God's Paper, had made them
and had never forsaken them. Always He was wanting them. And
now she wanted Him. As she dipped her gourds into the water
at the river's edge, she paused to look up again.

"Do You want to enter the pit of my stomach today, Father?"
And Yoshwi knew that He did.

One after another the Wai Wai were receiving Christ. Among
the men now were Elka, Yakuta, Mawasha, Kirifaka, and two
older boys, enough to start a special class for the teaching of God's
Paper to believers. It was to meet at Kanashen on a day they had
learned to call Wednesday. In one of their earliest sessions they
memorized the translation of Jeremiah 33:3: "Call unto Me, and I
will answer thee, and show thee great and mighty things, which
thou knowest not." They were taught to expect God to perform
miracles in their midst. When He did they were not surprised,
but thankful. Learning to read was stressed so that they could
study God's Paper themselves. Bahm and Kron taught the men
to help their families stand firmly for Christ, even in the un-
wholesome atmosphere of communal living where many still were
not companions of Jesus.

"After a while I'll be up," said Yukuma to Kron one day in an
offhand way, referring to the Wednesday class in which he was
beginning to take an interest. He was shocked when Kron hesitated to admit him among the believers. Kron said that to be
obedient to God he would have to give up either the mother or
the daughter he had as wives. Though not so definite on ordinary
plural marriages, Kron said, God's Paper did condemn this ar-
rangement. Yukuma decided to give up Tochi and keep Rataru.
Kron still hesitated, suspecting an insincerity in Yukuma, and he
went to Elka.

"What about Yukuma?" he asked.

"Yukuma? He's a good hunter," replied Elka.

"But is he a companion of Jesus? He wants to come to the believers' class."

Elka fell silent, thinking about his old rival. Yukuma had caused him much grief.

"Hnnnn," he said presently. "He's almost a companion of Jesus. Let him come to the class."

Having found a new kind of love for his people, Elka was now able to pick out Yukuma's good points rather than the bad ones. He could see that Yukuma was trying to please God, through this unstable fellow was finding the way difficult.

Elka knew his people better than the missionaries ever could, so Kron accepted Elka's verdict. Yukuma joined the group. In time, others were admitted to the Wednesday class who had not yet become companions of Jesus. They were interested and could be said to be on their way to faith.

Kron and Elka started a similar class at Yaka Yaka for the women. In tribal gatherings the women were usually spectators, so it was with uncertainty of feeling that special teaching was begun for them. Would they be interested enough to come? Could they make the effort to learn? A few showed up for the first session—Yoshwi, Ahmuri, Feya, and one or two others. Later the class grew and was turned over to women leaders among the Wai Wai, with general supervision provided by the missionary women.

By 1956 both the men's and the women's classes, the latter now meeting at Kanashen on Fridays, saw newcomers arriving almost every week to make public confession of their faith in Christ. The front row of benches, near the teacher, was reserved for those who wanted to declare that they had become companions of Jesus. All who sat there were questioned about their faith, the men by Elka, the women by Yoshwi.

"You came, Little Brother?" Elka would say at the start of a Wednesday class.

"I came," would be the scarcely audible answer of one who looked shyly down at his feet.

"Why did you come?"

"Because I have received Jesus."

"How do you see your sin?"

"I see it as bad."

Elka or Mawasha or one of the others would then admonish the convert to pay close attention to the teaching and to apply it as he walked in the forest or in the fields or as he sat by his fireside at home.

There were many new things for them to learn. Kworokyam had been lax about rules for living. Except for observing the taboos, the people had done as they pleased unless someone interfered. When that happened, they contrived to work around the interference. But to live for God, they must learn forgiveness and forbearance, mercy, patience, overcoming the habits of lying and stealing, purity—all these and other things to learn.

One young man said of the teaching one day,

"We're ignorant. Tell us again."

So it became the custom to introduce a new subject at the Wednesday and Friday classes and to repeat it on Sunday afternoons. Hearing it again made it easier to "get ears."

"We're still ignorant," the young man would sometimes say after the second hearing. Then the same lesson would be extended over two weeks.

Mawasha, Kirifaka, and Yakuta soon seemed fitted by faith to join Elka in spiritual leadership. One day as Mawasha cuddled in his arms the daughter he once had meant to kill, he and Elka discussed the life of their people. In talking over the tribal dances they decided to discourage night dancing, which led to immorality. They also agreed to begin any festive gathering with a lesson from God's Paper.

"Other people should see us as different ones now," Mawasha said.

Yakuta was certainly one of the "different ones": he had stopped stealing other men's wives. It had not been easy for him to make the change, but his earnest desire to become a companion of Jesus finally won out over his lust for women. He married a girl near his own age, and he loved her and remained faithful to her.

Elka looked at Ahmuri, his Christian wife, and his children, and smiled. His wife might not be all he could wish, but neither was he. However, making God's Paper talk, singing the songs, and praying in their hammocks every night before sleep would help them to know God better. Clearly, God was blowing His breath of life and blessing on the Wai Wai, and Elka felt that a special comforting breeze had blown his way.

Believers were still few compared with those who held to the old way. In the house at Yaka Yaka filthy talk, stealing, and wife-trading continued. Because of this, Elka was beginning to feel the need to give his family something better. The question was resolved one morning as his young son, Kulanow, stood in the middle of the dark, smoky house chewing on a cane of sugar. Leathery old Kurum lay in his hammock, groaning now and then, though not too sick to call obscenities to Elka. He talked that way simply because he felt like taunting his son-in-law for having become a companion of Jesus.

Elka stood up. He put away the arrow points he had been carving and walked out into the bright sunlight. His mind was made up: he would build a house for just his own family.

Elka's decision surprised and even offended the villagers, but the men helped him build the house anyway.

"Don't you like us any more?" they would ask as they brought palm leaves and poles from the forest.

"Of course I like you," was Elka's invariable reply. "I like you lots."

"Then why do you leave us to live alone?"

Elka would then try to explain that he did not want their bad talk to reach the ears of his children and that he wanted a place where he could be alone with his family when they talked to God.

"Hnnnn," was all they would say.

The new house, round like the communal dwelling but with sides made of palm slats instead of thatch, stood a half-dozen paces from the main house. The door Elka had made from sawed planks usually was ajar: traffic in and out was heavy. People wanted to sit before Elka's blackboard and learn letters or to watch him study at his new desk. They also wanted to see the strange wall made of split palm, which divided the house into two halves. Guests were welcome in the outer half. Behind the wall, the family ate and slept.

Elka's people came to understand that he was not angry. But they themselves, even the Christians among them, would not build separate houses; it was the way of the Wai Wai to live together, and change comes slowly. Elka gave up trying to explain why he thought his way was better. Little did he know that he was about to receive unexpected help in his effort to convince them, and at the same time his own faith was to be tested severely again.

One windy day in the dry season Ahmuri sent little Tamalkuku to the main house to get a burning brand to start a cooking fire in their house. The child was careless; coming through the doorway of the communal house she touched her brand to the dry leaves. In a flash the doorway and a large area at the front of the house burst into flame.

Because the house was large, it had been built with two openings, and the women, children, and pets escaped without injury by way of the rear entrance. Elka, coming from the landing where he had bathed, first heard screams, then saw the raging flames. He ran as fast as he could to the doomed house. Other men converged from the nearby fields. Entering the house by the rear door, they cut down a few hammocks and snatched some crowns of bird plumes before falling chunks of fiery leaves forced them to retreat. They had saved all they could, and it was very little.

Elka looked at his own house. Even as he breathed a prayer

of thanks to God that his family and the dog were safely outside, he found himself wondering why he had built so close to the other house. A strong wind was blowing, and the flame it fanned was expanding. The fire could easily jump the space between the two dwellings and devour Elka's home with the same insatiable appetite with which it was eating up the main house.

Sparks shot from the inferno and landed on Elka's roof. He needed water to wet down the dry leaves. Rushing into his home, he grabbed two water gourds near Ahmuri's baking plate and raced out again. Just as he started to douse the front of the house a gust of wind whirled the roaring flames directly over his head. He dropped the gourds and ran.

"Your house will burn, too," several of the villagers cried.

They were right, it would burn. How could he expect it to escape?

But there still was God! Elka had read in His wonderful Paper of the miracles that God performed. God could perform a miracle today if He knew that Elka really needed it.

Elka knelt down before a stump, burying his head in his arms. "Father in the Sky, this is old Elka. You can see the burning house. It will be lost. You can see my house and it hasn't burned. But look at the flaming bits landing on my roof! All I own is in my house. My hammocks, my bow, my gun, my desk, my wife's cooking pots. Do You want those saved?"

A new scream went up from the people. Elka raised his head to look. The fire had spread to the village workhouse, also close to the big house. And a small leaf shelter used for cassava preparation was burning.

"Father!" Imploringly he raised his face toward heaven. "I'm Your child. I am needing You. I'm looking to You now."

The main house was now one big flame. Elka prayed and watched. The fire roared like a chorus of howler monkeys. Its heat rivaled the sun's.

The workhouse and leaf shelter burned rapidly and were soon

heaps of smoking ash. A few timbers still stood, blackened and smoking. An occasional flame licked at them, dying out only to puff up again when fanned by the wind.

In contrast, Elka's house remained intact. Brown spots of scorch showed plainly, but none of the sparks had ignited the tinder-dry leaves of his roof. Intense heat had curled them, but strangely, the house was spared.

"Why didn't my house burn?" Elka later asked Bahm. "Did God send an angel to guard it?"

"Maybe He did," replied Bahm. There seemed no other explanation for the miraculous escape.

The big house was rebuilt, but some of those who had seen Elka's house spared were impressed that God had preserved it. They had a new respect for privacy. Slowly, others followed Elka in putting up their own houses. It was the beginning of a new closeness within families. As they moved to their own homes the Christians among them were better able to apply the teachings of God's Paper to their lives.

Once more God had vindicated Elka's daring to stand alone.

13

Trial of Faith for Elka

Further trials were in store for Elka in the days following the great fire. A wave of sickness enveloped his family. First Elka suffered many large, painful boils. Then one of his wife's teeth became infected and bled dangerously for a day and night. A daughter fell suddenly sick. Clomp, clomp, clomp, Elka in loin-cloth and Kron's big cast-off rubber boots went to Achi with his child during a torrential rain.

"Achi, my girl is hot! You must do something."

In her medicine room Achi looked at the child. She prayed. Then she reached into her medicine box and drew out some pills that she was sure would work. Elka hoped they would. It hurt him to see his child sick. And at home, he knew, was Ahmuri, whose faith often stretched so thin that it nearly broke, ready to say, "I told you we should never have given up our taboos."

But now, as before, she had no opportunity to say it. The girl got well.

Then came the sickness of their only son, Kulanow, to try Elka's very soul. The little seven-year-old struggled pathetically to breathe. He wheezed and panted. He cried and complained of pain in his chest. His heart pounded fast and hard. Elka felt each cry of the boy, this flesh of his flesh, as he would the stab of an arrow in his breast. One night he and Ahmuri took Kulanow to Kanashen.

Since Achi was away, they asked Bahm to stick him. Bahm gave him a shot of medicine and suggested they stay in an unoccupied leaf shelter at the edge of the mission so as to be near medical care should more be needed. A second shot was given next day, but Kulanow was no better. He seemed likely to die. Bahm got on the radio to Kron, who was then in Georgetown.

"Claude, get hold of a doctor and send him in by charter plane," he said. "I don't know how else we're going to save Elka's son."

There was no plane available. The best Kron could do was to describe the boy's condition to a doctor—the symptoms spelled out severe asthma—and relay medical advice over the air. While Elka prayed, Bahm tried to give the capsules the doctor had prescribed.

When Ahmuri saw that their son could not swallow the pills she took Elka aside.

"Maybe we should blow on a bowl of water and give it to him," she said quietly.

"No," Elka said. "I don't blow any more."

"But it would not be blowing the way you used to do," she assured him. "Muyuwa told me once it is just a way to make medicine. Maybe it would work; I don't know."

"I don't know, either," Elka replied doubtfully.

"Ask Bahm to try it."

"Hnnnn. I don't believe I want to."

"Go ahead. It's only a way to make medicine."

"No."

"Then you'll let our son die. Don't you love him?"

How Elka loved his boy! When he saw that the lad could not swallow Bahm's medicine, he went to Bahm's side and tried to help him get the capsules down the boy's throat. It was no use.

Then, rather hesitantly, Elka asked,

"Does God's Paper say anything about blowing on a bowl of water to turn it into medicine?"

Bahm's face clouded. Elka knew the answer then and wished he hadn't spoken, but it was desperation that had make him ask. His only son was near death, this boy who was his delight, who he hoped would some day take his place to lead another generation. Was he now to die? Was God going to turn his back on him as Kworokyam had done with Little Crab?

Did God ever let a child die?

He had asked the question before. The first time he asked it he thought he knew the answer, and it made Elka think kindly of God. Now he didn't know. Had he followed Jesus only to have his son snatched from him?

Bahm's answer to his question came quietly but firmly.

"Blowing is sorcery. God's Paper speaks against witchcraft."

Bahm spoke with tenderness; he could guess at how great the temptation was for Elka. His words were punctuated by Kulanow's heavy breathing.

Elka's faith should be in the will of God—not in the life of his boy. It was a hard doctrine to expound to the father of a boy near death. But it was basic.

"God doesn't always give us our desires," Bahm told Elka above the boy's labored breathing. God was not to be manipulated like the spirits Elka had once invoked with his sorcery. Instead, God was to be trusted to give His best to His people. Could this be said of Kworokyam?

As Bahm spoke Elka recalled how he used to work and work to persuade Kworokyam to reverse his evil just a little. Not so with God, Bahm was saying. "God aches to do good for us. He gave His own beloved Son for our good. He always wants to give us His best. We must trust that He will—whether it is life or death for our children."

"Hnnnn," Elka said pensively and, looking at his son, sadly.

During the night, the rainiest and stormiest of the year, Elka sent Ahmuri to call Bahm and Ferochi out of their sleep, for Kulanow was worse. The missionaries dashed to the hut through the driving rain. Elka now lay in his hammock, his son in his arms. He shielded the boy with his body from the chilling mist that blew in under the leafy eaves. Elka looked at Bahm and saw despair on his face. But Ferochi was not ready to give up.

"Let's try the capsules again," she insisted. Kulanow struggled. It seemed to take an age for them to get five capsules down that one troubled throat.

"Father," Bahm began to pray. Elka looked first at Bahm and then at his son. "Father, if the medicine works, thank You. If it doesn't, we can do no more."

The missionaries left; the rain passed. The familiar noises of the nearby jungle sounded again. Slowly, ever so slowly, the dawn came for the burdened parents in the leaf shelter. Before the sun rose, Bahm came hurrying toward the hut.

"Elka! God showed me a verse this morning that I feel is just for you. It's in Psalm Twenty-one: 'He asked life of thee, and thou gavest it him.'" Bahm bent his tall frame to enter the shelter as he spoke. "How is Kulanow?" he continued.

"A little bit better," Elka replied.

The boy had relaxed. His breathing was easier and he was able to take a new dose of medicine with little effort. Elka was weary after three sleepless nights, but Bahm's message pumped new life into his tired body. He was grateful for this encouragement, and he was confident now that his son would live.

Bahm was about to leave when Elka stopped him for a moment.

"I prayed during the night, Bahm," he said, smiling faintly as he spoke. "I said, 'Father, if You want to take my child, *okwe*, how sad, You go ahead and take him. If You take him, I'll still love You. I won't give You up. I'm giving my son to You, *oklee!*'"

14

Trial of Faith for the Wai Wai

The faith of Elka and his people began to reach out beyond the banks of the Essequibo.

Elka was concerned about the Wai Wai who still lived across the high mountains on the Mapuera. He wanted them to learn the way of Christ that his people now knew. As chief, he sent his brother Yakuta with a *shim-shim* to invite those on the other side to come and live with him. This was how they could best learn God's way.

Mawasha volunteered to go far down the Mapuera in search of the Shedeu, a people much like the Wai Wai. In years past the two tribes had freely intermingled, but many rain seasons had passed since the last visit.

When a party was formed to carry trading goods across the mountains to the hills where the Mawayana lived, Elka encouraged Kirifaka to go along to tell them about God.

The first to arrive back were the Mapuera Wai Wai. Among them was Mafolio, the happy old witchdoctor who had inspired Elka to serve Kworokyam. Elka was glad to see him. Mafolio was as ugly as ever, but his face wore the same bright smile. Elka, drawn to the old man in love as earlier he had been in awe, told him how Christ had triumphed over Kworokyam.

194

"Working good charms is not enough, Grandfather," he said.

Mafolio looked at him quizzically. How could Elka make the old sorcerer understand that God was the source of goodness?

Soon the Mawayana people were brought back by Kirifaka. He had found them in deep trouble. Many calamities had struck. The most recent was an attack by a jaguar which had decapitated a young boy of the village.

The lad had been at the edge of the clearing when the jaguar sprang from behind a tree.

"His aunt saw the attack," a villager said. "She screamed and we came from gathering sticks for our fires. One of our men put an arrow in the beast, but only in his shoulder. He will come back to avenge the injury."

Their old witchdoctor had gone to the sky to learn who made the jaguar spring upon the boy.

"It was Muyuwa who sent his spirit over the mountains and into the cat," the sorcerer told Kirifaka.

They had burned the boy's body amid wailing. Bone fragments were raked from the ashes and placed in a clay pot. With these bones the old sorcerer made ready to perform *farawa* against Muyuwa. It was at this moment that Kirifaka arrived. He listened to their story and then said,

"I wouldn't call on the spirits for revenge."

"Muyuwa will kill us all," someone protested. "He will tell the cat to kill us one by one while we are sleeping in our hammocks."

"Muyuwa is getting ears about God," Kirifaka said, reassuringly. "You need to know God, too. He wants to help you."

"How can we know God?" asked the sorcerer. "We've never seen Him."

"Go over the mountains with me," Kirifaka replied. "Elka will give you ears about God. Elka is missing you. He wants you to live with him. He'll help you plant fields and show you good hunting trails. We'll all help you. Kron and Bahm will teach you, too."

After much muttering all but a handful went with Kirifaka. On their way back they stopped in the only other large Mawayana village and persuaded the people there to go with them to Yaka Yaka.

The villages along the Essequibo—particularly Yaka Yaka and Kanashen—began to bustle with activity. They were strange places, mixtures of old and new, of faith and fear. The contrasts were even more pronounced when the first group of Shedeu people arrived on the heels of Mawasha.

As with all new people, their entrance was marked by ceremony.

Upstream from Kanashen they stopped on a rock to apply fresh paint and feathers. Then they paddled on, whistling and shouting and pounding their canoes until they rounded the last bend and sighted the landing. By this time someone, having heard their signal, had already dashed down the path to Yaka Yaka to bring Elka to Kanashen.

The sun shone brightly. Yellow butterflies fluttered over the landscape. Some of the canoes stopped at the village landing, others went beyond to a point downstream. At a whistled signal the Shedeu left their canoes. The men first, then the women, climbed the footholds in the bank. In two single files they walked from the points of debarkation into the mission yard, coming together under the big mango tree.

Elka was there waiting for them. Resplendent in paint and feathers, he looked every inch a chief. His queue, reaching his waistband, ended in a duster of toucan feathers. He wore khaki shorts in place of a loincloth. Arms folded across his chest, he surveyed the newcomers as they seated themselves before him, picked out a number of acquaintances, and smiled at them all.

"You people have come," Elka said when all had assembled. He spoke with dignity, yet his sincerity overcame any likelihood of cold formality.

"It is good to us that you have come. You will see us as different ones," he continued, using his expression for spiritual rebirth. "We want you to become God's children. I will teach you. Mawasha will teach you. So will Bahm and Kron and Kirifaka and Yakuta."

He assigned the Shedeu places to live.

"Elder Brother," he said, pointing his lips to an older man, "you will live in my village. I want you close to me so I can teach you about God myself. Little Brother," he singled out another, "you started to get ears from Mawasha while he was in your village. You stay here at Kanashen with him. Uncle, where would you like to be?"

The new people found their surroundings strange. Nothing was stranger than the mission houses standing on legs. To reach the upper levels, fearsome steps had to be climbed. On his first day in Kanashen, a Shedeu man climbed up warily. Hnnnn. That was fun. He did it again and again.

Late in the afternoon Achi, working in the house and hearing voices, looked over the half wall next to the kitchen where she was preparing supper. Seated on the floor of the porch were the Shedeu climber and Yakuta, talking earnestly.

"This is how it was, Elder Brother," Yakuta was saying. "In the beginning God created . . ." The Christian Indian began telling the age-old story to one who had not heard it. Yakuta progressed through the account of creation to the tribulations of the Israelites, likening them to the experiences of his own people. Abruptly he broke off and stood up.

"That is all for now, Elder Brother," he said. "I'll tell you more another time."

At later sessions Yakuta spoke slowly and carefully of the crucifixion of Jesus, pointing out to his listener that Christ had died for his sins. With the help of Kirifaka and others, Elka taught him—at the desk in Elka's house, on the hunting trails, and while shooting fish in the river. Before the next full moon came, this Shedeu leader—a man who had killed children in his own country—bowed in repentance to God.

Elka urged all the Shedeu to attend the Sunday lessons at Kanashen. They were astounded to hear him say one Sunday that a Wai Wai witchdoctor was throwing away his charms.

The witchdoctor was Chiriminoso who, years before, had seemed likely to become the first Christian Wai Wai, but turned away after the death of his young wife. In sorrow he had gone back over the mountains, but something drew him back to Kanashen on frequent visits. One day, after coming to the mission to stay, he heard a murderer, one of the Mawayana, tell how he had become a different one.

"I love my wife and child now," the Mawayana had said. "I don't want to harm them." Then he asked Chiriminoso, "How do you see Jesus, Father?"

"With desire," had been the old man's answer. He was impressed that Jesus could change this notorious wife- and child-beater, this murderer of infants, into a loving husband and father. In a few days Chiriminoso sat on the front bench of the men's Wednesday class.

"Why have you come, Father?" asked Elka.

"Because I have received Jesus," replied Chiriminoso. It was not long before he decided to throw his witchcraft basket into the river. He was the second witchdoctor to choose Christ over Kworokyam.

Muyuwa was the third. The old chief, still called by the title but considered a leader no longer, had fought hard for the evil spirits against the way of God. But he had lost. He was a man who had known power most of his days. Kworokyam had power; that was why he had served him. But listening to Bahm and watching Elka, Muyuwa came to acknowledge that Jesus was more powerful than Kworokyam. He moved to Yaka Yaka to be nearer to Elka, this one who seemed so close to God.

"Jesus is the all-powerful," Bahm had taught. "Though evil spirits abound today, Jesus will destroy them."

It was Jesus, then, whom Muyuwa wanted. He had served

Kworokyam out of fear. But if he was to serve Jesus, he learned, it would have to be out of love. Love was hard for the old man to understand. He wanted to forget his fear; maybe he was not too old to learn love.

Elka often took Muyuwa aside to teach God's Paper in *oho* style. After many days of listening he decided to become a companion of Jesus. He also wanted to take the next step—to give up his charms. Elka suggested that the old sorcerer cast them away in the river.

Muyuwa brought his basket of charms to the Sunday lesson. Kron said they would all go to the river soon, but first he wanted to tell them something. He had sent Muyuwa's picture, he said, to friends in his country. These people had talked to God about Muyuwa. They had prayed that Muyuwa would become a companion of Jesus. Their prayers, Kron said, had been answered.

The old man wept. Elka thought it strange, wonderfully strange, to see tears welling in those eyes that had been so flinty from the first time he had seen Muyuwa at Old Baking Plate. He thought he saw the hard lines soften around Muyuwa's mouth. The old man brushed his thinning hair with his fingers and smiled. He said he was ready to go to drown his charms.

"Are you afraid?" asked Kron.

"No," he replied. "I saw Little Brother give up his. He has remained strong. I will give up mine."

Once again Elka's resolute actions—renouncing Kworokyam, killing the wild pigs and eating them—had won a victory for God.

The landing was crowded as Muyuwa stepped carefully down the footholds to a canoe. The people began a song they all knew: "Jesus is strong, he is stronger than all . . ."

The song ended. Elka called for quiet. He looked down at the old man in the canoe, then he lifted his face to the sky. He asked God to protect Muyuwa from any retaliation by the spirits. Elka knew the trials that lay ahead for one who had served the Devil so effectively. He finished praying. Muyuwa moved to the far end of the canoe and opened his basket.

He took from it a headband made from the hair of the ant-eater and dropped it into the water. Then came a wristband of feathers from the white crane. Next were the chestbands, representing the spirits of many birds. Tobacco came next, then little sticks used in blowing or sucking. He tossed out a whistle that had called his pets, and a gourd rattle. Last of all came the small smooth stones of the river, which, with one shake of his upturned basket, he sent tumbling back into the water from which they had come. For good measure, Muyuwa threw in the basket.

The Wai Wai stood around the landing in silent awe. What a thing had happened this day!

Elka heard Kron call this the "year of release." God's Paper told of the release of the Hebrew slave after seven years of slavery; the Wai Wai were finding their own release from spiritual bonds just seven years after the first penetration of the Gospel into their country. Since Elka's triumph over the wild pigs, many Wai Wai, and now some Mawayana and Shedeu, had taken a stand for Christ. Old problems had lightened: stealing, lying, the drunken madness of the dance. Witchcraft and fear were still present, but in community life they moved into the background.

The number of companions of Jesus increased to the point where Kron said it was time they chose their own spiritual leaders.

"They will be 'look-afters,' " Elka explained to some twenty men gathered in an old house at the edge of the mission settlement. "We need someone to look after God's children. What should the look-afters be like? Let's ask God. He will tell us."

They prayed for guidance. Kron read what Paul had told Titus about elders. They talked about the desired qualifications.

"Whom do you want for your look-afters?" Kron asked.

"Elka."

His name was shouted by nearly everyone. Others names were called out.

"Mawasha."

"Kirifaka."

"Yakuta."

A few more were suggested, Yukuma among them.

"These are more ripe than we are in the things of God," ventured one in the support of those suggested.

The candidates were sent away during the discussion.

"How is their conduct?" asked someone.

"This is how it is: They don't take other women, they don't talk bad. They work hard in clearing fields. They are good ones."

"How about Yukuma?"

"Hnnnn."

"What about Kirifaka?" asked Kron. "Isn't he young to be a leader?"

The people were not concerned about his age, only his qualities. Elka, Kirifaka, Mawasha, and Yakuta were selected unanimously.

Shortly after this the Wai Wai themselves began preaching.

Kron had spoken on Sunday afternoons while Bahm was on furlough in the States. One day, however, he came down with a cold. By Saturday he was unable to speak above a whisper. In answer to a call from Kron, Elka went to the missionary's house. Kron said hoarsely,

"I can't speak. What can we do?"

He was plainly worried. But Elka saw no reason for Kron to be upset.

"Hnnnn," he said. "I'd like to preach myself."

Elka preached that Sunday. He told of Daniel and how he did not fear even in the face of conniving enemies. He contrasted Daniel's faithfulness to his own faithlessness. He said that after he had given up his witchcraft under the mango tree Muyuwa had prevailed on him to blow on his sick grandson. He told how he had deceived Kron by circling around Kanashen on the way home and entering the mission as if he had come from his village of Yaka Yaka.

As he confessed, Elka looked at Kron, who sat dumfounded at this revelation and amazed at Elka's ability to speak with such a ring of conviction in his voice.

Kron's voice returned the next day. Could it be that God had deprived him of it in order to shift the burden of preaching to the Wai Wai? The missionaries reached a decision. Never again would it be necessary for one of them to preach in the Sunday meeting. They would teach the elders through the week, and the elders would speak to the people.

Each of the four elders developed his own way of preaching and teaching. Elka felt a burden for the everyday life of his people; he emphasized the practical. He related the principles of God's Paper to their lives. He devoted one sermon to the sin of stealing and often spoke out against witchcraft. In talking about the stoning of Stephen at Jerusalem he reminded his people how they used to carry sticks to club their enemies while walking the forest trails. Once, to illustrate the crucifixion, he held up one of his children against the rafters of his house.

Mawasha was a man of deep sincerity and purpose that showed in his preaching. Seriously he urged his hearers to walk God's way and beware of snares in the path. "Satan wants to throw us," he would warn, drawing his figure of speech from their wrestling.

Kirifaka was a great storyteller. As he spoke, his hearers could almost see before them the woman who gave her mite or the hungry masses fed by Christ. For their understanding he talked as if the events had taken place in their own villages. Kirifaka said God loved the Wai Wai because he gave His Son for them.

"My girl is dear to me," he said. "I wouldn't want to give *her* up."

But it was Yakuta who became the most eloquent preacher.

He walked up and down before the people as he spoke. He used many gestures and rolled his eyes toward the heavens whenever he said "Jesus." His imagination was fertile. When he spoke of Paul's first missionary journey and his encounter with the sorcerer, he digressed:

"Maybe the witchdoctor painted the children red as we used to paint our children red to keep the evil spirits from seeing them."

At the beginning all preaching was patterned after the *oho* palaver, with questions aimed at one man. Newcomers from across the mountains or ones who had heard the Gospel but had not yet responded were called on to reply. This was done by grunting assent to each statement the preacher made. After his message, the preacher reviewed for all to hear the sins of the one he had addressed. He then explained that he himself used to do these evil things, but God had fixed him fine and would fix his hearer that way if only he would let God do it.

Kirifaka was most anxious for his wife to get ears for the gospel. Before making an important point in his preaching he would call out to her, while all were listening,

"My wife, you stop looking at the baby and look up here at me. I want you to catch this truth from God's Paper."

Others who had learned to read studied the translated Scriptures and occasionally preached. One day one of them told in his sermon how bad the Wai Wai had been before they knew God. He said he had been in a group cutting trees with Bahm and that they had cut down a giant tree with the intention of killing him.

Again Kron was dumfounded by a confession.

Elka well remembered the attempted murder. How changed the Wai Wai were! Looking around he picked out those who had been involved. Most of them now were companions of Jesus. Kron noted the change, too, and wrote of it to friends in his country. The Wai Wai looked the same and their daily routine was what it had always been. But what a change within!

Everyone who testified told of dropping his burdens of fear and hate. The Wai Wai were beginning to know a love based on giving, not getting. Like Elka, the men had begun to help their hard-working wives. In turn, their wives smiled oftener and attended to the chores with less grumbling. Once out of respect to their leader the people replaced Elka's old rusty gun with a new one. They learned sacrificial giving, too, when one day they offered possessions toward the cost of building a church in Georgetown where Bahm's brother, Mlayla, was the minister.

They were also learning that faith did not depend on material gain. In his preaching Yakuta once said, "God is the one who gives us our meat. Sometimes He doesn't. I love Him just the same."

Teams of men went to villages up and down the river to conduct services between Sundays. Elka brought the people of Yaka Yaka together every daybreak for singing and praying. Sometimes days of prayer were called. Even the shyest believer learned to pray aloud. Occasionally three to five days would be set aside for tribal games and teaching of God's Paper. Christmas came to be spent in this way.

By this time most of the old fears of the jungle had dissolved, not only for the Christian Wai Wai but also for those who, though not yet believers, had been influenced by the Christians. Even the anaconda, once feared more for its evil spirit than its physical menace, no longer frightened them. The backwaters they once avoided because of the snake became sought-after fishing grounds. Yakuta even led a group of men to capture one of the legendary serpents alive for shipment out of the jungle, for he had heard that some white men would like to have one.

How far had they moved from their old ways? Far enough to snare and cage without trepidation the "parent" of the one they once had called their creator.

The numbers on Kron's calendar read "1958." That year severe sickness—Achi called it "Asian flu"—came with the heavy rains. One of the first victims was Mafolio. His old body could not resist the effects of the new epidemic that swept through the tribe. He died within a few days. Since coming to Kanashen the old witchdoctor had practiced no sorcery: there had been no call for his services. Some believed he had laid aside his witchcraft to become a companion of Jesus, but no one knew with certainty.

"Hnnnn. Maybe he did," said Elka after helping to bury his old friend, for he noticed that Mafolio's death had been without the agony suffered by some witchdoctors.

One morning Kron told Elka that more than two hundred were too weak to rise from their hammocks. Elka tried to guess how many that was. He looked at all his fingers and toes, then at those of his brother. He knew it would take many sets of hands and feet to number the sick.

But the flu waned sooner than Elka had dared to hope. It took only eight fingers to number those who died. People grew strong again and life surged anew. The Wai Wai turned again to learning from God's Paper.

As one person told another about his new faith, the number of believers increased. The day came when the Wai Wai erected a new building—God's House. It stood at the edge of the mission settlement, round like a Wai Wai house, large enough to seat more than a hundred worshipers. Only those who were companions of Jesus had had a part in its building. The workers began their task with enthusiasm and a song, and those who were not Christians came by to watch.

"Why are they building a house just for God?" they would ask. "Is God coming down here to live?"

One Sunday soon after the completion of the church, excitement filled the air. The first baptism among Wai Wai was to take place. Kron had taught them what God's Paper said about believers and baptism. Elka agreed with Kron that only those who showed Christ in their lives should be baptized. The elders met to consider the candidates.

"How does he walk?" Elka asked about one man.

"He walks true," came the reply.

"How about Yukuma?" Elka asked when his name was presented.

"Hnnnn. He is like Samson. He is strong and he is weak."

They spoke next of one who "used to be lazy, but God has made him useful."

Twenty-six were accepted by the elders for baptism in the flood-swollen creek at Kanashen.

On the day appointed for the baptisms the people gathered in the church to hear a visitor preach. Leonard Harris came originally from London. He had been a pioneer missionary in Brazil and had started to pray for the Wai Wai in 1926, the year he first heard of the tribe. A kindred spirit flowed between the Wai Wai and their guest. He talked to them of Naaman of God's Paper. He said that in baptism they would go under the waters to show they had died to the old life. Coming up, they would testify that they had come alive to the new.

After Harris' message the people walked quietly from the church to the creek. Kron and Bahm baptized the four elders. Elka was first, then came Kirifaka, Mawasha, and Yakuta. After that the missionaries left the water and the elders continued the rite. They baptized first the men, then the women.

Baptizing Muyuwa, Elka said to the old chief,

"Father, once we both were witchdoctors. We served Kworo-kyam. Now it is God we are serving."

To another he said,

"Obey God. What will you do when Satan speaks to you? Do not answer at all. Be just like a dead one. You see, if a person is dead he does not answer. But to God, let us be as risen ones."

Mawasha asked his father, Chekema, Elka's older half-brother,

"How do you look upon your sin?"

"I look upon my sin as bad," he replied, for Chekema with the forthrightness that was his nature had examined his life.

The sun sank behind the houses across the swollen creek, and still the baptisms continued. Finally the last person came up from the water. Mawasha then exhorted the nonbelievers and the Christians who were spiritually immature.

"There are those of you who would like to be baptized," he said. "You must let your sin go now. Love Jesus much and don't love your sin. Don't imitate us; imitate God. Don't hear God's Paper as a lazy one."

Before he said goodby, Harris expressed amazement at the spiritual development to be found in a tribe so recently strangers to God and His ways.

Then a new disaster struck the Wai Wai. One Sunday, about a year after the flu epidemic, Achi was called to Kirifaka's house at Kanashen. A man was there who had been sick for a week downriver. He had been cutting jungle away for a new field when he started to sniffle and wheeze. He gave no thought to the fact that his itching eyes and running nose came after he had eaten and shared a drink pot with Wapishana Indians just in from the savannas. Then he had come on to Kanashen and hung his hammock in Kirifaka's house.

Achi took one look at his infected eyes and throat, and her heart sank. She knew she was facing her first case of measles among Indians, and she was alone at the mission station, for the other missionaries were away temporarily. The flu had brought much physical distress, and even death to a few with low resistance, but measles had an added dimension of terror: the knowledge that whenever it had struck jungle people it killed off the entire tribe. This disease of "the bumps" had wiped out the Taruma Indians, neighbors of the Wai Wai.

"You're going back to your camp downriver," Achi insisted to the sick man. "And I'm going with you."

She told him to stay inside the house until she would be ready to leave the next morning. As she left the house, she met several persons coming along the path.

"Don't go into Kirifaka's house," she warned. "Don't go near it. If you do you'll get itchy and hot."

When Elka came for the usual Sunday service, she took him aside to tell him about the outbreak of measles.

"Tell the headman of each village to take his people home and stay there," she urged. "Don't visit around. And you'd better start building huts here for the ones who will be coming down sick."

. How odd that Achi should want them to separate. They had never done this in illness. Elka knew of only one man who was sick. Achi was being too hard on them.

Early Monday morning Kanashen was strangely quiet. All canoes but the sick man's were gone. Achi, afraid to think of what might have happened, helped the measles victim into his canoe, rounded up two paddlers, and the four of them set out.

"Your wife should have sent you to me earlier," she told the measles victim. "No telling how many you exposed before I saw you."

They had paddled some distance downstream when, rounding a bend and coming on a point of high ground where the trees had been cut, she saw some fifteen canoes tied at the landing. Above them on the hill was a company numbering at least a hundred. Elka and his people were there as well as other villagers. In the midst, standing out because they wore clothing, were the Wapishana. They had paused in the hot work of field-cutting to pass pots of cooling cassava drink.

Coming alongside the beached canoes, Achi jumped into the nearest one and from that one into the next one, and so on until she reached land. She clambered up the bank without a thought about her lack of dignity.

"What are you people doing?" she asked sharply.

The drinking pots were lowered as if by command. The people had not seen her coming and she startled them. Elka was more than surprised; he was ashamed. Achi had told him to separate the people yesterday, and here he was today with a whole group. He had disregarded her instruction.

She seemed angry, but actually she was frightened.

"Didn't I say you'd all come down sick if you gathered in a group like this? Don't you realize what sickness we've got? Measles! Measles! Don't you know what happened to the Taruma?"

"Meesoo!"

They all repeated the word. Yesterday they hadn't been impressed. But today, with Achi standing there on the edge of the hill, fists clenched, they began to share her shock. They knew only too well what had happened to the Taruma. They had all heard how those poor people jumped into the river to cool their burning flesh, to no avail. They knew how the Taruma had gone blind and stumbled around, not even able to find their hammocks; how they had lain on the ground and died.

"You go back to your own villages and stay there," she directed. "Unless you get sick. Then come to Kanashen right away."

Elka stepped forward and said what he should have said the day before.

"Everybody go to their houses and stay there," he ordered.

It required only the time to gather up axes and knives, hammocks, pots, and food supplies, to leave the disease-carrying Wapishana and split off into village groups. Some went upstream, some down. Soon the last of their canoes had disappeared. Achi went on with her sick passenger. She hung her hammock with those of his family, hoping against hope that he would be her only patient.

He was not. In a few days she had to move back to the medicine room under her house at Kanashen. The huts that Elka built filled up with folk complaining of headache and sore throat or aching ears. The splotches looked funny on others, as if somebody had started a new design for skin painting. They looked funny until the bumps appeared on one's own skin. Then they became a serious concern.

Strong men and babies came down with measles. Fevers burned high. A terrible weakness came over the most able, who lay languidly in their hammocks. The ever-present threat of chest complications, so dangerous to Indians of low resistance, caused Achi much fear and strain. She radioed for serum from the States.

Hard rains and mud added to the misery. Alternating with cloudbursts were hot, moist days that made the sick look longingly at the waters of their river.

"Don't you go down to the river to cool off," Achi warned. "You'll get pains in your chest and you might die."

They might die. And if some did, would the others remain faithful to the Father in the Sky to whom they prayed, asking that he make them well? The troubled times of the flu were still fresh in memory. No definitely known companion of Jesus had perished then. If one did now, would the Wai Wai murmur for the old ways of witchcraft?

Elka understood that it was not always the will of God for the sick to be made well. For him this had been settled when he cradled his son in his arms, thinking the boy would die, and found himself willing to accept life or death at God's hands. But did his people understand it? Would their faith surmount the suffering that was coming on them again?

As some started to mend, others got sick. Convalescent begged to go to the landing to sit in the water when the sun was in the middle of the sky.

"Would it hurt, Achi, just to stick my toes in for a while?"

Mothers who had not noticed such things before complained that their unwashed children were smelly. Against such pleading Achi relented some. She permitted mothers to pour water over their children in the warmth of the sun. And though the women would have liked to go beyond this, they did not. Her patients were obeying her every word. She had accurately forecast their sickness. More than this, over the years they had come to trust her.

One day the radio brought word that the serum had come. It was being held in Georgetown, however, because it was the wrong type; somehow the emergency order had been garbled.

Elka knew that disaster threatened. But he knew, too, that there was another resource, one he turned to in times of distress as Achi did now.

"Father," she prayed, laying her burden before God, "if our people, especially our babies, are to live, You will have to be the one to keep them alive."

Miraculously, the disease abated—without the loss of a single life. When word finally came that the right serum had been on hand after all, the emergency had already passed. The absence of medicine seemed to stress their complete dependence on God. The faith of the Wai Wai had passed its hardest test. They remembered that the Taruma had turned away God's messenger a few years before they died. The Wai Wai were grateful they had received a faith strong enough to bring them through any crisis.

"Not one of us died," said Elka to Achi, mulling over the recent events. "The Taruma died from the bumps. They couldn't talk to God, though, could they?"

15

A Slow and Uncertain Process

As the faith of the Wai Wai grew wider and deeper, they began
to think less about themselves and more about other tribes in the
jungle around them. Just as the missionaries had come to the Wai
Wai with the news about God, so the Wai Wai, Kron had said,
should carry it to others. They had made a start by inviting the
Shedeu and the Nawayana, people very like themselves, to come
and hear the Gospel. But there were strange tribes farther away,
people they did not know or people they had always feared, who
still lived without hope in fear and suspicion, hatred and killing.
They needed to hear the words from God's Paper—and who
would tell them if not the Wai Wai?

Elka liked the idea of going to tell them. He had found peace
and victory of soul. He knew others could find the same release.

Mistokin, who had left to prepare the way, sent back word
that the remote regions of northwest Brazil were being opened
for missions. This good news led Bahm and Kron to make plans
for the first trip, to the Waica people. Bahm asked for Wai Wai
volunteers to go with him.

For the Wai Wai it was a hard choice. They would have to
leave their familiar land, travel across the savannas they hated,

pass through the strange towns of the white man's civilization, and risk entering another forest to meet a people they did not know. Who could guess what might happen to them on the way? Who knew whether they would ever return?

But Elka and Mawasha had a confident faith, and they had learned what God could do if they followed His way. They volunteered to go with Bahm.

On the day of departure all went out to the new landing strip recently cleared on a jungle hillside near Kanashen. The Wai Wai had seen the missionary sky canoe land and take off before. But now Elka and Mawasha entered it themselves, the first of the Wai Wai to fly. The engines roared and the sky canoe trembled. Soon they sped across the land, faster than a deer, and in a moment they were soaring up over the trees. Elka and Mawasha exclaimed in amazement to see the forest spread out beneath them. What a great wide forest it was, stretching as far as they could see.

Suddenly, however, the forest ended and they were over the open savannas. The sky canoe circled and brought them down to a place where other white men were waiting. The Wai Wai went from the sky canoe to a "land canoe," a big box with wheels.

"Oh, this thing goes fast!" Elka gasped, as the car sped across the open savanna.

More days of travel brought the mission party to a new and different forest. They journeyed on foot and by dugout far up a tributary of the Rio Branco in Brazil. The rapids and waterfalls were treacherous, and once they lost their food supply when the canoe overturned. Razor grass cut their legs as they slashed new trails, and their bodies were covered with the bites of flies and mosquitoes. They were sometimes threatened by ambush by hostile Indians, and were in frequent danger of being caught in the crossfire of warring tribes.

Finally the small party reached the land of the Waica. They had feared they might meet with suspicion or even violence, but the people welcomed them to their small scattered settlements. The tribe was loosely organized, without strong traditions or customs that drew them together; their poverty led them to covet the supplies of the missionary party. But they tried to help Bahm and the Wai Wai to learn their tongue, and many came to listen when Sunday lessons began.

Elka and Mawasha worked hard during their stay with the Waica. Each day they labored to hack an airstrip out of the jungle growth. They led services and held prayer meetings, trying to reach the hearts of the people with the Gospel, in spite of the strangeness of Waica ways and language. In their unfamiliar surroundings, the two young Wai Wai were often homesick, sometimes ill. But they remained steadfast through the long weeks, never complaining or shirking the task for which they had volunteered.

Elka sent back to his own people letters that read like the letters of Paul in God's Paper.

This is what I say to you, uncles, brothers, fathers, cousins, everybody; that is, only God's children. Just have God in mind; don't have in mind to become mature of your own accord. God is the only one who makes us mature.

Now you, those who are not God's companions, . . . I feel a lack in you, because you don't know that God is the completely strong one. Receive Jesus right now so that God's spirit will be your spirit.

He exhorted the Wai Wai church:

Say to God there, "Father, make the Waica love each other." The Waica are afraid of each other; they get angry and want to fight with those of other villages. God carried us through some people who are bad, who want to kill other people. We are all right, but are just like weak ones because of the mosquitoes' teeth, ouch!

I miss you all because I am far away. Anyway, I am peaceful because I know that God is with me and because I am his child. Satan says in my mind, "Let's go on back quickly." But God has made me not to be an obeyer of Satan, but an obeyer of God."

To his own children he wrote:

Be sure and learn how to make papers talk back to you, that's the way I want you to be. You be that way, too, Kulanow. Get ears, Little Body.

To Ahmuri:

Be sure and have God in mind there, my wife. Teach our children about God. Don't scold our children in your anger; scold as a smiling one when they don't obey you.

And this further word to his son:

Kulanow, mind your mother.

The Waica language was a difficult one, and the missionaries had not been able to say much that the people understood. But by the time they left, after being absent four full cycles of the moon, they felt they had made a beginning in sowing the first seeds of the Gospel. Elka knew the Waica had heard enough about God's way to make them hunger for it. On the journey homeward he thought of the many other tribes who still needed to be told how to forget fear and find faith.

When Elka and Mawasha arrived at Yaka Yaka, they found that their fields had been planted for them by fellow tribesmen. Their people had chosen that way to express appreciation for the work they had done.

Elka had many stories to tell his people about the Waica Indians and about his own experiences with the Indians and in the white man's settlements. They were amazed to hear about the strange way white men bathed in a "shower," and they could not believe it when Elka described the white man's "bed." No, said Elka, he hadn't been able actually to sleep in it. How could you sleep in something that didn't sway? And perhaps one or two Wai Wai caught something of Elka's vision as he talked about the need for visiting other tribes and telling them about God, showing them how they might exchange their fears of evil spirits for faith in Christ.

Although Elka dreamed of ways to reach other Indian tribes, he still had to deal with problems among his own people. Most Wai Wai professed to be companions of Jesus, but many of them continued in their old ways. Others weakened after a strong start in the faith.

As the Christian leader of his people, Elka carried a heavy burden.

"If a man sins, he is poisoned by his sin," he preached one Sunday. "And the poison spreads to all of us."

For this reason Elka dealt with offenders publicly. Among the more frequent sins Elka had to handle were immorality and gossip. One punishment was to ban wrongdoers from the weekday classes for a while. To tell a person that he must stay home while the others were meeting together usually brought an early repentance. Wai Wai nature still rebelled at being set apart.

One day a baptized believer was reproved for unchaste conduct.

"Haven't I taught that a man must leave the wives of other men alone?" Elka asked sternly. "Haven't Bahm and Kron and Kirifaka taught you this?" At the end of his rebuke, which lasted long enough for the sun to move along several degrees, Elka sighed, and added, "It's just as if you didn't have ears to hear."

He looked on witchcraft as the worst of sins. One time a rejected suitor asked a former witchdoctor for a magic song to make his girl unattractive to his rivals. The elders closed in swiftly on the culprit, warning him of tribal censure.

"We've known the Devil's power in witchcraft," Elka said. "I is bad to us that you play with it."

Some problems in the new faith and practice arose from the young people. The older ones remembered what tribal life had once been like and they wanted no part of it. For the younger ones the past was only a matter of hearsay. Witchcraft and the orgies of the dances held no terror for them. On the contrary, they possessed a certain glamour.

Now and then would come the suggestion that the "good parts" of the old dances could be renewed without danger of reverting to the morals of pre-Christian days. But always someone would ask, "Where will this lead to?"

A shortage of girls in the tribe caused some young men to lose hope of ever having homes of their own. Kirifaka could have told them that even in supplying a wife God was able to do the impossible, but theirs was not a faith that left such matters to God. They still abandoned themselves too easily to fatalism.

There was a certain youth to whom this wifeless prospect appeared worse than death. One morning he pulled his long arrows and even longer bow from a rafter in his house.

"If I don't come home, it's all right," he told his mother moodily as he walked out.

When he did not return by nightfall, his worried mother went to Elka.

"For days he has walked sad," she said, weeping, and told of his cryptic farewell.

Elka got out his flashlight. With the men of Yaka Yaka and Kanashen he searched the fields and forest around. The next day the youth's body was found in an old field near Yaka Yaka, an arrow in his breast. Apparently he had been shooting arrows into the tall tree above him—some were still stuck in the high branches. Among those that fell again, one had plunged into his waiting body.

The impetuous, the immature, the headstrong—there were many among the Wai Wai, and Elka had to deal with them. For families in which Christian parents tried to train their children, the problems of youth were manageable. It was in the homes of tenuous Christian influence that the threat of cleavage arose for this Christian society.

There could be no substitute for home training. But to help bridge this gap Achi started a Sunday School, and the elders began morning devotions each day at Kanashen and Yaka Yaka.

Great hope was placed in another new venture: a day school. The missionaries had said the children should be taught, and parents asked for a school. Katherine Pierce—Kitty—who had been a missionary in Brazil's Mato Grosso and on the Guiana savannas, came to start the new learners. Jean McCracken, who had taught on the savannas, took those who could already read. The men built each teacher a schoolhouse, round and thatched like the village homes and church. Parents of the eighty-odd pupils took an avid interest in the school program.

Once Elka visited a classroom to hear his son, Kulanow, recite. On leaving he appeared a bit miffed.

"Hnnnn," he said gruffly, but failing to hide an inward smile, "my boy is getting to know more than I do."

Little issue was made over plurality of wives except with Yukuma, who had taken a mother and daughter. Most men with more than one wife gave up all but one. A certain villager at Kanashen felt he ought to relinquish one of his two wives so that another man could give her a home. But he put off doing it. The wife died. Full of remorse, he said that what he should have done maybe God was forced to do.

It would take a full generation before family lines were clear and straight and all brothers and sisters united under one roof with a single set of parents.

The Wai Wai and those who attached themselves to the tribe grew in numbers to 200, then 300, and eventually to 350. Achi compiled a census. In it were 125 children under twelve years of age. Of these, 34 had been born to persons who lived on the Essequibo when the missionaries first entered the Wai Wai country. One hundred twenty-five children! Just a few short years before, there had been only five persons on the river too young for armbands.

Malaria, which had caused so many fevers and splitting heads and deaths, was brought under control by distributing medicine in church. But if the people became lax in taking their pills, it always flared up again. Dysentery had become less serious. Resistance to colds and to pneumonia was building up. Childbirth was becoming safer; infections and the diseases of infancy were causing less alarm. Body parasites could be eradicated at will, but those who carried them around in swollen bellies seldom willed, except when Achi insisted.

Achi, however, did not give sole credit to the miracles of medicine. She said to Elka one day,

"Your people are now strong because their bodies have become houses for God to live in."

Some of the Wai Wai developed tastes for food the missionaries imported, which Indians could not afford. White flour was one of the most wanted items.

"Are you hungry?" one woman was heard to say to another, within earshot of Ferochi and Maramara, the missionary wives. "Why don't you go home and bake yourself some bread with white flour?"

Ferochi thought the missionaries should give up their white flour. She and Maramara found they could use cassava flour. By the same token, the missionaries refrained from installing electricity in their houses.

Was this a solution or merely a delay in the march of civilization to the jungle? How could anyone know, when the tribe seemed drawn in two directions—new goals calling for initiative and new ways, on the one hand, and contentment with old routines, on the other.

Some men had planted larger fields in order to feed their families better. This permitted them less time to preen themselves with paint and feathers. Others, however, seemed bent on playing or lounging about nearly all day, every day. Elka had to remind them of their obligations to their families.

There was no easy solution to the problems of Indian economy, which they were coming to see must not be dependent on the outside world but self-sustaining.

The teaching of simple arithmetic and the introduction of

money as a symbol of numerical values proved a stabilizer in trade with the savanna Indians. No longer could a Wapishana slyly trade a quart of easily obtained salt for a Wai Wai grater board that took a full cycle of the moon to make. But still the Wai Wai wanted products of the white man's civilization—clothing, for instance. The men wanted shorts, which they found more practical than a loincloth, and they could afford to buy them.

"They save a lot of scratches while walking the trail," explained Mawasha, who sewed a pair for himself and became the first of the tribe to wear shorts regularly.

Then the women asked for dresses. Here the problem was more than saving a few dollars from the sale of an otter skin, as the men did. Elka agreed that dresses should be attractive. This meant obtaining large amounts of serviceable cloth. Each woman needed at least two dresses if she were to keep dry in the moist climate. And somehow money must be found for replacements as well as for the soap needed to keep the dresses clean.

But dresses remained beyond the reach of Wai Wai economy.

More and more, civilization was thrusting its head into the jungle: a jet plane streaking across the sky; visitors coming from the outside world. In 1961 the Wai Wai met up with politics. A candidate for district office brought his plane to a harrowing landing on the Kanashen airstrip. Shaken, yet inspired by a crowd of constituents, he hopped out of the plane and pumped hands all around. He passed out his campaign buttons, which the Wai Wai pinned to their neck beads. On election day the Wai Wai carefully cast the first ballots they had ever seen. But, asked Elka rather sharply,

"Why don't those people out there choose their own chief? Why do we have to help them do it?"

The day came when all the missionaries were absent from Kanashen for a six-week period. For Elka and his fellow elders it proved a testing of their leadership.

During this time additional members of the tribe came to sit on the believers' bench. And it was in this period that the first church wedding among the Wai Wai took place. Elka performed the ceremony at a Sunday lesson-time.

"Little Brother," he called at the beginning of the service.

Slowly the young man to be married got up from his seat, walked to the front of the church, and leaned against a post.

"Little Sister," Elka summoned the girl.

For several moments she did not move. He waited patiently, smiling a little and humming softly to himself, until finally the bride in simple red-and-white bead apron came to take her place at the front.

Elka asked them both to look at the people. They did, but only for a glance. Hastily they lowered their eyes again to their feet.

"I'm going to talk to you now, Little Brother," Elka began. "Do you want a wife? What do you answer to God?"

Barely heard was the young man's "Um-hum."

Elka asked the same of the girl. Her answer was even less audible.

"That's the way God wants it to be—a man and woman to be husband and wife," Elka said, addressing the congregation. To the couple he said,

"Talk to God together. Don't scold one another. Little Brother, when your wife is sick, don't scold her for being weak. Little Sister, when your husband does not bring back meat from the forest, don't scold him.

"Don't be concerned about anyone else. Little Brother, you cannot let her go even if she is bad."

"*Taa,* all right," they both assented.

"Both of you should learn to make God's Paper talk to you clearly. Later on, God will give you children. When you see them, say, 'God is good to us!'

"That's all I'm saying to you."

He sealed their simple vows with a prayer and told them to

sit in the front row. Then he went on to teach the day's lesson.

Kirifaka's elopement had helped remove Wai Wai marriage from the realm of trading a girl for the profit of her father or brothers. This marriage ceremony performed by Elka lifted it from the furtive, haphazard custom it had been into a part of Christian living.

Each day brought its problems for the elders. There was, for instance, old Muyuwa's lapse into immorality. The elders said they would rebuke him in front of the Christians.

"If you scold me, I'll give up Jesus," he threatened.

Elka sought out his former adversary. He dealt patiently and humbly with the old man. Elka pointed out his own sins, adding, "When I am bad, I want to be told about it."

Muyuwa found it hard to reject the love and understanding that flowed unstintingly from the depths of Elka's being. He said he did not really want to turn his back on God. With good grace he submitted to the reprimand.

Others were disciplined for gossip and abusive conduct. They acknowledged the right of their leaders to strive for righteousness within the tribe.

This time of testing showed how soundly established was the Wai Wai church and how capable and dedicated were its elders. Kirifaka, Mawasha, and Yakuta had gained the respect of everyone. Yet no one of them could stand in Elka's place.

Spiritual and temporal leader of all the Wai Wai as well as of the Mawayana and Shedeu allied with them, Elka had gone far since the day he pledged himself to serve Kworokyam. It had been his desire then, as now, to help his people, but the difference lay in whom he served—God or the spirits of evil. He loved his people. No longer might he satisfy himself that warding off evil was all he could offer them. Now he wanted God's best for them.

By the example of his own life he won many of his people to Christ. When there was work to be done—maybe a jungle to be cleared—Elka was right there ready to do it. He did not order the men to work; he went himself and others were drawn to work alongside him.

People sought his approval for long trips to hunt or to find wood for making bows. They asked his permission to take a wife. With the help of the other elders he judged in matters of personal grievance and took steps he thought necessary to promote the best interests of the tribe.

Elka had his temptations. There was pride to fight: He had been outside the jungle, undergoing experiences others would never have; he was in a unique position as leader of his people; he had been a key factor in God's working with them. Elka prayed now for humility. He was grateful that Bahm and Kron and Achi had told him their friends far away were praying for him. If they stopped for even a day, he realized, he stood in danger of spiritual defeat. This he felt clearly when a longing surged within him to commit an adulterous act. He faced the temptation; even allowed himself to approach it. Then, refusing, he turned away. If desire, however, was sin, he had sinned. He confessed it. Through prayer he sought and found restoration to God.

Within Elka's family the Christian faith was also growing.

Chekema, for example, had come across the high mountains from Big Falls on the Mapuera to be taught by the missionaries and to sit before Elka's desk. He had seen his younger half-brother develop over the years—from the shy lad holding back the tears while the ants stung his legs to a puzzling, gangling youth, then to a handsome, personable man of great abilities. He could see that as a witchdoctor Elka had been feared and obeyed. As a chief filled with God's spirit he was trusted and followed.

When Chekema became a companion of Jesus his sense of exactness told him that God merited the best and that the Wai Wai had not given Him their best. He urged them to build a new House for God. The one they had made, he said, was just thrown together as they would have done for anyone. Elka said he was right, and eventually the people did build a bigger, better church.

Tochi was another one to find faith. It became easier for her to live with Kurum, her sickly old husband, and to give up her claim on her younger daughter's husband, Yukuma. She still talked bad, but not quite so bad, about people. She was a beggar by nature, but now she did not *always* insist on knowing whether someone else had been given a bigger or better thing. She was up and down—still able to deliver a tongue-lashing, but often showing a pleasant side.

Kurum, too, received Christ. For him, spiritual growth was difficult. "Father," he once prayed sincerely but with despair, "why don't I understand Your Paper?" And nearly in tears he added, "It's just as though I'm one who doesn't love You." But Kurum kept trying.

Ahmuri was another who had gained spiritual depth. Passing through the dark valley of their son's illness had humbled her once-proud spirit, and she had grown more tender toward Elka and her children. She began to give up her superstitions. At church services she no longer sat haughtily on the elders' bench, as once she did, showing off her position as wife of the chief and leading elder. Life under Elka's roof began to improve.

As the missionaries returned from various absences, they would find a strengthened Christian community. Many new believers had been baptized. The people had grown in understanding of God's Paper and they were more respectful of their own leaders. The roots of Wai Wai faith were now deep and firm.

New people continued to arrive in the Wai Wai villages. The rest of the Shedeu came from the Mapuera. They were followed by people of the Hishkaryana tribe. They were entirely unexpected, and their coming embarrassed Bahm, who had encouraged two missionary friends to settle in this tribe far down toward the Amazon. He had expected the Hishkaryana to learn God's way from them.

But their coming was no problem to Elka.

"We didn't ask you to come," he said, greeting them under the big mango. "But if you want to stay, we'd kind of like to have you be here with us."

The Hishkaryana had had contact with traders in rosewood. Guns and other goods from outside the jungle were not new to them. One day a man of that tribe asked Elka what the Wai Wai could give him that the traders could not.

Elka thought for a moment. Then he replied,

"The news about Jesus, God's Son."

"Hnnnn," said the man thoughtfully. He nodded. Elka had spoken the truth.

Yoshwi became, next to Elka, the newcomers' best friend. Strongest leader among the women, she was completely transformed in the use of her tongue, which had been as biting as Tochi's, and in her spirit. She visited the new families to help the women with their babies or their baking and to tell them gently and patiently of the difference God had made in her own life.

The new Wai Wai way of life held great attraction. Nearly fifteen men who had been village headmen or chiefs gave up their positions in order to live under Elka's leadership. No fewer than a dozen witchdoctors—among them were some of the chiefs— renounced Kworokyam when they learned that God's Paper spoke against sorcery.

The peace and happiness generally prevailing in the tribe had given the Wai Wai a reputation that fanned out in all directions. Some of the fame of their "new way" was discovered by Kirifaka when he led a party of Indian missionaries to the Tunayana tribe. The Water People lived over the high mountains, east of the hills where the Mawayana had once lived. Kirifaka had heard that the Tunayana might be hostile, but he felt compelled to find them and share with them the good news of eternal and abundant life. Before his party caught sight of the Tunayana people, they saw the visitors paddling up the river—a headwater of the Trombetas —and rushed to the landing with clubs in their hands.

"Who comes?" the Tunayana called out. Several paces separated them from the Wai Wai, who were beaching their canoes.

"It's us," Kirifaka replied. The Tunayana gripped their clubs and raised them ready for use.

"Are you killers?" one of the men demanded bluntly.

"Are you Katwena?" asked another, calling the name of a fierce tribe that lived below them on the Trombetas.

"No," replied Kirifaka. "We are Wai Wai. We are God's children."

Hearing that their visitors were Wai Wai, the Tunayana dropped their clubs. They ran to Kirifaka and his companions and threw their arms around them. Kirifaka later reported to Elka,

"Even the women ran to us and hugged us, *gicha!*"

Kirifaka taught God's Paper to the Tunayana. Eventually the time came for the Wai Wai to leave. They invited the Tunayana to go back with them. At Kanashen and Yaka Yaka, they said, the Tunayana could learn more about God.

"We want to come but we can't come now," said their chief. "We've planted our fields and can't leave them. Come back next dry season. Some of our people will go over the trail with you and learn about God. Then they can come back and give ears to the rest of us.".

Meanwhile Yakuta and another Wai Wai went with Kron for a second visit to the Waica of northwestern Brazil. The party was unexpectedly stranded in the Waica area without plane transportation. It was not what they had planned or desired, but spending a longer time with the Waica enabled them to influence the tribe more effectively for Christ.

When they did return and Yakuta stepped out of the sky canoe, there was laughter from some in the welcoming crowd. What had happened to Yakuta? His hair was cut short, as Kirifaka's had been years ago, and people had called Kirifaka a buzzard. Some were teasing Yakuta now, but he did not seem to mind their jests.

Elka smiled with brotherly pride—and thankfulness—as Yakuta explained his shortened hair.

"The Waica men wanted us to cut off our pigtails and look like them," he explained. "At first we didn't want to. It would take many rain seasons to grow long again. But then we felt it was no sacrifice at all, if by cutting off our hair we could make the Waica know that because of Jesus we loved them."

Elka looked at his brother with new admiration. And in the following months he often looked at the boy's bamboo tube, which for a long time hid the shortness of Yakuta's hair. He thought of the youth's unselfish love of God and bowed his head in thanks for the day when God had placed him over the body of his newborn brother, to shelter him until he was lifted up and saved.

The day finally arrived when the Wai Wai said goodby to Kron and Maramara. The couple had decided that the time had come for them to move to the Trio tribe in neighboring Surinam, a tribe which had never heard the name of Jesus. Bahm and Ferochi also made plans to leave Kanashen. They were to locate on the savannas to give Bahm more time for the translation of God's Paper.

There was urgency in putting God's Paper into the Wai Wai tongue. Their Christian faith rested squarely upon it. Evangelizing the tribe, the initial task, was nearly completed. Now there was another mission: helping each weak one to become strong, and each stronger one to become Christlike in all his life and practice. For this the Wai Wai had to have God's Paper in his own tongue so it could become a part of him.

There was no other way.

To translate the whole of God's Paper might require the lifetime of the translator. The Wai Wai could not wait that long; they needed their guidebook now, and they needed it in the language they spoke in the fields and on the river and in their hammocks around the night fires. Already they possessed one of the Gospels, the Old Testament narratives, and scattered scriptural portions. At their stage of development they needed to learn the lessons learned by the first Church. In a sense, theirs was a first Church too. By making the Acts of the Apostles talk back to them, they could profit by the triumphs and pitfalls of their earlier counterparts.

Bahm was soon to take his family to the States for furlough. He hardly knew how to get the translation of highest priority done in time. But Elka's thirst for these new lessons opened the way.

Bahm had started teaching Acts orally. He hoped the people would remember enough to make use of it in their lessons while he was gone. After a few chapters had been covered, Elka asked for a thick pad of paper. He didn't want the teaching to escape him. He wanted to write the lessons down. Bahm knew this should be written translation, for then the Wai Wai teachers could study the lessons and teach them in their own language. Elka, however, was a slow printer; he could never copy down Bahm's lessons.

"Elka," Bahm said one day, having hit on a plan, "you speak the lessons I taught back into my talk-box and I'll write them down the way you tell them. Then not only you, but all the people will have the lessons to study at home as well as at church."

Into Bahm's recorder Elka and Yakuta recited in their own vivid detail the accounts of the early Church and Paul's missionary journeys. When they came to the passage about the great missionary's capture and imprisonment, Yakuta shook his head sadly and said into the talk-box,

"Oh, I hoped that wouldn't happen."

As time passed, Elka, leader of a people who had chosen to serve God, was finding much to encourage him. And then again when he looked at his people, he would ache in the pit of his stomach. Sometimes it seemed that for every step forward made by one believer there was a backward step by another. To him, their turning to God was a slow, uncertain process. Fearing that God might lose patience, he prayed, like Moses, that his Father would spare his people. At times his burden became so great that it lifted only after he had gone into the forest alone to talk at great length with his Father in the Sky.

Elka knew that his people had, on balance, walked forward with God. Yet he sensed a threat to the progress they had made, a threat not merely for stragglers but for all of them, including the leaders. Lurking like an enemy beside the forest trail was the specter of complacency. If this enemy wrestled with them and prevailed, they could be pushed backward along the spiritual trail they had come. Not all the way back, for God placed bounds even on his wayward children; but back far enough for them not to care any longer about going forward.

Complacency could appear as contentment that they had been "lifted up" by God, that nothing further was needed. Wasn't this message of salvation familiar to all in their villages and accepted by most? What more, complacency would ask, was there for God to do in their midst?

Complacency could lead them into boredom; into casualness about sin; into perfunctory reading of God's Paper around the family fire, praying and singing before meals, meeting together in God's House.

There were weapons against this insidious enemy: There was prayer. They could pray for themselves, and others could pray for them still, as they had already done, faithfully and specifically over the years. There was the daily feeding on the words of God in His Paper. For this they needed diligent schooling and continued translation. And there was the sharing of their knowledge of God with others who did not yet have ears for Him. In this they had made a start. Witnessing, however, was a spiritual exercise that had to be kept up in order to reap its benefits.

Complacency could throw them, as sour drink once had. Or it could be routed by dedicated zeal.

Much depended on the way the leaders went. Elka knew well the tremendous responsibility that rested on him. Ahead was a crisis—or an unending series of crises—as great as any he had ever faced.

16

"Let Us Go Far"

A crisis came, indeed, with every opportunity to go to another tribe with the good news about God. Would the Wai Wai respond? Would there be those willing to risk personal danger and hardship and long separation from home and loved ones, to tell fearful and sometimes savage Indians that peace awaited them at the foot of a Cross?

Thus far there had been many who volunteered to go. This carrying of their new-found faith to other people had become a challenge to the Wai Wai, and their best contribution to God and to the world lying beyond their own villages.

They helped reopen the trail to the Trio Indians of Surinam who lived under the sunrise. Years before, some of the Trio people had entered the hills of the Mawayana to trade. One day a few of the visitors were killed. Their wives were taken in forced marriages. Further killings followed when the morning *Onhariheh* was called and drink pots were unsuspectingly lifted. The trail to the east had then closed, apparently forever.

More than one child of the Trio now lived among the Wai Wai. One of them, part Trio, part Mawayana, volunteered to take his wife and son and go with Kron, now at another station, to the Trio people. Though Kron and his family had left Kanashen, their influence lingered. A number of Christian Indians made the arduous trip to Kron's new place to demonstrate to the Trio tribe how Christian faith had brought welcome changes into their lives.

For a trail that had been all but lost, it certainly was active now.

Elka and his fellow elders urged their people not to hold dear their homes and fields or even their families, but to be ready to leave them all if God should call them to go tell another tribe about their Father in the Sky. In sermons and informal talk they spoke of other tribes living as they used to live—in continual fear of evil spirits, talking bad about each other, suspicious, truthful only when convenient, killing by club or sorcery. Elka spoke strongly of how ignorant they themselves had been.

"Shall we just let other people near us stay on in their ignorance and sin?" he would ask. "Shall we let them alone? No! How would we be if the missionaries had said that about us? How would we be if Jesus had said that about us and had never come from His home to earth to save us?

"Jesus came far. So let us go far, too. He died for us. We haven't yet died for Him. Let us die for Jesus."

By 1962 the Wai Wai had gone on as many missionary trips in all directions as a man had fingers and toes. A few of the trips were with the white missionaries. Most of them were on their own and by themselves. Occasionally the party would include a man who hoped to come across a long-lost brother in a forest village; or one who sought relatives in a tribe from which he had been separated in childhood. Yakuta led a group through difficult terrain only to take a wrong turn and, disappointingly, end up at home instead of the place he was heading for. This did not discourage him. He set out again.

Some Wai Wai travelers ran out of food. Others got sick on the trail. Once Kirifaka was being flown from a distant tribe by the pilot of another mission. The plane took off from the jungle airstrip, but stalled in the climb to avoid the taller trees, and crashed. The plane was damaged beyond repair, but neither Kirifaka nor the pilot was hurt.

After that experience Kirifaka might have been expected to stay at home. He did not. Neither he nor others counted their lives dear when God's work needed doing.

One day news came of a building project planned by the Brazilian government just across the high mountains. Some construction was required. The Brazilians asked the Wai Wai to build the installation and, after it was built, to live near it and keep the jungle at bay. If they did, it would mean that certain families would have to leave the Essequibo and build homes, a church, and a school over there. Maybe it would also mean the selection of a second chief. Who could know? Perhaps he would become a second Elka.

From time to time the Wai Wai talked of trying to get in touch with the Karafouyana, the giant People of the Bow. In the dim past the Bow People had been their mortal enemies. Coming from under the sunset, these big fellows had raided villages, burned houses, killed old men and children, carried off women. After one such raid the Wai Wai gathered from all their villages and, mustering courage, pursued the marauders. Superior in numbers (there were so many, legend had it, that the earth rattled as they walked), the Wai Wai attacked one dawn, inflicting heavy losses. The invaders, however, dealt the last blow. They performed *farawa* for their dead.

As a result, every Wai Wai who had killed a Karafouyana died by this black magic.

Reports came occasionally that the Karafouyana were still fierce and unfriendly. To the mission-minded Wai Wai, they were no longer a race of frightening giants but simply another people to seek out and win to Christ.

The Katwena were another tribe to be sought. Yakuta began making plans for a trip to find them. After them would come the Chickayana. Then maybe the Cashuana.

Who knew how many other tribes were hiding under the thick foliage of the vast forest?

Once more the *tali tali* locust sang, heralding as it had year after year another dry season. Kirifaka made ready to go back to the Tunayana. He was anxious to get started. Word had come that a wild tribe to the south had attacked and killed three of the Water People.

"The Tunayana might scatter from fright," Kirifaka said. "They might retaliate and both sides suffer many killings."

The next Sunday at church Elka spoke of Kirifaka's plan to return to the Water People. Two of the men who had gone before were now living with the Trio people. Replacements would be needed. A party of seven would be just about right, he thought. Who would go?

He called Kirifaka to the front of the church. Would anyone come and stand with him?

It was a serious thing, a trip over mountains and through dangerous rapids to go to a people who might even have to be flushed from their hiding places in the jungle. Elka spoke of the danger of falling trees, of snakes and jaguars, and of the possibility of death by drowning or by the arrow of some concealed Indian who would not know why they were coming.

"The new moon will come again this many times over their camp," he said, holding up four fingers. "I don't want anyone going who will walk sad or whose spirit is weak."

Slowly and with full realization of what their decision meant, first one and then another rose from his seat and came forward to stand by Kirifaka.

Wisho was one, he whose lust and cruelty had made him a terror to all; whose stock in trade had been the vengeful *farawa*.

Through the grace of God he was now tender and compassionate, especially to the children he had once despised.

Tamokrana was another, Tamokrana who had killed his own children, but who in less time than it took the full moon to return had received Jesus after hearing of Him. He had spent whole nights praying for those in the jungle who did not know God. Now he was ready to go in search of them so that he could tell them about their Father in the Sky.

A young man simply called "Wai Wai" volunteered. Tunayana blood flowed in his veins and he had wept when he heard of the murder of his kinsmen. Another was Wahni, father of twins. While still in the bonds of superstition, he had made plans to kill his children. He was prevented and became a companion of Jesus. His twins were old enough to walk now, and it saddened him to think of leaving them. Elka had never before known "Wai Wai" or Wahni to walk with enthusiasm for God—and here they were offering to go to the Water People!

Emehta would go along; Achi had taught him to prick the arms of sick ones. Chayukuma, not long in his armbands, completed the group.

Elka then called for men to help carry food and supplies over the mountains.

"About this many are needed," he said, holding up most of the fingers of both hands before the people. He got all the volunteers he needed.

Donations of cassava bread and fruit for the trip were brought to the church. The piles mounted higher each day. A box had been tied to a post in the front of the church. Into this the people dropped their offerings to finance the journey.

What were the expenses of a trek through the jungle? Beads and knives were needed for trading, just as white men had to invest in trade goods when visiting Indians. The Wai Wai would trade their goods for food when they reached the Tunayana. They might have to buy a canoe if theirs should sink. A trip could not be made without sacrificial giving.

The young man whose exploding gun had gashed his arm on the Mapuera several years earlier, showed up at the church with only one armband.

"Where is your other one?" someone asked him. He pointed his lips at the offering box and felt his naked arm, which still bore the scar. His big eyes danced as he said,

"I thought Kirifaka might need it."

The following Sunday Elka called the seven Wai Wai missionaries to the front of the church. He spoke first to Kirifaka.

"Your going is good to me. See the Water People, see them fine. Tell them God's Paper. They are different from us. They are afraid, they drink, they dance. But they will see you as different ones.

"Now, look for lots of people. Where maybe could they be? Look at one village and then another and another. Don't be afraid of the people even though you may think they want to kill you.

"That's the way to be, Kirifaka."

He stopped for a moment and then continued in a serious tone,

"This is what I would like you to say: 'Elka loves you. Don't you want to go and show yourselves to him there?' That's what to say to them. I want you to bring three or maybe four back with you. You come back in your canoe and they will come in theirs. They may become unhappy on the trail, so ask only strong men to come. Say to them, 'Elka wants to see you. He really loves you. He wants to be good to you.' Say to them, 'Therefore, let's go to him.' Say this."

To the seven men he promised,

"We will talk to God without stopping about you."

He spoke to the men as if they were his sons—and indeed, some were his spiritual sons.

"Walk with Kirifaka," he said. "Don't walk alone when you

are over there. Show yourselves as two walking together. You are going to show God to the people through His Paper. If the people see you as bad ones God will not use you to show them. So all go concerned with God's Paper.

"Now, if you are going to drown, God will help you. If you are climbing and about to fall, God will help you. Maybe a snake will bite you. God will help you. God fixes us all fine."

He turned from the men and talked to the people.

"People, these are the ones going. They want to go. This many wanted to go." He showed all his fingers. "There isn't a canoe over the mountains big enough. There isn't food enough for the trail. That's the way it is, so I don't want you all to go—only these seven.

"Talk with God about them. Every day without fail talk to God about them. Meet each dawn by being concerned about them.

"They are leaving their wives here. We should take care of their wives. Give them meat. What maybe will you shoot? If you shoot a bush hog, if you catch a *haimara* fish, give them a piece.

"They are leaving their children behind. They will get hungry for meat, the children will. The women do not shoot arrows. Only men hunt for meat. Therefore, let us be hunting their meat.

"This is the way to be also. Don't gossip about their wives. If we talk about them they will be sad. They will say, 'They're scolding me when my husband doesn't know it.' Let us be good to them.

"That is all I'm saying to you. I am finished now."

He then called Mawasha, Yakuta, and Melsha, a newly appointed elder.

"Come up here, you elders," he said.

Mawasha was holding the infant son he had long hoped for. Handing the baby to his wife, he took his place with the others. His head of heavy black hair, decorated today with just a swatch of downy white, stood out above the rest.

When they were assembled, Elka said,

"This is the way Paul and his friends did a long time ago. They sat down on their knees in front of those who were sending them. So let us be that way also. And now you who will make the trip, put yourselves in a circle close together, sitting on your knees. And you elders, put your hands on the crowns of their heads. Like this Paul was. This is how they fixed them, the mature ones did.

"Now, let's talk to God."

Monday was a day of prayer in behalf of the missionary journey. On Tuesday excitement filled the air even before the sun drove the mist from the village. The smoke gently seeped through the thatch of the Kanashen houses, showing that families were up and busy preparing to see their husbands and fathers off, or an uncle or brother or neighbor. By sunrise they had woven baskets in which to carry the bread and fruit that now was stacked high in the church.

Little groups made pilgrimages from the village of Kanashen, or along the trail from Yaka Yaka, to the white clay-bank of the river landing. A number of canoes from other villages up and down the river were already there. There was something of a holiday spirit, yet there was the sadness of men saying goodby to their wives and children.

Young boys ran around carrying food baskets or bows and arrows, or rounding up canoe paddles, or slashing palm branches from the trees to make more baskets that were suddenly needed. Men stayed close to their families, talking in near whispers, giving last-minute instructions, assuring them that all would go well or asking those left behind to pray for them.

One canoe and then another filled with the contingent of copper-colored missionaries and their carrier helpers. But as fast as they filled, they were emptied. Somebody had forgotten his hair oil, or his vanity basket, or felt he should take along another arrow or a second knife. It was hard to tell where there was more activity—at the landing where the canoes were being loaded, or in the paths to the villages where articles were being retrieved at the last moment.

Oblivious to all, Elka sat on a log bench under the big mango tree. He was writing a letter. He had folded a paper on his knee and with some difficulty was printing a message on it with a pencil no longer than his little finger. For a long minute he looked at what he had written. His lips moved slightly as he made the paper talk back to him.

"It's done!" he finally exclaimed with a smile. He got up and walked through the mission gateway and along the path to the river landing. Kirifaka was still on the bank. Elka handed the paper to him.

"Make my paper talk to the Tunayana chief," he instructed Kirifaka. "I am telling him that God is making me love him and his people. You say to him, 'Old Elka wants you to come and learn about God. God is the good one. He is good to the Wai Wai people. He wants to be good to you, *oklee!*' Say this to him."

As the canoes rounded the first bend and were lost from sight, Elka turned back along the path to Yaka Yaka. He had a lesson to teach the men the following day; it required careful study and private prayer. A day or so later he must lead a group of men to a spot in the forest to cut away growth for a new garden field. There were new people—the Hishkaryana—to counsel and encourage in their first gropings toward God. And sometime, when he could find a moment, he should go hunting and fishing to provide food for his growing family and to share with those whose men had gone on the missionary journey.

Achi and Jean and Kitty, the teachers, had stayed at Kanashen after Bahm and Kron left. Elka worked with them in teaching and caring for his people. Yet there were duties which, as chief, he and no one else could perform. The demands on him were heavy. He did not mind; this was his life—to serve his people.

A call came for him to preach to the Wapishana. Again he

set aside his chieftainship for a while to take up the role of evangelist to people other than his own. He was downriver on a hunting trip when the word reached him. Achi dispatched a messenger to ask him to come back, and he came. She told him that her radio had brought a request from a missionary doctor on the savannas, who wanted Elka to accompany him on clinic trips to distant points in Wapishana country. The doctor would treat; Elka would preach.

He had gone on clinic trips before, as Yakuta had, along with the Wai Wai who spoke Wapishana as a second tongue and who interpreted for them. Long looked down on by the Wapishana as inferior, naked savages, the Wai Wai now had something to give their civilized savanna brothers. On his tour with the doctor, Elka told the crowds that gathered that they, too, could enjoy decent, peaceable, purposeful lives. Wherever he went he looked up the village headman to witness personally to him of his satisfaction with Jesus Christ.

Always, a silent throng stood by, listening, drinking in the words of this unusual jungle Indian.

These opportunities of witnessing to his faith refreshed Elka. From his own experience he knew that if his people fed on God's Paper and pursued an ever-broadening ministry to needy souls about them, there would not be boredom, self-satisfaction, or pride. He was prowman in their journey. Before he could lead them safely through treacherous courses he had to be sure of the way himself.

Each new dawn brought a new challenge: Would he be the man God needed him to be that day?

Elka knew that for the most part his place was at home among his people. Yet the call of missions was strong. He heard of a man among the Trio who had heard the teaching "just a little." How Elka longed to go and tell him more.

Others wanted to go, too. He stepped aside and sent them. Maybe he could go some day. And maybe a call would come again from the Wapishana. Surely he knew of no greater challenge than the Wapishana, unless it was the people in his own villages.

Elka knew that some people in the jungle made war, with a little destruction, and that sometimes people outside the jungle made war with a great destruction. He knew that everywhere there were people who feared death as the Wai Wai used to be afraid to die. He had heard that others felt there was no use in living, as the Wai Wai used to feel there was no use, but with a feeling not so strong as their fear of dying. He saw a former chief of the Shedeu suffer a long and painful sickness and then become the first of their companions of Jesus to die. But he saw his brother in Christ die radiant. One day this man of the Shedeu had surrendered the fears and hate and the burdens of a guilty life and from Christ had received in their stead faith and unshakable joy and peace. His encounter with the Son of God had made all the difference—in life and in death.

If Jesus Christ could do this for a man who had walked the darkest jungle trails, as the Shedeu had done and as he himself had done, asked Elka in meditation one day, could He not do it for anyone anywhere who asked it of Him?

He could, *oklee!*